ADVANCES IN LIBRARY ADMINISTRATION AND ORGANIZATION

Volume 10 • 1992

ADVANCES IN LIBRARY ADMINISTRATION AND ORGANIZATION

A Research Annual

Editors: **GERARD B. McCABE**
Director of Libraries
Clarion University of Pennsylvania

BERNARD KREISSMAN
University Librarian, Emeritus
University of California, Davis

VOLUME 10 • 1992

 **JAI PRESS INC.**

Greenwich, Connecticut   *London, England*

CONTENTS

INTRODUCTION

It was with a sense of disbelief that the editors of *Advances in Library Administration and Organization* realized, in late 1990, that the next volume in the series was to be a tenth anniversary issue. It was hard to realize that ten years had elapsed since our first spare volume of 1982. In retrospect, however, came the realization that a lot of life and library activity had flowed past in the last decade.

The first volume noted that two librarians originally destined to co-edit ALAO had both met accidental deaths. Many other highly respected colleagues had also passed on, Metcalf and Downs among them. We watched several library schools die away.

In the intervening years the first editor changed directorships from Virginia Commonwealth to Clarion University, and the second editor retired. The first editor, in the last decade, has written and edited several works, all well received, on the smaller library and on library buildings. The second editor has established a successful publishing house with his atlas of the California environment.

From the outset, ALAO has been widely cited and it now enjoys a secure niche in the library publishing world as the vehicle most receptive of the long research article. Back issues of ALAO continue to be sought by the librarians of the country, and supplies of the earliest volumes have all been exhausted. Reprint volumes may be made if the demand continues.

The title, *Advances in Library Administration and Organization,* has become somewhat controversial over the last ten years, as the series has moved into its present eclectic mode. It is probable that a name more indicative of ALAO's contents could be developed. However, the serial has gained its reputation under the current title, and the editors would be loathe to lose that identification for any possible advantage a more descriptive title brings. Besides, serials librarians hate name changes. Thus, it is with a sense of pride in a decade of accomplishment that the editors bring you our tenth anniversary volume.

Strategic planning, a subject of earlier papers in ALAO (Ostler, Volume 8; Stephens, Volume 9) is the theme of a major research report for the Council on Library Resources prepared by Robert M. Hayes, former dean of the University of California at Los Angeles Graduate School of Library and Information Science. While the report focuses on that university and is intended to assist in planning for the future of research libraries, the report provides much of interest to academic libraries of all sizes. One such area of interest is the provision of library information to users regardless of their location through online access. Libraries with integrated library systems now allow dial-in access to databases, and the report envisions even greater access to information stored in libraries through the medium of remote access.

Many academic, public, and special libraries have manuscript collections, but many more are in private hands or those of dealers. How may serious scholars find these materials and obtain permission to use them for their research? Patricia A. Etter, in a paper prepared for this volume, describes the Manuscript Society Information Exchange Database. The database allows owners of many rare and unique manuscript materials to make their treasures available to legitimate scholars, and the current capabilities of computers make such research possible. The larger the volume of information, the greater the accuracy of historical research. We all benefit because so many more original sources now can be located.

James R. Coffey and Theodora T. Haynes follow with a paper that approaches bibliographic instruction from a distinctly different viewpoint. All academic librarians in public service will want to read this paper.

Librarians facing rising periodical subscription costs will find Sandra E. Goldstein's paper of more than passing interest. Her study of citation analysis can be especially effective for the arrangement of serials by the small academic library.

Justification—a word we hear so often in management, especially in terms of persuading others that what is proposed is worthwhile, is the focus of Thomas J. Waldhart's paper on justifying cost. More and more today, the proposals of librarians for improving services and buying equipment or new technology must be defended in terms of usefulness and the significant benefit to the community that the library serves. Waldhart explains the process through which this is done and his insights should be useful to many readers.

At a 1989 preconference of the Library Administration and Management Association in Dallas, Texas, Ellsworth Mason presented a paper on library lighting. The respected and distinguished librarian and building consultant enthralled his listeners with his wit and coverage of the subject. While the printed page cannot convey the enthusiastic reception of the audience, the editors are grateful for the opportunity to present Mason's views.

Larry Hardesty presents the full length report of a study he helped to prepare for the Council on Library Resources. It is reassuring to know that academic deans think well of the librarians who serve their campuses. It is less reassuring to realize that librarians must do much more to keep academic administrators aware of library services and the heavy dependence of all faculty and students on the campus library. In an age of limited fiscal resources, librarians must be prepared to justify, on hard rational grounds, why new services or systems are necessary.

Rashelle Karp appears again in the pages of ALAO with an annotated bibliography on general education, with co-authors Sandra Yaegle, Faith Jack, and Polly Mumma. With growing concern for general education in academia, the appearance of this bibliography should provide major assistance, particularly for librarians who may be called upon to produce reading lists.

Another supplement to his "Bibliography of African Librarianship" has been prepared by Glenn Sitzman. The bibliography attests to the vitality of our profession as practices in Africa. The compiler and the editors hope that additional compilations of writings on African librarianship will be forthcoming..

What lies ahead? Neither of us is willing to look ten years down the road; in the near future, however, if the demand for individual articles continues, the editors may consider a "reader" of articles on a common theme drawn from the issues of ALAO. We are also hoping for greater representation of research papers from public and special librarians. There is also the possibility that we may publish special issues of our serial devoted to a single subject. We are also interested in publishing the first papers of library school doctoral candidates or, even, particularly noteworthy masters dissertations. Library school deans and professors should be aware of our particular interest in the best student work. We invite your correspondence if you wish to share ideas with us.

To be candid, however, the editors wold be quite pleased if the next ten years of ALAO are as good as the last ten years.

Gerard B. McCabe
Bernard Kreissman
Series Editors

LONG-RANGE STRATEGIC PLANNING FOR LIBRARIES AND INFORMATION RESOURCES IN THE RESEARCH UNIVERSITY

Robert M. Hayes

INTRODUCTION AND SUMMARY

This is the Final Report to the Council on Library Resources (CLR) for the UCLA Project on *Strategic Planning for Libraries and Information Resources in the Research University.* The project was undertaken at UCLA to explore means by which a major university could carry forward strategic planning for library and information resource management, with specific emphasis on involvement of faculty.

Background

The project was one outgrowth of a conference held at the UCLA Lake Arrowhead Conference Center in December 1981. It brought together university

Advances in Library Administration and Organization,
Volume 10, pages 1-50.
ISBN: 1-55938-460-3

administrators, academic librarians, and library educators for the purpose of identifying the effects of technology on the future of universities and of the research libraries within them. But there was one vital element missing from that conference—the community of research scholars, the persons depending on libraries and information resources for their research and instruction.

During the ensuing months, discussions between staff of the CLR and of UCLA led to the proposal for an effort in planning that would directly involve the research faculty as well as librarians and administrators. As a result, a four-year project was funded for a total amount of $400,000. It was titled "Strategic Planning for Libraries and Information Resources in the Research University."

This is the Final Report on the project. In it, we will present specifics of the approach taken, of the results obtained, and of the final accounting for expenditures. In this section, we will describe the context and objectives and summarize the remainder of the report.

The Project Objectives

To set the context for the details, though, it is important to identify the objectives intended for the project, aside from simply involving faculty, administrators, and librarians in a planning process. To do so, the broad perspective will be taken as that of strategic *management*, which of course includes strategic *planning* as a necessary component but by no means as the total story.

Scopes of Consideration

Strategic management in general must consider a range of contexts, both internal and external, and at various levels of detail. With respect to university libraries and information resources in particular, one must simultaneously deal with at least three levels:

- the "library," taken narrowly as the traditional collection of books, journals, and a wide range of other media, with its inherent set of facilities, operations, and services;
- the "library of the future," taken broadly as the entire set of information resources and facilities, including libraries taken narrowly but adding to them computing centers, media centers, film and data archives, museums, and telecommunication networks; and
- the "research library network," consisting of the entire set of libraries and other kinds of information resources acting as a cooperative and integrated whole in support of scholarship.

It is not easy to keep these separate, and the pressure to slip from one to the other is great, sometimes without realizing that one has done so. But all three were explicitly identified as encompassed within the scope of the project.

At each level, one must deal with issues of concern to the institution and its management, with issues of politics and social policy, with legislative and legal constraints. One must deal with legislative and legal constraints. One must deal with cooperation and competition among universities and their libraries, with relationships also cooperative and competitive with publishers and other suppliers of information resource,s with the changing effects of technology and the economics of equipment. One must deal with the range of services and products to be provided and with the market for them, the constituency of users to be served.

The Issues of Concern

In undertaking this investigation, several issues were seen as paramount in importance: (1) effects of technology, (2) economics of libraries, (3) changes in the academic enterprise, and (4) changes in patterns of publication.

Effects of Technology on Academe. The first, effects of technology, is surely the most dramatic. The question to be faced is, how should the university and its libraries respond to those effects? It was in fact the primary focus of the 1981 Lake Arrowhead Conference.

The continuing increases in functional capabilities, capacities, and speeds of computers, combined with equally spectacular decreases in cost, have revolutionized our entire society, the university as much as any other institution. Today the microcomputer is ubiquitous in the university, replacing mainframes in virtually every area of routine and user managed data processing. But at the same time, the supercomputer is adding new dimensions to research, conceptualization of problems, and the means for processing overwhelming quantities of data.

The capabilities for data acquisition, data storage, and data display have also spectacularly increased over the past decade. Sensors, scanners, and other means for raw data entry now provide means for acquiring amounts of data orders of magnitude greater than previously possible. Optical disk formats— CD-ROM, WORM, videodisk—have increased our ability to store data, again by several orders of magnitude. Displays now provide storage resolutions that rival the best of printed pages. Indeed, these areas of technology have recently developed at a pace far greater than computers.

The growth in telecommunications capabilities has paralleled that of data acquisition, storage, processing, and display. The result is that the data can be transmitted at rates commensurate with the processing capabilities—today at 100 million bits per second, tomorrow at even higher.

All of that technological development clearly is affecting the university both in what its faculty and students do and in what administrators and librarians must do. What are those effects and how do we deal with them?

Economics of Academic Libraries. A separate concern is the economics of academic libraries. In part, of course, this concern is related to technological change. Libraries have been forced to make major investments in automation of operations and services, programming, installation of equipment, conversion of catalogs and other files, training of staff and the students and faculty being served. Those costs have been of great magnitude, both for capital investments and for operating expenses; they will continue in the future as obsolescent and even obsolete equipment and related software must be replaced. Libraries have been forced to deal with costs incurred in new means of data access—the online computer data bases. They must respond to the demand for new media, such as optical disk stores, that must be acquired to serve the needs in instruction and research; the costs will place additional burdens on the budgets for acquisition of materials.

Indeed, the pressures on the acquisition budget are almost certainly the most pernicious economic problem faced by academic research libraries. They are creating conflicts within the library in fighting the diversion of funds from books to journals to data bases to external services. They are creating conflicts between the library and the faculty and even among the faculty members, as different choices adversely affect different disciplines. The past decade and more has seen rates of inflation in journal prices, especially those from foreign commercial publishers, that threaten every other commitment of the acquisition budget. Those price increases, because they largely focus on journals, affect not merely today's budget but force commitments of resources for the indefinite future.

Another major economic concern is with the collection itself—its storage, its preservation, and the tools for physical access to it. Major research collections for good reasons will still grow, so buildings must be built to house them—whether on campus or in depository facilities. The capital costs represent 50- 100-year commitments. The collections of every major research library are in states of disintegration, some of it due to deficient buildings and lack of environmental controls that have exacerbated the problem of embrittlement. A major capital resource of the university—its library collection—is falling apart before our eyes.

How do we deal with these economic pressures?

Changes in the Academic Enterprise. The university itself is continually changing. How should libraries and other information resources respond to those changes?

Even though the labels on departments may be the same today as yesterday, the substance is dramatically different. The subjects taught, the means for instruction, the foci of research—these all undergo change in response to internal development within each discipline. They also must change in response to external pressures from society—changes in the demography of students, governmental priorities, and the means for funding of programs.

How do we identify these changes in academic program and determine what needs to be done to support them with adequate information resources?

Changes in Patterns of Publication. Primarily as a result of the impact of technology on publishing but also in part as a result of changes in the disciplines themselves, there are changes occurring in patterns of publication. The new media—computer data bases, online access to them, electronic mail and facsimile, distribution of data and images in optical disk formats, desktop publishing—these all provide new means for communication of scholarly information. How will they affect the traditional means? At what pace will they develop? What changes will they make in the substance of what is communicated?

How do we determine what are real changes in publishing and when those changes will be meaningful to operations of libraries and other information facilties?

Goals and Objectives

Early on in the project, an effort was made to identify more specific goals and objectives that would relate information resources to the academic program as explicitly as possible:

1. Increase the reputation and national visibility of the university, especially as that may depend on or be affected by information resources:
2. Improve the quality of instruction at every level, especially as it may depend on or be affected by information resources;
3. Increase the research productivity of faculty as it may depend on or be affected by information resources;
4. Expand the role of information resources in obtaining funding of academic programs for both instruction and research;
5. Increase the information literacy (i.e., ability to use information resources) of students and other users;
6. Increase the amount of information available to students others;
7. Maintain the position of the university at the forefront of developments in the information resources field itself—educational, professional, technical, and technological;

8. Develop the means to assure that faculty and students have access to the technical information support needed to use information resources effectively;
9. Increase the level of cooperation with foreign countries and institutions, both generally and specifically with respect to information resources;
10. Increase the effectiveness in use of expenditures throughout the university in acquiring, producing, and using information resources;
11. Increase the degree of cooperation among academic units in the use of information resources;
12. Develop single point access to the full range of information resources in the university;
13. Deliver information directly to workstations and PCs;
14. Provide support to personalized data base systems for faculty and students;
15. Establish equitable personnel policies for the full range of staff concerned with information resources; and
16. Protect the university's interests with respect to external policies affecting its ability to use information resources in support of its academic responsibilities.

Strategic Management

The project under CLR sponsorship was intended, then, to experiment with means for responding to these questions and to determine how best to meet the goals and objectives, with specific emphasis on involving faculty in identifying their own needs. One point, though, became evident at the outset. Planning in this area cannot keep pace with developments as they actually occur. The most dramatic evidence of this fact was the initiation, about six to nine months after the start of the CLR project, of a UCLA planning effort for the entire campus academic program. Suddenly, the primary element for planning of information resources—the academic program—was itself the focus of a vastly greater effort.

Furthermore, the UCLA library itself is a highly dynamic organization, constantly at the forefront of developments of every kind. The planning effort repeatedly was faced with the reality of implementation of services and facilities within the library, not at some planned future time but today. Conversely, the very means used by the project stimulated demands that presented the university library management with immediate problems.

It became painfully clear that something more than "planning" was necessary if this kind of dynamic environment was to be dealt with. The answer, once found, is evident and is represented by a simple though vital change in one word. We need to be concerned with strategic *management* within which planning may play a role, but at most a supportive one.

Strategic Management is a concept of increasing importance in modern industrial management. The following is a definition of the term as it will be used here:

> *Strategic management* is that part of general management of organizations that emphasizes the relationships to external environments, evaluates the current status of them and the effects of future changes in them, and determines the most appropriate organizational response to them.

With this definition, a distinction is made between such externally focused management and that which is internally focused, which will be characterized as either "tactical management" (concerned with the most effective deployment of resources within the organization) or "operational management" (concerned with assuring maximum effectiveness in use of the available resources).

It is important to note that at UCLA strategic management and planning within it are facts of campus policy, long embedded in procedures of both campus and library administration. The CLR strategic planning project is therefore at most an ancillary support, a means for providing data that would be of potential value in the ongoing management and planning efforts.

However, it is also important to note that the campus commitment to this kind of management provides a context within which the CLR strategic planning project could be initiated not as an isolated activity but with full commitment of the campus and library administration. The timing in fact was especially fortuitous, given the initiation by the UCLA administration of its campus-wide academic planning efforts some months after initiation of the CLR project. The result was that the two efforts could be mutually supportive.

A direct result of the combination of activities was the assignment of coordinative responsibilities for information resources on the campus to a Vice Chancellor and the establishment of the position of Assistant Vice Chancellor for Library and Information Service Planning. It institutionalized the entire process of strategic planning represented by the CLR project.

Summary

In the remainder of this Final Report, we will discuss the Strategic Planning Project as it actually developed; in doing so we will assess the degree to which the identified methodology did or did not succeed.

The Project Methodology

In the next section—The Strategic Planning Project—of this Final Report, we will discuss the methodology proposed for this project. To summarize, though: First, it was proposed that Disciplinary Task Forces be established in as many areas of the total campus academic program as was feasible; it was the aim to use them as a primary means for identifying future needs for information resources in their respective academic areas. Second, it was proposed to carry forward small-scale studies as appropriate to support the work of the Disciplinary Task Forces. Third, it was proposed to undertake research investigations arising from the work of the task forces or from the identification of problems by individual faculty from throughout the university. Fourth, to carry forward this work, it was proposed to establish a small administrative structure, an Advisory Committee, and a program of communication both internal and external to UCLA.

Was the methodology successful? In the overall, no; in specific respects perhaps yes. On the negative side, as will be discussed later, there were substantial problems in establishing the Disciplinary Task Forces, with only a few actually becoming effective, so the primary methodology simply was less successful than had been hoped. On the positive side, as will be discussed in the fourth section—Specific Results, the small-scale studies and research projects were reasonably successful and did indeed provide a rich picture of current and future needs for information resources on the campus.

The Project Results

In the third and fourth sections, we will discuss the specific results, first with respect to administration and second with respect to studies as subprojects. To summarize, though, perhaps the most important result, especially as a long-term effect, is establishment of the position of Assistant Vice Chancellor for Library and Information Services Planning. In a very real sense, it institutionalized the means for carrying forward this kind of planning effort. Another result was establishment of an ad hoc administrative committee that involved faculty from throughout the campus to be concerned with monitoring federal activities, such as copyright legislation and administrative policies that affect the university's academic programs. A number of preliminary data bases were created covering persons, academic programs, facilities, projects (both within the scope of this project and separate from it), and external environments. They provide a starting point for a continuing maintenance of the data necessary for effective planning.

Several of the subprojects led to substantial proposals to funding agencies for continuation of the work initiated as a small study. The total resulting funding of information activities or research efforts generated as a result of the subprojects totalled about $800,000. The subprojects themselves served as means for identifying real, rather than hypothetical needs for information resources. In the fourth section, we will list some seventeen specific needs, together with descriptions of their implications for future planning and of the evidence provided from the subprojects.

The CLR project provided the Graduate School of Library and Information Science with a heightened visibility on campus. It also had impact on the faculty of the school and on the program of instruction. Finally, the material created from all of these efforts provides a basis for development of a text on "strategic management of academic libraries;" it is planned to develop that text in publishable form for use by both practicing librarians and library educators.

THE STRATEGIC PLANNING PROJECT

The Methodology

The Proposed Components

The project, as proposed by Graduate School of Library and Information Science GSLIS, was to be based on six major components:

1. an administrative component, to be responsible for management of all aspects of the Research Program, including the necessary logistical arrangements for the other activities;
2. an Advisory Committee to the administration of the Research Program, starting with members of the UCLA "Committee on the Library of the Future" but augmented with additional faculty and outside representatives, to be responsible both for advice with respect to the overall conduct of the program and for specific concern with those issues relating to the organization and management of information systems and services in the university including the identification of research that may need to be undertaken to resolve those issues;
3. a set of "Disciplinary Task Forces," involving faculty from specific academic areas, to be responsible for identifying the needs for information resources in their areas of interest or, as part of that work, identifying research that may need to be undertaken in order to establish those needs and the related ways in which information resources will be used;
4. a set of study activities, parallel to the Advisory Committee and the faculty task forces, to provide immediate support to their work by obtaining and analyzing currently available data concerning specific issues identified by the Advisory Committee and Disciplinary Task Forces;
5. a set of research projects, to be initiated as a result of the identification of needs for research by the Advisory Committee, the Disciplinary Task Forces, and/or the supporting study activities; and
6. an active program of communication for the purpose of making the process involved in the work of the Research Program and the results

obtained in it widely available, including a newsletter, seminars, conferences, and formal publication of both articles and monographs.

In this structure, the Advisory Committee and the Disciplinary Task Forces were to serve as the primary means for involving faculty from the broad range of university interests; the supporting studies were to be focused on meeting the needs in those groups for specific information to carry out their work. The research projects that arose from their work were to reflect gaps in the data immediately available or, it was hoped, specific research issues that were identified by participating faculty as important in their own right.

Actual Results

In principle, this methodology was followed. We will discuss specifics in subsequent paragraphs of this section of the report.

Assessment

Was the methodology successful? In the overall, no; in specific respects perhaps yes. On the negative side, as will be discussed later is this section, there were substantial problems in establishing the Disciplinary Task Forces, with only a few actually becoming effective, so the primary methodology simply was less successful than had been hoped. On the positive side, as will be discussed in the fourth section, the small-scale and research projects were reasonably successful and did indeed provide a rich picture of current and future needs for information resources on the campus.

Time Schedule

Proposed Schedule

The Research Project was proposed for four years, starting on January 1, 1986 and lasting until December 31, 1989. The first year was to be spent in developing the administrative and methodological structure and in initiating the work of Disciplinary Task Forces, studies, and research projects. The following two years, 1987 and 1988, were to be devoted to continuation of the work of the Disciplinary Task Forces, supported by specific studies, in the same pattern as planned for 1986. Beyond that, though, the major focus was to be on carrying forward work on research projects generated out of the ongoing activities. The final year, 1989, was to focus on completion of the project and any ongoing studies or research efforts.

It was proposed that there would be a conference held during 1986 to bring together a number of persons involved in projects parallel to this one.

Actual Results

The first year, calendar 1986, indeed was focused on establishment of the administrative organization, the Advisory Committee, the Disciplinary Task Forces, and the supporting study activities. Of those, the first two were virtually already in being, so the principal activities related to the substantive work in establishing task forces and supporting studies. More specifically, the first year (January 1 through December 31, 1986) was devoted to meetings with deans and faculty committees in each disciplinary area.

At the mid-point of 1986, UCLA served as host for a Research Conference at which representatives of a selected group of other universities joined with UCLA and the CLR in a discussion of the general issues of concern to the Council on Library Resources. As part of the background and content of that Research Conference, UCLA presented the approach as proposed for this project and the results obtained during the first six months. This provided a frame of reference for representatives from the other universities to explore similar, though different, approaches to the same areas of study.

By the end of 1986, while the Disciplinary Task Forces indeed has been established, only a few of them were active and effective. Attention was therefore focused on involvement of individual faculty. As a result, a number of concrete research projects were defined, to be carried out by faculty in both the substantive disciplines and the Graduate School of Library and Information Science (GSLIS). Those projects served as the focal point for work in subsequent years of the Research Program and in many cases as the basis for proposals to funding agencies.

In summer 1988, a second conference was held at UCLA bringing together about forty of the CLR Senior Fellows. It had the objective of speculating about future development of academic research libraries by creating a set of scenarios.

Assessment

In principle, the schedule as proposed was followed. The relative lack of success with the Disciplinary Task Forces, though, led to a reorientation of the focus of efforts during 1987 through 1989.

Administration

Assigned Responsibility

Administration of the Strategic Planning Project was the responsibility of Professor Robert M. Hayes, then Dean of the GSLIS. Support was limited to a part-time secretary.

Actual Results

In the third section, the means for administration will be discussed in detail, but to summarize, the project was administered as proposed, with varying amounts of time committed by Professor Hayes to it. During the first year, about 50 percent time was spent (Hayes taking a year-long sabbatical for this purpose); during the subsequent three years, the time varied from 20 percent to 25 percent, given administrative responsibilities as Dean and teaching workload as a faculty member.

Entering the final two years of the project, Hayes recommended that the administrative responsibility for the project be transferred from the GSLIS to the campus administration, specifically to the Vice Chancellor for Academic Administration. That was effected, followed shortly by the creation of a new position, Assistant Vice Chancellor for Library and Information Services Planning, subsequently to be filled by former University Librarian Russell Shank.

Assessment

It is evident that assignment of responsibility for administration of a major planning effort to a faculty member or a dean is not appropriate. Given the scope of the tasks and the centrality of the responsibility to campus and library administration, it should be vested in a full-time, continuing position. Otherwise, the pressures of other primary administrative tasks and/or teaching and individual research take precedence. Furthermore, it is only with the imprimatur of identified administrative responsibility that there is any basis for persuasion of faculty and other administrators that the work is of campus importance.

Fortunately, the planning responsibility was institutionalized in the creation of the position of Assistant Vice Chancellor for Library and Information Services Planning so that future activities will carry the weight of that position.

Advisory Committee

Membership and Proposed Role

Central to the Advisory Committee were the members of the UCLA ad hoc committee on the Library of the Future. Therefore, Executive Vice Chancellor Schaefer wrote to them asking them to serve—as persons and not as part of their responsibilities on the ad hoc campus committee. Other faculty were added to the Advisory Committee so as to assure that the objectives of extensive involvement of faculty in the project would be met. To that end, Executive Vice Chancellor Schaefer wrote the Chair of the Academic Senate, requesting nomination of faculty to serve; from the list of nominees, three were selected.

In much the same vein, it became evident, through discussion with the librarian community on campus, that added representation of librarians on the Advisory Committee is essential. To that end, Executive Vice Chancellor Schaefer wrote a letter to the Chairman of the UCLA Librarians' Association of the University of California, and two librarians were subsequently appointed.

The Advisory Committee was to serve two purposes. First was indeed that of providing general advice and guidance to the project. The second was to provide the means for review and recommendation with respect to funding of research proposals arising from the project.

Actual Results

During the first year-and-a-half, those purposes were well served. Indeed, the assistance of the Advisory Committee was crucial in dealing with the problems, as will be recounted in a moment, in gaining wide-scale faculty involvement; they were also crucial in reviewing the proposals for substantial investigations at the Disciplinary Task Force level that were initiated during the eighteen-month period. However, during the remaining two-and-a-half years, the Advisory Committee did not play a significant role.

Assessment

It is evident that an Advisory Committee of administrators, faculty, and information professionals brought together to review and recommend is crucial to a planning effort for information resources in any university. It is consistent with patterns of university administration as well as with the substantive needs in assuring broad input. That was clearly demonstrated in the first eighteen months of the Strategic Planning project.

Disciplinary Task Forces

Proposed Role

The Disciplinary Task Forces were to constitute the core of the Research Program, providing the means both for gaining faculty involvement and for learning what academic needs are or the means by which they may be determined.

The major effort during the first year of the project was indeed devoted to establishing the several working groups. The means for doing so was to meet with each of the deans on the campus, both in the Divisions of the College of Letters and Science and in the several professional schools. Each was asked to appoint a number of faculty to serve and, if possible, to involve appropriate staff from the library or other information activities of importance. It should be mentioned that the reception was universally positive. Each dean expressed the view that the objectives of the project were consistent with their own concerns in strategic planning. Subsequently, meetings were held with each of the faculty Disciplinary Task Forces as they were established.

Each Disciplinary Task Forces was asked to deal with the following types of questions, with specific attention to each area of academic program.

1. What are the current and expected future needs for information resources?
2. What are the current and expected future changes in publication and distribution of information?
3. What are the different media of importance, both currently and as expected in the future?
4. What role do the different media play in research, scholarship, and education?
5. How do faculty and students use information resources and how will they do so in the future?
6. What are the means used for access to and use of information resources?

These questions were intended to be representative, not complete or prescriptive. It was felt that some of them could be answered from the knowledge of the members of the Disciplinary Task Forces or their colleagues; some of them might require supporting studies which could be funded within the framework of the Strategic Planning project; some, though, it was expected would require the formulation of a research proposal for consideration as a formal project, funded either by the Strategic Planning project or by an external agency.

The task forces were to try to consider the "20-year context" for the following issues:

- the future needs for library and other information support in the specific academic program area;
- the future of publication and communication in that area;
- the future role of the library and its collection;
- the future of computers, communication, and other technology;
- the future for information personnel;
- the future for facilities and equipment; and
- the future for economic resources.

And within that 20-year context, the task forces were asked to consider the following specific concerns for the coming 5-year period:

- collection development, management, and organizations;
- facilities and automation development; and
- financial requirements.

Actual Results

It must be said that in only a few cases were the Disciplinary Task Forces effective and even in those few cases it was because of the efforts of single individual faculty or of the librarians and other information professionals. To be specific, the Disciplinary Task Force in the Anderson Graduate School of Management led to the study of integration of libraries, computing, and telecommunications in the design of the new AGSM building; it was undertaken by the director of the AGSM computing facility and the AGSM librarian. The one in the School of Architecture and Urban Planning led to the study of the needs for information resources for the school by a faculty member. The one in the School of Medicine was especially effective as a part of that school's overall effort at strategic planning, and the Biomedical Librarian played a central role in that planning effort.

But those were the only cases in which there was effective result from the Disciplinary Task Forces.

Assessment

It must be said that in proposing this approach, there were high hopes for it as a means to gain faculty involvement in a strategic planning process. The lack of effectiveness reflects the reality of academic life. Faculty must focus their attention on their specific teaching responsibilities and on their own, self-identified areas of research. Issues of importance to campus administration, to management of libraries and computing facilities, and to long-range planning for information resources are regarded by most faculty as "part of the woodwork." It is only when they experience personal problems that they will want to devote attention to the perceived cause of them.

This problem of involving faculty in activities that librarians and administrators may perceive as vitally important is not unique to UCLA. Just to illustrate: Among the subprojects was one concerned with the impact of "copyright policies" on faculty interests. That study obtained copies of about 150 policy statements from both librarians and administrators of about 100 major universities, and analyzed them in terms of relative restrictiveness and the means for formulation. Of them, despite the vital effect of such policies on academic programs, only six directly involved faculty in their formulation.

(Speaking as a former dean, I must in retrospect say that I should not have been so naive. I already had ample evidence of the fact that faculty will focus their attention on their own responsibilities, and rightly so.)

Supporting Studies

Proposed Role

It was expected that, in cases in which an ad hoc study might be able to serve the needs of the Advisory Committee or a Disciplinary Task Force, the Strategic Planning project would establish a supporting study, with graduate students as Research Assistants working under the direction of faculty of the university carrying forward the study. Some studies might involve staff of the University Library System, the Office of Academic Computing, and other facilities responsible for archives of various kinds.

A supporting study was expected to involve assembly of a bibliography or of relevant data, a statistical analysis of available data, and a brief survey (such as a polling of faculty with respect to a question). It might involve writing to external sources to obtain data that is available for them. It might involve a brief experiment to determine the effectiveness of some tool. It might involve preparation of a position paper, with identification and evaluation of alternatives. It might involve an analysis of transaction data from online catalog operations.

The point is that a supporting study was expected to be brief in time, limited in scope, and based on readily available data (frequently on data that are published). It should be within the capability of graduate Research Assistants, working under suitable faculty direction.

Actual Results

Two categories of Supporting Study were ultimately identified: generic studies and specific studies. The first category included studies that appeared to have wide applicability across the campus; the second included those that were specific to particular disciplines.

The generic supporting studies included: (1) a survey of scholarly and professional publishers for the purpose of determining their current plans and future expectations with respect to publication in CD-ROM (i.e., "compact disk, read-only memory") formats which clearly affects disciplines across the entire campus; and (2) a review of the impact of copyright and contractual limits on the scholarly use of information resources which involved identifying the administrative policies implemented by various universities to deal with constraints on the ability of faculty to use such resources.

There were no supporting studies generated as a result of the needs of the Disciplinary Task Forces, even though it was expected that, as the Disciplinary Task Forces began their own work, a number of specific supporting studies would be requested and initiated.

Assessment

Supporting studies have value in the context of the central administration of a planning effort, not in a dispersed responsibility.

Research Projects

Proposed Role

The development of research projects under the direction of faculty and/ or librarians or other information professionals at UCLA was one of the primary objectives of the project. This reflected the hope that there would be identification of problems of substantial interest to faculty from a variety of disciplines.

Because the funds directly available from the project budget were limited, it was expected that they would be used for relatively small projects or for the pilot phases of larger projects (as preparation for proposals to other funding sources).

It was expected that proposals would grow out of the work of the several Disciplinary Task Forces or from discussions with individual faculty and/or information professionals on campus. It was felt that other proposals might result from the need for pilot studies to develop projects in response to opportunities provided by other funding agencies.

Actual Results

As the lack of effectiveness of the Disciplinary Task Forces as a means for conduct of the planning process became evident, the Advisory Committee recommended that direct approach be made to the campus-wide faculty. Based on that recommendation, two direct mailings were made to every member of the faculty of the campus. Each of them identified the objectives of the project and announced the availability of funds to support individual investigations. Two levels of funding were described: small projects (on the order of $1,500 to $3,000), suitable for a graduate student working under faculty direction, and larger projects (on the order of $15,000 to $30,000), involving major efforts by the faculty member(s) involved. Expenditures were not generally allowed for purchase of equipment, travel, or augmentation of faculty salaries but if a suitable proposal demonstrated real value in such expenditures, they would be funded. They were allowed for graduate student support and for expenses involved in the conduct of investigations.

The result was submission, during an eighteen-month period, of about forty proposals, most of which were approved. They will be summarized in the fourth section of this report.

Assessment

It should be said that these efforts were not "cutting edge" studies as far as advancing our knowledge of information technologies, information services, or librarianship is concerned. They were all very pragmatic, current, and immediate. This does not diminish their importance, though; instead it highlights the necessity of distinguishing between the perceptions of the information professionals and those of the faculty as users.

This is a valuable and effective means for determining from faculty what their real needs are. It is relatively inexpensive, especially if most of the efforts are in the "small project" funding range, but it does provide concrete evidence of needs. Furthermore, it can be very effective in generating proposals for funding from external agencies.

Communications

Proposed Role

A central objective of the project was to communicate both the process and the results in ways that would assist the university community at large in determining how to proceed with this kind of strategic planning. To that end, a variety of means for communication were to be implemented.

Actual Results

A publicity release was distributed to appropriate media—professional and general. Another form of general publicity was represented by the Newsnotes in the *Library Newsletter/UCLA*. A different form of general publicity was provided by opportunities for formal talks given in various professional contexts. These included presentations to the OCLC Academic Libraries Advisory Committee, IFLA, a number of professional library meetings, librarians in academic libraries, and faculty of library schools. Perhaps thirty such talks were given during the past four years. Generally, the title of the talk was: "Strategic Planning for Information Resources in the Research University: A Report on a Project and its Implications."

Every effort was made to communicate the nature, purpose, and current status of the project throughout the UCLA campus community, both academic and professional. Presentations were made to the UCLA Academic Senate Library Committee, the ad hoc Committee on the Library of the Future, the Office of Academic Computing, UCLA LAUC, faculty and professionals concerned with the several "media archives," faculty and staff in specific areas of instruction, and groups of faculty identified by each dean. A newsletter was distributed twice, as part of the effort to gain the participation of individual faculty.

The GSLIS has a continuing program of colloquia and other formal talks presented by distinguished academics and professionals. Some of these were closely related to the objectives of the project. To be specific: colloquia were presented by Visiting Professor Donald Lamberton from Australia on "Information Economics;" a colloquium was presented by Edward Huth, editor of the *Journal of Internal Medicine*, on the topic "Electronic Publication."

There was a conference in early September 1986 for the purpose of discussion among a few interested universities on possible approaches to long-range, strategic planning for information resources in the research university. The UCLA project was to be used as an example, but the primary purpose was to gain the benefit of general discussion. A second conference was held in summer 1988 involving about forty of the UCLA/CLR Senior Fellows in a three-day examination of alternative scenarios for strategic planning for the future of academic libraries.

MANAGEMENT OF THE CLR PROJECT

The CLR sponsored project was carried forward as a campus effort, though administratively centered in the Graduate School of Library and Information Science. It involved the university administration at the level of Vice Chancellors (for Academic Affairs and for Research); it involved the university library at the levels of University Librarian (Russell Shank and now, Gloria Werner), Associate University Librarians, and major unit heads. It led to creation of the new position of Assistant Vice Chancellor for Library and Information Services Planning.

The actual administrative responsibility for the CLR project, however, was centered in Professor Robert M. Hayes, who served as Principal Investigator. The management staff was minimal—one part-time administrative assistant— so the overhead costs for administration were minimal. Administration involved two component efforts: overall management and management of project studies.

It is important to reiterate that the CLR project was not the means for conduct of the campus program in strategic management and planning. In fact, campus and library planning continued as they had in the past, as conscious active efforts. The project in that respect was merely ancillary, providing a means by which specific studies relating to overall planning could be initiated without complicating ongoing campus planning activities.

Management of Subprojects

Actual Results

The CLR Project was carried out through a large number of individual studies, each the responsibility of a faculty member of the university or a professional librarian or information professional. Specific subprojects will be reviewed in the fourth section, along with other sources of data for assessment of information resource needs of academic programs.

The projects fell into two categories: small (with funding on the order of $1,500 to $3,000) and large (with funding on the order of $15,000 to $30,000). The former were approved based on simple proposals—a letter or a one- to two-page description; approval of them was made at the discretion of the Principal Investigator. The latter were approved on the basis of a more extensive, but still fairly limited, proposal; they were reviewed by a subcommittee of the Advisory Committee and then approval was based on their recommendation and the discretion of the Principal Investigator.

Conduct of any project, including the mechanisms for reporting results, was treated as the responsibility of the faculty member or librarian conducting the study. Financial accounting was handled either by transfer of funds, in the amount approved for the project, or by the administrative offices of the Principal Investigator. (Most of the accounting was handled by transfer of funds in order to reduce the bureaucratic burden.)

It was the hope that subprojects might lead to the development of proposals for much larger levels of funding from other agencies. That turned out to be the case in at least the following subprojects.

- The project with the School of Engineering, in the area of information needs for research on Hazardous Substances, led to inclusion of an information center as part of the proposal to the National Science Foundation; that large program was subsequently funded by NSF, including explicit funding for the information center, at a level of $120,000 per year for the five-year period of the contract.
- The project with the Center for Medieval and Renaissance Studies, concerned with the information resource needs of the potential program for preparation of the *Repertorium Columbianum*, was an integral part of the work in preparing the proposal to the National Endowment for the Humanities for support of that project; the work for the first set of volumes, including the information support tools, was funded by NEH.
- The project with the Anderson Graduate School of Management, concerned with means for integrating the library, computer facility, and telecommunications of AGSM became a central component of the architectural planning for the new AGSM building.
- The project with the Center for African Studies, concerned with development of a bibliography in the area of politics, led to a proposal for funding of that effort by the Defense Intelligence Agency; that project at a level of $80,000.
- The project within the Graduate School for Library and Information Science, concerned with the need for materials to instruct Latin American

librarians in the use of microcomputers, was funded by Unesco at a level of $20,000.

- The project within the Graduate School for Library and Information Science, concerned with university and academic library copyright policies, was incorporated in a project of the Association of Research Libraries. It also led to creation of an administrative committee at UCLA to review federal activities is such areas.
- The several projects concerned with data conversion led to a project funded by the National Agricultural Library within the Graduate School for Library and Information Science funded by the National Agricultural Library at a level of $20,000, concerned with evaluating optical scanning equipment and CLR software.

The preparation of proposals for such major funding was certainly one of the major benefits of the overall project.

Assessment

Overall, the several studies and research efforts were successful both in their identified objectives of involving faculty in the strategic planning efforts, in the generation of proposals for more substantial funding, and in providing the data on which strategic planning could be based.

Project Data Files

Actual Results

To manage the UCLA Strategic Planning project, a number of data files were established that served as means to control the exceptionally wide range of activities involved.

Persons. The data file on Persons served both as means for management of the project, for identifying the roles of individuals, and for communication with them. Each record in the file included data for name, title, address, telephone number, and links to all other files (Academic Programs, Facilities, Projects, and External Environment). The linkages to other files, in a relational database structure, permit bringing together relevant data for each person that is contained in them, without redundancy or inconsistency.

Academic Programs. The purpose of the Academic Programs data file is to provide means for identifying individual units (schools and departments, organized research units, and others). Each record included data for name, responsibility, budget, and staff. Links with the other data files (Facilities,

Projects, Persons, and External Environment) again permit bringing together relevant data; of special importance is the linkages to the Persons file, in the identification of the responsible manager.

Facilities. The purpose of the Facilities data file is to provide means for identifying several information facilities (libraries, computers, media centers, archives, and other kinds); for each of them, recognition of system, department, and other categories was provided for. The records in this file identified the name of the facility, the responsible person (by linkage to the Persons file), budget, and staff. Linkages to the other data files (Persons, Academic Programs, Projects, and External Environments) provided means for relating relevant data.

Projects. The Projects data file was the most central for management purposes, given the methodology used. Its purpose was to provide for means of identifying relevant research projects, wherever they may have been carried out, and tie-in of Principal Investigators or possible researchers of the subprojects of this particular Strategic Planning project; it also provided means for distribution of communications. Each record identified the project by name and identified the responsible person (linking to the Persons file), the assigned budget, and related staff (again by linkage to the Persons file). Some records in this file were specific to subprojects within this project (both supporting studies and research efforts); others related to projects funded elsewhere. Of course, links to the other files (Persons, Facilities, Academic Programs, and External Environment) provide means for relating relevant data.

At a very early stage in the Strategic Planning project, data were obtained from the UCLA Office of Contracts and Grants for all funded projects on the campus that related to information needs. Of the some 2,500 total grants to UCLA, over 10 percent either generating information files (in the specific sense, not in some generalized sense) or were acquiring them for purposes of analysis. The funding of that 10 percent or more was an even greater percentage of the total external contract and grant funding.

External Environment. The data file on the External Environment has the purpose to tie-in data about relevant literature, technological forecasting, political and societal forces, the status of publishing, and so forth. The records provide both bibliographic references and technical details. Again, links to the other files provide means for relating relevant data.

Assessment

It is absolutely essential that any strategic planning effort be based on adequate current data files using the most sophisticated data base management software.

SPECIFIC RESULTS

Internal Top Management Concerns

Administrative Structure

A paramount strategic concern is the administrative structure for information resource management. Does the campus establish a "czar" for information, with operating responsibility for the entire set of resources and facilities? Does the campus subsume the computing facility under library management, or vice versa? Does one merge film archives or data archives into the library? Does one assign responsibility for management of the media center to the university library?

There are good arguments for any of these alternatives or perhaps others. For example, establishing an information czar would be consistent with the view that information resources are essentially substitutable for each other. Placing computing and libraries under one manager makes great sense if the perception is that electronic means for information distribution will become the dominant form in the future. Merging various kinds of libraries and archives makes sense if one looks only at the similarities among media.

The arguments for distributed management, leaving aside the issue of management style which we will examine in a moment, seem exceptionally persuasive. First, the different kinds of information resources require different kinds of management and technical expertise; there is no reason, in principle, to expect that one person will be insufficiently expert in each of them. Second, most information facilities, the library and the computing facility among them, are already major bureaucracies; there is no reason to expect that there would be returns to scale in combining them. Third, most of the information resources are closely tied to specific academic programs; the political and operational problems that would be created by combining them in some overall agency far outweigh the advantages to be gained from doing so. Fourth, the acquisition budget of the library must be carefully protected from a wide range of forces that would dissipate it; if the library were to be combined with data archives, film archives, media centers, and the wide range of other resource acquiring agencies, the result would be a dramatic increase in those pressures.

The facts, though, are that the administrative structures reflect the style of the institution rather than the logic of similarities. Where the style is hierarchical, with strong lines of authority, one might expect to find an information czar. But where the style is for distributed decision making, one would expect to find independent administrative units working within a coordinated, cooperative framework.

At UCLA, the style is for delegation, for distributed responsibility in decision making with the requisite authority. The result is that the several information agencies on campus function either as independent administrative agencies or under the management of the relevant academic unit, school, college, or department. In such a distributed style of management, coordination is important, of course, so the Academic Vice Chancellor has been assigned that responsibility, together with the Assistant Vice Chancellor for Library and Information Services Planning. Each of these assignments has been made within the past two years, reflecting the recognition that planning must be institutionalized at the highest level of administration.

Personnel Policies

Another concern of campus administration should be appropriate personnel policies. There is need to assure equity across the range of information professionals—librarians, media specialists, computer staff, and archivists of every kind. The need is especially acute in a decentralized administration, because independent units may otherwise make appointments and promotions that meet the needs of the local unit but are at odds with overall equity and even with real needs in performance.

Generally, the standards for professional librarians in this respect are quite well established and effectively applied. But in most universities there are no comparable policies for other categories of information professional. This is an area of administration that needs to be carefully examined in every institution.

Needs of Academic Programs

Paramount among management concerns is the relationship to campus strategic planning and the role of information resources in it. To what extent do the objectives of the institution and of the units within it depend on each kind of information resource? What are the needs of the constituencies to be served by the information resources? Normally, in market analyses, one is concerned with stimulating or creating demand, with renewal and revitalization of demand. In the academic environment, though, the objective is to identify the needs in specific areas of academic responsibility: instruction, research, public services, and service to local industry. Indeed, the faculty needs, in instruction and research, were the primary concern of the CLR project. Of special interest were the effects of changes in the process of teaching and research, changes in the process of disciplinary communication, and the needs for new forms of information. It is those issues that were the primary concern of the CLR project at UCLA; they will be summarized in later subsections.

External Top Management Concerns

The other crucial component of strategic management is the external environment. In the following sections we will describe the environment for strategic planning for information resources in the research university in the following categories: (1) publishing; (2) political, social policy, legislative and legal; (3) cooperative programs; and technological. Each of these environmental elements is so some extent supportive of the interests of the university and research library, but each of them is also to some extent resistant to those interests.

Publishing

Print. While the role of the publishers may appear to be self-evident, it is important to recognize that print publication is still the primary source of information resources. Of paramount importance is the dependence of the library on the decisions made by publishers about what will be published and about its format. In a later subsection we will comment specifically on the implications for print publishing.

Other Media. The library community has been at the forefront in development of new formats, with the experiments by the Library of Congress, the National Library of Medicine, and the National Agricultural Library as specific examples. To explore that, a CLR subproject was conducted early in 1986 on CD-ROM publication. It revealed that three years ago, in 1986, about 75 percent of CD-ROM publications were specific to library operations (i.e., abstracts and bibliographic data files); in 1988, it was 60 percent; it is estimated that by 1990 it will be less than 40 percent (according to a ComputerWorld report on June 5, 1989). Text files and raw reference data (such as pricing and financial data) are rapidly becoming the dominating kinds of content.

The federal government is moving rapidly into this form of publication. For example, the Defense Mapping Agency is mastering six disks per day; it will published 860 CD-ROM titles in 1989/1990. The Defense Logistics Agency is publishing hazardous materials information in CD-ROM format; the U.S. Patent and Trademark Abstracts will be distributed to Patent Depository Libraries six times per year in CD-ROM format.

The implications are clear: Optical media promise to become significant means for publication of materials important to academic functions. The pace of growth needs to be continuously determined, and this study provides a starting point for doing so. The range of disciplines shown in the study presents some issues of tactical importance in planning for acquisitions, equipment support, training, and other operational support. There are also implications for the design and use of workstations.

Still, though, the mainstream publishers of books and journals are moving into this form of publication very slowly, very cautiously. That means that there is much uncertainty about when, or even whether, library materials will be available in this form.

Pricing Policies. The CLR project did not consider any of the effects of the pricing policies of publishers, but they have such critical importance to strategic planning that we must make note of them. The massive rates of inflation experienced in the price of journals, especially foreign commercial journals in the physical and biological science, has produced a catastrophic situation for every major research library of the country. It has even resulted in a court case—"Journal Publisher Sues Author of Price Study" (*American Libraries,* September 1989, pp. 717-718)—as at least one publisher has tried to counter reports that profits of publishers increased exorbitantly.

The implications of this for strategic planning are multiple. They get to the heart of allocation of resources among academic programs, as commitments of acquisition budgets to journals of value to the sciences force reductions in purchases of the monographs of value to the humanities. Furthermore, the nature of serial publications is that they represent commitments not just for today but for the foreseeable future.

Political, Social Policy, Legislative, and Legal

In areas such as copyright, federal policies on access to governmental information, privatization of governmental functions, the actions of Congress and the president create the environment within which academic responsibilities must be carried out.

Campus Committee on Federal Communication. In the course of the project, several issues were identified that related primarily to factors outside the university itself and yet which have dramatic effect on the ability of faculty and information professionals to use information resources effectively in carrying out the university's responsibilities. These external factors need to be identified and means created by which the university's needs and obligations can be recognized in the political processes that lead to policy decisions at a national and state level. Recognition has been given in the UCLA administration of the need for UCLA to establish means for such strategic planning, with the establishment of an administrative committee.

Copyright. Intellectual property rights are of two-fold importance to the academic community—as owners and as users of copyrighted material. The development of policies to deal with those rights is a matter of current concern in universities throughout the country.

As CLR subproject determined the policies of major universities with respect to copyright. A survey was sent to all Association of Research Libraries (ARL) and AAU institutions, to both the library and the university's legal counsel. Replies were received from all but two of those institutions and, in most cases, from both the library and the counsel. The results became the basis for a SPEC Kit distributed by the Association of Research Libraries. The subproject was, to some extent, triggered by the effects of a University of California system-wide policy greatly restricting off-air taping of audio and video broadcasts. The question was whether such policies adequately reflected the needs and responsibilities of the academic enterprise, on the needs for information and the effects of copyright policies on academic research and teaching. As I have indicated one of the revealing facts was the minimal role played by faculty in the formulation of these policies, despite the crucial effect they have on teaching and research.

Access to Information. During the past decade, the policies of the executive branch of the federal government have been to reduce access to and availability of information of virtually every kind—from scientific and technical to economic and demographic. The effects on libraries and other information organizations have been so severe that the professional associations have felt forced to take stands on access to information." The Information Industry Association, the Medical Library Association, the Association of Law Libraries, the Association of Research libraries—each has come out with official policy statements of concern about federal restrictions. The restrictive policies affect not only the information provided but they stifle scholarship. The Handbook of Labor Statistics, International Economic Indicators, Federal Statistical Directory, Vital Statistics of U.S., American Education, and electronic databases—have all been affected. Beyond that have been conscious efforts at control of information, film censorship, and even efforts at disinformation (lying). It has been characterized as "less access to less information by and about the U.S. government" by the ALA.

At the same time, the commercialization and privatization of government information has led to other means of control, as federal agencies have pressed data base firms to curb access to "sensitive" information.

A CLR subproject in the Graduate School of Library and Information Science was focused on the effects of limits placed on academic access to information resources. It led to the establishment of a First Amendment Information Resources center. The view was that of all external policies, those that deliberately restrict the scope and freedom of inquiry are the ones that strike at the very heart of the academic enterprise. It is essential that there be a complete awareness of those kinds of political, social, and judicial restraints. The subproject established means of maintenance of files that will document the facts about restrictive policies.

Cooperative Programs

The library community has a long tradition of cooperation. It is represented by interlibrary loan, by the development of cooperative cataloguing through the Library of Congress and the bibliographic utilities (OCLC and RLIN), the Center for Research Libraries depository center, the preservation program, and a wide range of consortia and networks.

These cooperative enterprises have value, as represented by the sharing of resources through interlibrary loan, but they also have costs, both financial and in loss of institutional prerogatives.

There were no CLR subprojects concerned with any aspect of cooperation.

Technological

It hardly seems necessary at this point to comment on the role of information technologies in modern information distribution. They pervade every aspect of library operations and services; computer facilities embody them; other kinds of information facilities either use them or represent them.

In the same vein, the implications of the information technologies for strategic planning have dominated this report. There is need to consider the changes occurring with computers, as they become ever more capable, smaller, yet less expensive. The changes occurring in data storage, in data input and output, and in data communication all need to be considered.

There were no CLR subproject that specifically considered the technological environment; no specific effort was taken to predict or even to speculate on the direction or pace of future development.

Needs for Print Publications: Books, Journals, Manuscripts

Information Need

An issue of current debate is whether print form publications will continue to be viable and an important means for information distribution. Some have claimed that we will become a "paperless society," with electronic means for communication replacing print. Others have pointed to the fact that the effect of the computer, FAX, and other new media has been to *increase* the role of paper, not diminish it.

There was no explicit CLR subproject that answered this question. But, as we will detail, the implications of several subprojects are clear, direct, and unequivocal: *Print is still an essential medium for scholarship and scholarly communication.*

It is also evident that the information technologies and the new media must be considered in planning, not only in their own right but as essential adjuncts and supplements to the printed formats.

Implications for Strategic Planning

The implications for strategic planning lie in virtually every area: Collection development policies must still deal with print media as the major commitment of acquisition budgets. Resources must still be committed to buildings. The qualifications of professional staff must still emphasize knowledge of print materials. There is need for equipment to relate print media with computer-based media.

It is important that we establish some basis for projecting the likely rate of print publication and of library acquisitions of them. Historically, as shown in the study by Fremont Rider in 1944 and by Purdue studies by Oliver Dunn and Keith Dowden starting in 1965, the collections of major academic libraries had for well over 100 years increased at exponential rates, doubling within 15 to 20 years. Will that continue to be the case? Well, a more recent update by Warren Seibert of the NIM suggests not. In fact, it shows that for the past 20 years that historic trend has changed dramatically. We have seen virtually a 'steady-state" in the rate of addition for medium to large ARL libraries (ranging from 1000,000 to 150,000 volumes per year), and an actual decline in the rate of addition for the smaller ARL (steadily going down from about 80,000 to about 60,000 volumes per year). The decline for the small libraries can be directly attributed to the effects of network sharing of resources, with the smaller libraries depending on the larger for guaranteed access.

To what can we attribute this change from historic patterns, and is it likely to continue? There are at least six possible explanations, with the likelihood being that all of them are operative. First, rates of inflation in academic acquisition costs have been substantially greater than the average augmentation of the acquisition budgets; that forces a reduced rate of accession. Second, many large institutions stopped construction of library buildings for that 20-year period; that probably forced librarians to be much more limited in their acquisition policies. Third, the great period in which collections were available to be acquired, which made it possible to easily increase the size of collections, seems to have ended; that means it is much more difficult to sustain rates of increase. Fourth, the increased dependence on sharing of resources, which served to drive so many of the technological and organizational developments of the past 20 years, has reduced the dependence on local resources, especially for the smaller institutions. Fifth, the effects of new, technological means for access has led some libraries to use the acquisition budget, to fund the costs of these newer means for information access, with the view that they substitute for the need for collection development; that clearly reduces the funds available. Sixth, there were significant changes in political policy that reduced the availability of publications, such as those from government sources.

The pattern of the past 20 years appears likely to continue for the coming decade at least and probably for the next 20 years. We will see steady-state levels of acquisition by all academic libraries—at 150,000 for large libraries, 100,000 for medium, and 60,000 for small. It is possible that increasing rates of publication from foreign countries, especially developing ones, may change that picture, but probably not for the coming 10 years at least.

CLR Subprojects and Other Relevant Activities

What evidence did the CLR project at UCLA develop in response to this issue? It must be repeated that none of the projects explicitly considered the question: answers to it must therefore be derived by implications rather than direct evidence. Here we will list the subprojects in the CLR project at UCLA that to one extent or another relate to this issue and discuss the evidence from each that bears on this question: the Bibliography of African Studies, Rarely Taught Languages, the *Repertorium Columbianum*, Hazardous Substance Research, and Preservation.

Bibliography of African Studies. This subproject was concerned with development of computer-based methods for producing the newest edition of a *Bibliography for the Study of African Politics*. More generally, though, it provided an illustration of a serious problem for researchers concerned with area studies—the difficulty in getting access to materials from the countries of the developing world. The entire substantive focus of the bibliography is on print materials; there are no other media of current significance to it, though in the future other media may become important.

The crucial point with respect to the role of *print* as a medium for scholarly research and communication is that it is still essential. The source materials covered by the bibliography are in print, and for the foreseeable future will continue to be so.

A second relevant point is that new means for information distribution are also represented by this project, but in support roles. Specifically, the main focus of the CLR funded effort (which led to a proposal for a separately funded program) was on application of computer-based methods to the production and distribution of the data base for the bibliography. A standard data base language was used; data storage eventually was on WORM equipment, funded by the separate project; the campus ORION system served as a major source of bibliographic data (about *print* sources); the CD-ROM from *Dissertation Abstracts* served as a source of data about those print and microform publications.

Rarely Taught Languages. This project was concerned with means for obtaining access to materials from foreign countries needed to support instruction in rarely taught languages. While the full range of media, including video and audio tapes, was of concern, the major focus was on *print* materials.

Repertorium Columbianum. Throughout the *Repertorium Columbianum* project (to be described later), the entire substantive focus is on *print* materials: The sources for translation are in paper form, either print or manuscript; the final product was to be in print form.

Computer-based methods for information handling played a critical role in the project, and were the focus of concern in the CLR subproject, in fact, as we will discuss later. But the implication is clear: print and paper-based records are crucial to this project.

Hazardous Substance Research. This project was concerned with development of an information center in support of Hazardous Substance Research. While a full range of information sources was to be included—from computer data bases to image files—the primary concern was with printed journals, reports, and books.

Preservation. A pair of related projects, funded by the CLR, examined the magnitude of the problem of brittle books, the alternative means for solution of it and the related costs, and the benefits to be derived from ensuring continued access to them and their contents. The evidence from the examination of benefits was clear and unequivocal: preservation of these print materials is crucial to research throughout the university, from the humanities and fine arts to the sciences.

Among the alternative means examined by one of the related projects was the use of digitized images. Again, the new technologies serve as supplements to the print, as means for dealing with specific problems but not as replacements.

Integration of Library, Computer, and Telecommunications

Information Need

It is evident that libraries, computing facilities, and telecommunications must be integrated with each other. While that does not require or even imply single point management for them, it does require that they each function with conscious awareness of the others. It requires their parallel development be coordinated, and that policies be established that will encourage effective cooperation.

Implications for Strategic Planning

The strategic significance of three projects at UCLA is great. They each represented, in a microcosm, the comparable larger scale problems for the university as a whole. They each raised, and resolved, important issues related to organization (How does one bring together resources that have divergent administrative reporting paths?), facilities (How does one plan buildings and space around coordinated information resources?), and staffing (How does one manage a diverse array of information professionals in a coordinated set of services?)

CLR Subprojects and Other Relevant Activities

Several of the CLR subprojects and other relevant activities, especially those initiated by professional schools, were concerned with integrating the range of information facilities and resources specific to their interests. Three such studies are of special significance: the Anderson Graduate School of Management, the School of Architecture and Urban Planning, and the School of Medicine.

Anderson Graduate School of Management. A small supporting study was initiated as a cooperative effort of the Strategic Planning Project and the Anderson Graduate School of Management; it led to a formal proposal for a larger scale research project. The objective was to identify the needs of faculty and students of the GSM for an integrated information facility, combining library, computing, and telecommunications.

This study effort then related directly to the planning process for the new building for the AGSM; it involved solution of tactical issues in relating the library, the computer, and the telecommunications network of the GSM to the design of that building and to the needs of faculty and students.

School of Architecture and Urban Planning. This subproject was focused on the information resources needed to support teaching and research in the fields of architecture and urban planning. It represents a number of issues of strategic importance—integration of computer facilities and libraries with academic programs, special needs for graphics and computer processing, and special ties with community professionals.

School of Medicine. The strategic planning effort within the School of Medicine was carried out quite independent of the CLR project, without any identifiable contribution from it (except as might have been involved in subprojects to be described later). However, the implications of that effort are still relevant for the objectives of the CLR project. It dealt primarily with the academic programs of the School of Medicine, but the role of the Bio-Medical library, support to computer use, and telecommunications were explicitly recognized.

Interinstitutional Cooperation

Information Need

Much of academic research today involves cooperation among multiple institutions. This creates special demands for information support, in communication, in the use of shared data bases, and in access to common materials.

Implications for Strategic Planning

Interinstitutional cooperation implies commitment of resources and, to a significant degree, loss of independence. It also implies basing some of one's own institutional long-range planning on expectations that others will fulfill their responsibilities. An issue, therefore, is the extent to which the individual institution should support the National Research Network.

CLR Subprojects and Other Relevant Activities

Several CLR subprojects related directly to this kind of information need: the *Repertorium Columbianum* project of the Center for Medieval and Renaissance Studies, programs of the Center for Latin American Studies, and programs for Training Foreign Librarians.

Center for Medieval and Renaissance Studies. A subproject within the Center for Medieval and Renaissance Studies was focused on the needs for information resources to support development of the *Repertorium Columbianum*. A supporting study was initiated, involving a graduate student in the center, to examine those needs. The result was the decision to establish a collaborative effort between the Center for Medieval and Renaissance Studies and the Graduate School of Library and Information Science toward the development of proposals for the management of the overall project for the *Repertorium Columbianum* and for production of Volume 12, the index to the entire publication.

This project represents a major multinational, multi-institutional effort of substantial visibility and importance. It illustrates the needs for information resources not only as part of the substance but as the basis for management of such efforts. It will draw on both library and computer resources. There is clear need for development of a capability to support faculty with managerial tools for scheduling, financial control, logistical control, and intellectual control of large-scale projects. This is especially significant in the humanities, in which such projects are relatively rare. The *Repertorium Columbianum* project provides a clear example of the needs for information resource support to interinstitutional research projects.

Latin American Universities. There is an active effort at UCLA to build relationships with universities in other countries. A specific example is with those in Brazil, in which information resources play an especially central role— the development of computer communication with Brazil, the sharing of library cataloging data with the University of São Paulo, and the study in specific academic areas (as well be detailed later). More generally, these kinds of efforts have been initiated in several of the Latin American countries under the aegis of the Center for Latin American Studies.

Training Foreign Librarians. The Graduate School of Library and Information Science, together with the ORION User Services Office are repeatedly in the position of needing to provide institutional services in support of training foreign librarians. One of the subprojects of the CLR program has been focused on means for meeting those needs, using the example of librarians from Brazil. Another led to funding from Unesco of a training manual for the use of microcomputers in Latin American libraries and other information activities.

Department of Neurology. This subproject was focused on the development of a microcomputer-based system for management of a patient record file of data on surgery for epilepsy. It represents a context of multi-institutional cooperation, with the need to establish standards and procedures for the creation and maintenance of data files of critical importance to all levels of academic responsibility—teaching, research, and public service. It demonstrates that there is need for a consulting service for faculty needing to establish interinstitutional data files.

Acquisition of Foreign Materials

Information Need

The acquisition of information materials from foreign countries is a problem especially acute with respect to the world's "developing areas," representing large populations and vast geographic areas about which our knowledge is at best fragmentary. Academic interests require active research programs in several areas of concern with respect to developing countries: language and literature, society and economy, agriculture and industry, medicine and health, and the arts and sciences.

Implications for Strategic Planning

In the summary report on language and area studies, *Beyond Growth,* prepared by the Association of American Universities, library and information resources were identified as a crucial problem. Among the specific issues of concern were five that are especially relevant to strategic planning for information resources.

1. There is a shortage of staff with the professional competencies in both language and area studies, on the one hand, and library and information management, on the other.
2. Except for the activities of the three national libraries—the Library of Congress, the National Library of Medicine, and the National Agricultural Library—there is almost no sharing of foreign information resources between government and academic research programs.
3. There is no inventory of foreign materials in library collections, of periodical subscriptions, federal government information services, nor the extent to which any of these materials are covered by indexing and abstracting services or online information services.
4. There is no general information concerning availability of foreign information resources from governmental agencies or of restrictions on their use.
5. There is no evidence of the utilization by government agencies of foreign information resources available in university library collections or even of the awareness of such resources.

Beyond Growth recommends specific efforts be undertaken to deal with the problems, especially in recognition of the technological changes occurring in the means for acquiring, storing, accessing, and distributing of library materials and other forms of information resources. The report emphasizes the need to pay special attention to ephemera that tend not to be integrated into library collections.

The report focused on these kinds of problems within the United States, but it is important to note that they are even more critical in the developing countries themselves. Many of them lack adequate knowledge of the information about their own countries and their neighbors, not even to consider information about the United States. They have poor or nonexistent means to identify publications; they lack means for logistical support for modern information technologies; they do not have the professional information manpower to provide adequate information services.

CLR Subprojects and Other Relevant Activities

A number of CLR subprojects were initiated to examine this area: in the Center for African Studies, the Center for Language Education and Research, and the Center for Latin American Studies.

Center for African Studies.   As described above, the generic concern of the study undertaken in the Center for African Studies is on the needs for information resources in support of "developing countries research." This includes the needs both for academic research in the United States and for developing countries themselves. Issues include needs for professional staff qualified to develop such resources, statistical data about availability of information resources in the United States, in particular geographical areas and subject, the forms any kinds of information resources needed, and the use of such data in support of research and teaching.

This project has strategic significance, cutting across almost the·entire array of potential goals. There are immediate tactical implications in the need for further development of the UCLA Library's ORION system, both technically (to meet the needs in support of projects) and staffing (to provide training and consulting services). There are operational implications in the establishment of a capability to produce a specialized bibliography, using a mixture of personal computers, the ORION system, external data services, and UCLA library resources.

Center for Language Education and Research.   A focus of concern in the Center for Language Education and Research is on the needs for information resources in support of research and instruction in "rarely taught languages." Issues include the form and availability of such materials and the means for gaining access to them.

This project has multiple strategic significance, cutting across almost the entire array of potential goals. There are immediate tactical implications in the need for further development of the UCLA Library's ORION system, both technically (to meet the needs in support of projects) and staffing (to provide training and consulting services). Of specific technical concern are the problems of dealing with complex diacritics in the data files of the Center for Applied Linguistics; that is a problem that has much wider implications, though. There are immediate operational implications in the establishment of a capability to provide access to data files through the UCLA ORION system.

Center for Latin American Studies.   This subproject had several foci: the use of computer networks for communication with Latin American countries, the need for training materials for preparing information workers in the use of microcomputers and computer networks in Latin American countries, and the maintenance of statistical data files on those countries. One effort led to the contract from Unesco, through the International Federation of Library Associations, for the development of a training package for computer use by information workers in Latin American countries. Publication of *Statistical Abstract of Latin America* through the use of computer techniques has immediate tactical implications in the need for development of the means for assisting in the conversion of a manual system for publication to a computer-based one. As a result, this subproject has multiple strategic significance, cutting across almost the entire array of potential goals. To illustrate the breadth of information needs, the following lists specific interests of faculty and graduate students at UCLA just in the area of Brazilian studies:

- anthropology, Afro-American cults, race in formation of national identity;
- regional development, international development, environment;
- prevalence of AIDS, epidemiology of respiratory disease, ethnobotany and medicinal plants, public health in Brazil;
- Spanish and Portuguese literature, Brazilian literature, Afro-Brazilian folk and religious music, Brazilian art, nineteenth century Brazilian history;
- television industry in Brazil, computer communication with Brazil, development of automated library systems; and
- environment, community organization, trade and investment practices, international banking and finance.

Library Services

Information Need

The development of library services as tactical and operational responses to strategic needs is a continuing requirement.

Implications for Strategic Planning

These kinds of activities lie at the very cutting edge of transition from strategic planning into tactical and operational planning. They are the point at which wishes and hopes get translated into commitments of resources; they are the means by which experiments become realities.

CLR Subprojects and Other Relevant Activities

Several projects were carried on within the UCLA library system and its branches. Each was designed to experiment with a type of library service. Beyond them, though, are the results from ongoing activities in the tactical and operational development of library services; many of these are impossible to separate from initiatives of the CLR projects even though they may not have been explicitly supported by it.

Library Management Involvement.   In order to assure that the management of the University Library System was fully involved in the strategic planning process, a conference was convened bringing together all of the Associate University Librarians and major unit heads for discussions with the University Librarian. It provided the basis for internal management of the tactical and operational implications as well as for subsequent involvement of the library staff in the project.

ORION Data Bases.   Just this year has witnessed the addition of new data bases to the ORION online public access catalog, beyond the catalog of the UCLA library itself: Chicano Studies Library catalog, the Ethnomusicology Library catalog, the Film and Television Archive, the ISSR Data Archives, citations to journal articles on microcomputers, and the Water Resources Archives catalog. They represent exactly the kinds of materials that a single-point of access must include.

Expert Reference.   There is need to develop expert systems and generalized expert system approaches for applications in libraries. Developed systems should be easily transportable and made available for libraries for a variety of in-house local system uses. A subproject within the GSLIS was focused on this need, with specific concern to reference work. It has led to a continuing effort on the part of the responsible faculty member.

Ready Reference.   A project was initiated within the college library and then experimented with in three or four others. It involved the conversion of ready-reference files at a number of libraries, both on campus and elsewhere (at the Los Angeles Public Library, in particular), into computer data bases. The objective was to determine the feasibility of microcomputer support to the ready reference function on a shared basis. Initially, the database maintenance and search software was a quite expensive and sophisticated package; early on, though, it was seen that the functional needs could be met with a much simpler approach—the use of "personal file management software." Currently, the system is now operational (using a $60 package called *MemoryMate*) in five campus libraries; current experiments are with the means for update that will be both efficient and assure consistency of the shared files as well as meeting the individual needs of each library.

Current Contents Services.   A project was initiated in the Education/ Psychology Library to experiment with a current contents and journal delivery service. It is now completely supported by the fees paid by the subscribing members of the faculties served.

Inventory of Campus Data Bases. A project is continuing under the management of the UCLA Librarian to identify, to the extent possible, the full array of data bases available on campus. These include those that are formally acquired (such as in the ISSR, those that are associated with large scale projects, and those that are maintained by individual faculty. The strategic objective is to establish the basis on which catalog entries for databases can be incorporated into the ORION online public access catalog. For the ISSR data bases, this has already been done, but for the fuller array the inventory will be an essential first step.

Installation of CD-ROM Data Bases. CD-ROM data bases have now become an evident resource in the UCLA Library System. Initial experiments within the GSLIS were shortly followed by installation of *Dissertation Abstracts,* of the Agnelli Foundation's Videodisc Encyclopedia of Italian Civilization, and of numerous others.

Information Centers

Information Need

There are needs for activities that will focus on acquisition of information resources needed for specific academic programs. They require professional expertise in both librarianship and subject related analyses.

Implications for Strategic Planning

These kinds of activities require support tools in acquisition, staffing, and analytical tools.

CLR Subprojects and Other Relevant Activities

Several of the projects were concerned with the establishment of an information center specific to academic programs. While this brings a sense of deja vu, it reflects the fact that there is continuing need to establish highly focused resources, staff, and facilities to serve the needs of specific investigation, projects, and academic areas.

School of Engineering, Department of Chemical Engineering. As a result of discussions with the Dean of the School of Engineering and the Chairman of the Department of Chemical Engineering, needs were identified for information resources in support of Hazardous Substance research and in industrial partnership. The result was a set of specifications for establishing an operational service. Of special significance is the need for geographic indexing and retrieval

of textual, numeric, and perhaps image data. A proposal was submitted to the
National Science Foundation for a major research program on Hazardous
Substances; it was funded and initiated in May 1987. Included among the tasks
was establishment of a Hazardous Substances Information Center as the
operational service. This project has implications for virtually every one of the
potential strategic goals. Of special importance are two aspects: the development
of a geographic data base capability and the potential of a national service. There
are immediate tactical implications arising from the relationship between such
a substantive information center, the University Library, the ORION system,
the ORION User Services Office, the computing facilities on campus, external
sources of data, and the range of potential users.

School of Social Welfare. The School of Social Welfare has initiated a program
of Intervention Research. It requires establishing an information center to
accumulate the relevant data.

Institute for Social Science Research.   The Immigration Research program of the
ISSR has initiated an information center in support of that area of research.
Two subprojects were specifically concerned with the development of the
necessary resources.

User Interfaces

Information Need

Among the essential tools in implementing new technologies is effective
interfaces with the users of them.

Implications for Strategic Planning

Much of the intelligence and ease of use that can be incorporated into
interfaces for end users of information systems can best be done at the
workstation level. Microcomputers are the logical terminal/workstation
choice. Development of these interfaces needs to occur at several different levels
and on a variety of machines to support a variety of user needs. This implies
that library administrators must specify and require vendors to place more
emphasis on the development of intelligent microcomputer interfaces and
microcomputer integration as the foundation for the scholar workstation.
Library systems staff and/or computer center staff must begin to develop local
micro-based software for distribution to the campus community which will
assist users in maximizing use of the available information resources and will
provide the necessary navigation among local and remote services. Library
administrators should purchase microcomputers for installation and as
replacements for existing terminals as replacements are required. Library

administrators must commit resources to hiring and/or training staffing systems design and microcomputer program capabilities.

The underlying assumptions are that the academic world will see a universal use of computers. Personal computers therefore will be access means most readily available and responsive to needs. As a result, there must be at least minimal standards for interconnection and availability should be distributed in library facilities. However, it is necessary that operations recognize the sociology of user, the nature of "personal" computing, the range of work styles, and the need for self-service and self-sufficiency. Specialists and technical consultants are necessary, but expert systems technology may provide the means for supplementing them.

There is evident need for ability to produce hard copy, so printers must be widely available. There is also need for access to centralized library facilities and means for distributed video output, optical scanning facility, fax, and optical disk access.

CLR Subprojects and Other Relevant Activities

Two subprojects were initiated in this area of development.

Department of Psychology. The focus of this subproject was on the effect of technology, such as student workstations, and the process of education, one of the crucial issues in effective use of computer methods in learning. There is an example of the tactical and operational needs in the WANDAH facility at UCLA, an example of the type of learning environment to be considered.

Graduate School of Library and Information Science. The concern of this subproject was with the operational evaluation of "scholars' workstations" that combine access to a variety of information resources, including CD-ROM publications. An experimental workstation was received from University Microfilms, along with experimental databases (*Dissertation Abstracts* and *INSPEC*) and graphic files (*Engineering Index* journal page images) in CD-ROM form. It was evaluated in the GSLIS for operational capabilities. The vision of a scholar's workstation has existed at least from the time of Vannevar Bush's MEMEX; it has profound implications for the entire range of strategic planning concerns.

Digitized Images

Information Need

Without question, digitized images have become vitally important to academic programs across the entire campus. This new form of data poses both tremendous potential and monumental problems. The potential, of course, derives from the new means for conceptualization of problems that are created by this kind of technology. The problems arise from the fact that the amount of data that can be generated in this form—from satellites, instrumentation, publication, and conversion—exceeds by orders of magnitude that normally considered as a library problem. Yet all of the functional needs, for storage, cataloging, access, and processing must be dealt with.

At least three categories of digitized image data can be identified. The first results from conversion of source data to digitized image form; this arises in FAX transmission, for example; it arises in the preservation of brittle books by conversion to optical disk images; it arises in the conversion of motion picture film to optical disks. The second arises from algorithmic production of images, as from computer-aided design, architectural design, or cartooning. The third arises from the monitoring or observation of physical processes; this is illustrated by data from satellites scanning the earth and other planets; it includes data from scanning of persons, as in radiology and neurology.

It is the third category that raises truly awesome spectres of file sizes, because the magnitude of files that can be created in this way is orders of magnitude greater than any existing library.

Implications for Strategic Planning

Several subprojects were concerned with the issues in management and use of these kinds of data. Together, they raise some problems of strategic significance. Primary among them is the overriding concern with the management of the files themselves; here there needs to be fundamental research on the organization of such files and on the means for retrieval from them.

Almost equally important, though, are administrative concerns about access to facilities, resources, and equipment needed to acquire such data and to analyze it—spectral analyzers, monitors, and communication lines. Among the necessary supporting equipment are supercomputers, needed because the volume of processing required for use of digitized images exceed the capacity of even very large mainframes.

CLR Subprojects and Other Relevant Activities

Graduate School of Library and Information Science.   A project within the GSLIS was concerned with the use of digitized images for the preservation of brittle books.

College of Fine Arts.   A subproject in the College of Fine Arts was concerned with the use of digitized images in instruction in film.

School of Medicine. Three subprojects were supported in the School of Medicine: one was in the Department of Neurology, the second in the Department of Pediatrics, the third was in the Department of Radiological Sciences. Each was concerned with the problems in management of digitized image files that were growing so rapidly as to become unusable without careful organization.

School of Architecture and Urban Planning. In the same vein, the subproject within the School of Architecture and Urban Planning focused specifically on the needs for management and use of digitized image files.

School of Engineering. While there was not a subproject in the area of CAD-CAM specifically funded under the CLR project, it clearly exemplifies the kinds of needs that arise in digitized image management.

FAX Communication. There was not a specific CLR subproject focused on the importance of FAX communication. It is evident, though, that it has become a vital tool for communication. If nothing else, it has virtually destroyed policy barriers to international communication.

Administrative Data Files. The use of digitized image storage for administrative data files, while outside the narrow scope of academic needs, is worth consideration here as part of academic strategic planning. The concept is that scanned administrative documents can be stored in electronic form, with automated work assignment and scheduling, automated work-flow control, and automated indexing and file searching. The benefits arise from increased staff productivity, reduced costs for paper handling, improved control, and better response to needs.

This approach is feasible because the supporting technologies are all now here. The scanners are available and are inexpensive; the transmission capacity (now 100 M bit/sec) is operational; the processing power is now widespread, with microcomputers capable of meeting most needs; the software development is well in hand; the capacity for image storage (as evidenced by IBM's ImagePlus system) is available.

Use of this approach is likely when there are large amounts of data produced (crowded files, multiple documents, extensive use of microforms); when data cannot be keyed (for example, drawings, handwritten, signatures); when there is need for frequent access and retrieval (the same information being used by many different people, with frequent inquiries); when extensive processing (multiple view, complex routing, decisions) is involved; when the information is critical or errors costly; and when the organization is amenable (willing to change, able to visualize the benefits, understanding the effort required).

Management of Digitized Image Files. Given the extent to which it became increasingly evident that the management of digitized image files would become one of the most important areas for strategic planning in the management of information resources, a subproject was undertaken within the GSLIS to examine alternative means for doing so. It examined the range of options, from centralized management to coordination to laissez faire. It considered both data storage needs, equipment needs, and data access needs.

Off-Campus Users

Information Need

There are trends toward offsite storage and remote catalog access. They require better browsability of the online catalog. Bibliographic records should be enhanced with additional access points. There is increasing demand for easy user interfaces; often systems are good for the staff but difficult for the user. Administrators must require vendors to be concerned about user interface issues as well as technical aspects of their systems. Systems designers must think of the user as they develop automated systems for libraries.

Implications for Strategic Planning

Librarians should concentrate on making access to library information services nonlocation specific. This will require a reorientation of staff thinking and of job functions and organization. Information services should be available online and available remotely. Initial steps to begin, or continue, the transition process in all libraries might include: active promotion of telephone service for reference and document delivery; active promotion of electronic mail use for reference and interlibrary loan; and eventual incorporation of all electronic information services through remote access.

CLR Subprojects and Other Relevant Activities

School of Medicine—Drew Memorial Hospital. The focus of this subproject was on "the influence of new information resources on clinical teaching." It includes coverage of simulations, instant access to information through Medline, decision support, and use of computers in curricula. Issues include variations in needs and use across disciplines or across groups of faculty and students. This study relates to the impact of information resources on the quality of teaching; it deals specifically with the expected changes due to developments in technology.

Expert System Development

Information Need

The development of "expert systems" is defined here as the combination of four component elements; (1) an interface for communication with users in the formulation of queries; (2) a decision tree for determining how to interact between the users and the data bases, (3) a generic data base to support the decision tree, and (4) a factual data base. The evidence of the literature is that this will be an important area of research by faculty of the university in every academic discipline and professional area.

Implications for Strategic Planning

Implementation of expert systems will occur if the use of information resources requires professional staff expertise.

CLR Subprojects and Other Relevant Activities

School of Law. The CLR subproject in the School of Law was, among other things, concerned with development of expert systems in the law.

Graduate School of Library and Information Science. This subproject was focused on development of expert systems in support of ready reference in academic libraries.

Indexing and Abstracting Services

Information Need

Indexing and abstracting systems are the essential support tools for information access, whether in printer form or through online access. These tools are now well developed in the physical and biological sciences, engineering, and professional fields such as law and medicine. They are far less developed in the humanities and arts.

Implications for Strategic Planning

Production of these tools involves costs greater than a single institution usually can support. The implication is that a community of universities and academic research libraries needs to develop policy positions that will lead to interinstitutional cooperation or to commitment of national funding to the needs of the humanities and arts.

CLR Subprojects and Other Relevant Activities

Department of Dance. The CLR subproject in the Department of Dance has identified a need for an indexing service related to reviews of dance performances.

Department of Music. The CLR subproject in the Department of Music is concerned with indexing of sound recordings.

Desktop Publishing

Information Need

No subproject specific to desktop publishing was included among those proposed by faculty. Again, as with the importance of print publications, one must infer the need from the other projects. Throughout them, there is clear evidence of the needs to support this kind of activity. From the perspective of a faculty member there are evident values in speed of getting material into distribution, in control of the end product.

The most significant evidence of need is the dramatic increase in the use of microcomputer-based word processing by faculty. Five years ago, perhaps 30 percent to 40 percent were using this technology; today, it is certainly about 90 percent.

Implications for Strategic Planning

Equally clear are the problems that desktop publishing implies. From the perspective of departmental administration, the management of resources and the potential workload in a highly labor intensive operation were quite worrisome problems. (With all due respect to the virtues of the computer, data entry, formatting and design, editing, preparing for production, and final publication all require major efforts.) It can be consuming of faculty time—as long as they find it stimulating—and consuming of support staff and resources—when the faculty lose interest. From the perspective of a campus administrator the problems are likely to be monumental.

Beyond these institutional concerns, there are even larger problems in control. Indeed, "desktop publishing" is virtually an oxymoron that confuses the real role of the publisher with that of the printer. There are problems in quality control, in ensuring a publishable product, and in marketing and distribution. But most important are the scholarly aspects of control: refereeing, reviewing, and assuring integrity of reference.

CLR Subprojects and Other Relevant Activities

There were no CLR subprojects proposed in this area, important though it is. Evidence must be drawn from other relevant activities.

Online Electronic Journals. There is a slow but steady development of scholarly communication through electronic mail. Some has been formalized as "electronic journals," though most is still informal.

The Electronic Manuscript Project of the AAP. The Association of American Publishers, recognizing the increasing use by authors of microcomputer-based word processing, carried out a project to establish standards for encoding of electronic manuscripts to facilitate the communication between authors, publishers, and printers.

Department of History. A CLR subproject in the Department of History was concerned with the need to use computer processing on Aragon-Catalan script.

Department of English. While not supported by a subproject of the CLR program, interests in the Department of English at UCLA are highly relevant. The desire is to create a "Center for Electronic Text" in order to explore the personal computer as a rhetorical device. That is, what happens to written text, both literary and nonliterary, when it is displayed on an electronic screen? The concern is with such questions as "the history of electronic display, its present state and foreseeable future, the origin of electronic aesthetics in theory and practice of Italian Futurism and Dada, and inquiries into the implications for post modern aesthetics and literary theory of a volatile, electronic art object" (quoting from the syllabus for a seminar).

Data Base Development

Information Need

Throughout the university, faculty are creating data bases, but they frequently need help in doing so. Several of the projects have essentially represented needs for consulting support in design of data base structures, indexing of data files, and downloading data from external sources. This clearly represents a significant need, and doubtless one that will continue.

Implications for Strategic Planning

There is need for library staff to serve as consultants to data base development, including advice on data structures, features of relevant software, the availability of source data to be downloaded into personal files, and copyright and licensing requirements.

CLR Subprojects and Other Relevant Activities

Department of Neurology. This subproject was focused on the development of a microcomputer-based system for management of a patient record file of data on surgery for epilepsy. It represents a context of multi-institutional cooperation, with the need to establish standards and procedures for the creation and maintenance of data files of critical importance to all levels of academic responsibility—teaching, research, and public service. It demonstrates that there is need for a consulting service for faculty needing to establish interinstitutional data files.

Institute for Social Science Research. This subproject was focused on the needs in support of campus research related to "immigration." Funds were committed for two supporting studies: (1) establishing an historical archive, and (2) creating a visual archive to interface with the Museum of Cultural History. Research related to immigration is of special concern to UCLA, given the dramatic and rapid effects it has on the southern California community. The opportunities for community service to ethnic populations must be of strategic importance.

Department of Film and Television. This CLR subproject was concerned with the development of a television data base.

File Conversion

Information Need

As we move increasingly into computer-based processing of data, the need to convert existing data sources to digital text (or digital image) form arises across the entire campus.

Implications for Strategic Planning

Optical character reading equipment is now well enough developed that it can effectively be used in support of this functional need. Policies need to be established to ensure efficient use of such equipment, including inventory of equipment, announcement of availability, assessment of applicability, and allocation of use.

CLR Subprojects and Other Relevant Activities

Belt Library of Vinciana. The focus of this subproject was on the conversion of the catalog and index files of the Belt Library of Vinciana. Tests were conducted to determine the feasibility of using Optical Character Reading equipment for catalog and index conversion. A related project, under sponsorship of the National Agricultural Library, was for evaluation of OCR equipment for bibliographic purposes. The conversion test established procedures for ensuring image quality, registration, and avoidance of problems that reduce the quality of conversion. Data were accumulated on error rates, time for correction, and time for processing. They substantiate the general picture that OCR equipment is effective for conversion purposes if the reliability is greater than 95 percent; below 95 percent, it is not effective.

Department of Music. One subproject was concerned with the conversion of catalogs in the Department of Music.

Index to Christian Art. Nothing was done on this campus with respect to conversion of the files of the Index to Christian Art, but it still represents an opportunity of tremendous value to scholarship in all of the humanities.

Center for Folklore and Mythology. The files of the Center for Folklore and Mythology are all in manual form. In particular, the library of 6,000 volumes, 5 archives, including Ethnomusicology, is all manually cataloged. Again, nothing was done on conversion of these files, but it too represents an opportunity of value to many fields.

Project Management

Information Need

While the physical sciences and engineering have well established means for management of large-scale projects, the humanities, social sciences, arts, and even the biological sciences do not. Yet, there is increasing likelihood that such projects will develop in these other academic fields. There is need, therefore, for means for support to the management of such projects.

Implications for Strategic Planning

There needs to be consultant capabilities—in the computing center, library, campus office of contracts and grants, campus administration—to provide these kinds of project management support tools and consultative advice on use of them.

CLR Subprojects and Other Relevant Activities

Repertorium Columbianum.   The *Repertorium Columbianum* is a project that involves investigators from throughout the world. It requires communication of large amounts of information among them in order to ensure consistency in treatment of common standards in translation. It require coordination in order to maintain progress toward the objective of publication within a very tight time schedule.

COMPUTERIZED MATCHMAKING:
THE RESEARCHER AND THE COLLECTOR

Patricia A. Etter

In January 1990, the Department of Archives and Manuscripts at Arizona State University, Tempe, announced a dynamic new research tool: The Manuscript Society Information Exchange Database. The database lists thousands of items of manuscript material owned by collectors and dealers throughout the United States. The concept of locating material that has been isolated in hundreds of varied locations is an exciting one for scholars and researchers because it gives them access to unpublished documents in all areas of human endeavor that would otherwise be unavailable.

The opening of the database culminates two years of joint effort between the Manuscript Society and the Department of Archives and Manuscripts. Because this has been a pioneering project, I am going to focus on all aspects of it: the history of the idea, the database and its operation, the collectors, the documents, and the search results, I will also be taking a look at the kind of material researchers can expect to find and make some projections for the future.

The concept of sharing information contained in documents in private collections started with Ira Brilliant, Vice-President of the Manuscript Society, an international organization of 1,400 members. Brilliant is the ideal person

Advances in Library Administration and Organization,
Volume 10, pages 51-66.
Copyright © 1992 by JAI Press Inc.
All rights of reproduction in any form reserved.
ISBN: 1-55938-460-3

to promote such an undertaking. His collection of Ludwig Van Beethoven's first editions, manuscript letters, and other materials resides in the Ira F. Brilliant Center for Beethoven Studies at San Jose State University in California. This demonstrates his belief that he and others like him have a responsibility to share important and rare documents with others. "These are national treasures," he said, adding that "anything that exists only has value when it is used. Of course," he pointed out, "accessibility to knowledge is the key to its value."[1]

The Manuscript Society was founded in 1948, and its members are avid collectors of historical manuscripts and documents in a variety of subject areas. They encourage the use of manuscripts for research in history, literature, the arts, and other forms of culture, and they want to make it possible to facilitate the exchange of information among scholars, students, collectors, dealers, archivists, and librarians. The society sponsored a traveling exhibition of manuscripts for the United States Bicentennial celebration. In addition, they have published *Autographs and Manuscripts: A Collector's Manual* (Scribner's, 1978) and *Manuscripts: The First Twenty Years* (Greenwood Press, 1985). The organization also is concerned about preservation of manuscript material. Many members, because of their collecting interests, have become experts in their field and often have published books of their own that handle a subject in depth. This expertise can be of enormous assistance to researchers.

At first, Brilliant thought that the Manuscript Society should sponsor such an undertaking because it is a stable, known organization. But as the concept evolved and took shape, he began to believe that an institution such as a library would be in the best position to manage and promote any type of program on a long-term basis. Moreover, he also perceived the answer lay in the use of modern technology. As he saw it, the computer would organize the material into one place, even though it was scattered all over the United States. The important thing was that it would point to the existence and location of a particular document or manuscript.

ASU became involved by a lucky stroke of fate. Edward C. Oetting, Head of the Department of Archives and Manuscripts, had a chance meeting with George L. Vogt, former president of the Manuscript Society. Vogt spoke about the planned database, noting that the society was looking for a host institution. Oetting believed that ASU would be the ideal location for the database because of the Library's commitment to automation and its experience in managing an online catalog of close to two million titles on the CARL system (Colorado Alliance of Research Libraries), along with some twenty other automated indexes to maps, journals, statistics, ephemeral materials, and other specialized collections. Donald E. Riggs, Dean of Arizona State University Libraries enthusiastically supported the idea:

This worthy endeavor will marry twentieth-century computer technology with the centuries-old tradition of serious scholarship utilizing the finest of primary source materials. This unique collaboration between a private society and a major research university is a classic "win-win" situation; one which can only enhance the reputation of all participants.[2]

Dean Riggs asked Oetting to manage the program for ASU. Ira Brilliant, as Chair of the Manuscript Society Information Exchange, was to provide interface with the society and its members. Both organizations agreed to a six-year contract, which can be renewed. The Manuscript Society agreed to solicit material, promote participation of its membership, and act as a go-between with members of the society and staffers at ASU.

ASU agreed to develop, maintain, and publicize the database as well as provide printouts of submitted documents to each collector. A search fee was agreed upon. Oetting put the Assistant Archivist of Information Services in charge of working out the details of the program, supervising and training data entry, and operators and volunteer staff, and work with Ira Brilliant and members of the society.

Society members were to provide the basic core of documents. Brilliant estimated that this could amount to hundreds of thousands of pieces if all of the members participated. He faced some skeptics when he first proposed the idea to the society's Board of Trustees, but the concept took root and the material gradually came in as members realized the importance of sharing the information their rare documents could provide. The documents would remain with the owners, of course. The computer would organize the material and identify the various collectors (in code) all over the United States who had significant items about a particular person or topic.

As mentioned above, the collectors are not identified by name, because we are bound to protect anonymity. Brilliant assigns a unique number to each participant, and he or she is known by that number both in correspondence and conversation. If I need to contact an individual to discuss a collection, I simply write to "Dear 0007" and give the letter to Brilliant, who passes it on to the collector.

Such secrecy, of course, raises an important question for scholars. How does one cite the source? The answer is simple. We ask the patron to cite the database (see an example in note 5). A few scholarly eyebrows were raised at the idea at first. There is no doubt, however, that scholars will be seeing more and more of this as other databases of computerized information are cited in books, journals, and papers.

I cannot stress how important it is for researchers to obtain as much information as he/she can on a specific topic. As a result, material hidden in a private collection could be critical to a scholar's thesis. For example, my own research interests involve overland journeys to the Pacific by Southwestern trails, a topic little pursued by historians in the past.

In order to pursue my thesis, I needed as much primary source material as I could find. I tapped the usual references: *National Union Catalog of Manuscript Collections, National Inventory to Documentary Sources,* published guides from various repositories, and bibliographies. Still, I knew there was more material out there. But how could I find it? By chance, I heard of a collector who owned an overland diary, and, by another stroke of fate, we lived in the same city. The collector graciously allowed me access to the diary, which helped add definition to a specific overland route. In addition, I found a rare, delightful description of one of the more colorful Indian chiefs, the Seminole, Wildcat. I was able to use that material as well. But one cannot always depend on luck when there is research to be done.

At the same time, the collector, for personal reasons, asked me not to reveal the location though he did allow me to quote from the document. This kind of things adds a new complication because many scholars and researchers want to see the material for themselves. The ability to cite a database would have solved the problem. Ed Oetting sums it up very well:

> Researching primary source materials often resembles the medieval search for the Holy Grail. The idiosyncratic and elusive nature of individual repositories and their home-grown reference tools can prove as elusive as the many maps and clues that have 'pointed the way' to that holy artifact. The lack of consistent and comprehensive bibliographic tools noting the location and existence of manuscripts and manuscript collections turns most scholars into explorers and adventurers worthy of past crusaders.
>
> The metaphor of the Grail is particularly applicable to assuaging scholarly paranoia concerning that one fugitive letter that conclusively will prove (or more likely, disprove) one's central thesis. Scholars have tracked such elusive fugitives with cunning and quiet desperation for years, more often than not, to be thwarted by the private ownership of manuscript materials.[3]

We expect more and more academic researchers to query the The Information Exchange Database as time goes on and the word gets out. At the present time, documentary editors provide our most consistent user group because they traditionally make exhaustive efforts to locate every piece of information that various individuals have produced. Because these projects are ongoing and we continue to add material to the database, the editors would surely benefit if they consulted the database on a yearly basis.

A good example of this is the Lincoln Legal Papers Project: A Documentary History of the Law Practice of Abraham Lincoln, 1836-1861. The editors believe that "courtroom practice and legal logic shaped some of President Lincoln's distinctive habits of thought and rhetoric." In addition, they contend that a collection of this information will "give biographers and other students of Lincoln their first chance to fully understand and adequately interpret this important dimension of the man."[4] The Lincoln Legal Papers project is expected to last for a decade or longer as they try to locate then publish an expected 70,000 records scattered around the United States and beyond. We conducted a successful search for them, which added 37 rare documents to their growing collection of material.

Members of the Manuscript Society are also expected to provide a user group. Individuals may simply want to contact others who have similar interests or have documents that could add missing links to a collection. Not all letters are written or received by famous individuals, but we add all these names to our database. As a result, genealogists and those researching family trees may be rewarded by making a search.

Until now, we have been entering documents on an item-by-item basis, quite a departure from usual archival procedure of describing whole collections and creating a number of subject access points for them. We could, however, enter a group of letters as a collection. A good example would be some 6,000 letters written by as many individuals, north and south, over every day of the Civil War. By doing this, however, we would lose names of individuals and specific places. All of these items would be retrievable under the subject, Civil War, however. (See Appendix for sample documents.)

The database contains 16 fields corresponding with the fields illustrated in the Manuscript Society Information Exchange Database form (see Figure 1). At first, we asked the donors to complete this form, which contains a short annotation or description of the contents of the document. This is used as our data entry form and information is entered into the computer in the order it appears. Whenever a query arrives, we make the search and mail a printout of the data to the patron. And this is all he/she would have received in the beginning—the information contained on the printout and knowledge that a document exists. But scholars like to see original material if they can. So we had a new obstacle to overcome.

The solution was fairly simple. We created a form letter that asked the collector to contact the patron. This has worked quite nicely, because it turns out that the collectors are eager to know that others are interested in their holdings.

Because a number of the collectors have found it enormously time-consuming to fill out hundreds of forms describing their material, many are photocopying the original documents and the Department of Archives and Manuscripts completes the data entry forms. Moreover, the collectors have no problem with allowing us to photocopy the copies for the patrons who ask for material. We eventually hope to have copies of all the documents listed in the database, thus eliminating the need to contact the collector at all except to confirm receipt of his manuscripts by providing a printout of the entry. In addition, the patron need not make a long expensive trip. He can fill in and mail his Request for Search form then sit at home and wait for the mail.

Because we are now receiving copies of the material, and expect a great deal of it, we have also had to set up a way to store and retrieve it. Each group of material received from a collector is accessioned and processed. Because collectors continually add new documents to their collections, we expect to receive new material on a regular basis. This is organized alphabetically in folders arranged first by collector number, second by accession number. These folders are kept in archival boxes in numerical order. For example, 0002 collector may have sent in material in 1989, some more in 1990. The folders would be arranged something like this: 0002 89A-39, 89A-56, 90A-1, 90A-50, and so forth. How do we locate this material quickly. Say a patron asks for information on George Washington. We do a search and print out the results. These include collector number and accession number. So it is a simple matter to reach for the right box, locate the accession number, and pull out the manuscript from its alphabetical order for photocopying.

Because much handwriting is close to illegible and reading and annotating hundreds of documents is enormously time-consuming, the reader might ask, "Who does the work?" I have trained a data entry operator to fill out the forms and copy annotations that have been supplied by the collector. She also enters all data and prints out reports for the patrons. A library assistant with a history background helps read and annotate the material that arrives without any description. I add Library of Congress subject headings, for the most part, using our online authority.

From time to time, we have a good corps of volunteers who enjoy working with this material because they have an opportunity to be "voyeurs" for a short time and read some interesting historical vignettes. Let me give you an example. President Benjamin Harrison wrote a touching note to Senator Joseph R. Hawley in 1889: "I am alone and lonesome. Come down (if Mrs. Hawley will give her consent) and take a quiet dinner with me"[5] Certainly we cannot help but feel for such a man, whom we would assume to be surrounded by people and always in demand. Biographers like to find personal tidbits like this because it points out the humanity of the subject.

Another example concerns General Antonio Lopez de Santa Anna, who used a very special saddle and bridle in battle in San Jacinto. This gear may rest in a museum somewhere, its provenance unknown. It could be tucked away in someone's attic. Or, perhaps descendents of Sam Houston have been lovingly caring for it ever since it was given to him by a friend. In 1836, Houston sent it to his cousin Robert in Nashville, Texas. He wrote that he had "no ostentatious foible to gratify, or idle vanity, by becoming the owner of any of the spoils taken in Battle because they had once belonged to any particular individual."[6] He further added that his cousin could keep the saddle or give it to General [Stonewall] Jackson, if he so chose. The letter, of course, will not tell us where the saddle is today. But it lets us know it existed and also supplies a number of clues for us to start looking for it. In addition, the statement does not change the historic record but supports it; Houston was a man of integrity.

There are thousands of letters and documents like the above. We wanted to create a database that would allow us to retrieve as much information as possible, with a minimum amount of effort devoted to processing. Researchers of course, are interested in documents written *by* an individual and *to* an individual. We have added one more: *about* an individual. Whenever a name is mentioned in a document, we add it to our list of subjects. This can be quite useful. Say an author is writing about Sir Henry Shackleton, hero of Antarctic explorations. His name does not show up as an author or a recipient of a letter. A subject search in the database, however, turned up a letter written by Ernest Joyce, a member of Shackleton's 1917 expedition. Writing to Charles Rawson Royds, Joyce complains bitterly, believing that Shackleton was responsible for the fact that he lost his pension.[7]

Other search results are equally rewarding, and those individuals who have asked for searches have been greatly pleased. A search on George Washington, for example, resulted in 31 letters written by him, 8 letters received by him, and 17 letters that mentioned his name or talked about him—a total of 57 items. Even more impressive, a look into our records showed that this material represented 16 different accessions over a period of three years and was held by eleven collectors in as many cities over the United States. In the past, it would have taken years to track down this material.

A project editor wrote of her gratitude to the Manuscript Society Information Exchange Database. Because ASU did not have photocopies of all of the material listed in the database, we had asked the various collectors represented in the search results to contact the patron. They did. At the same time, each one offered information on material in their possession that had not yet been reported to the database. The editor of the George Washington edition wrote:

> The Exchange Database is performing a unique service to projects such as ours. We have found that manuscript collectors are almost unfailingly generous in sharing their holdings with scholarly projects. The problem has been in reaching them. When we see Washington material offered for sale in manuscript dealers' catalogues, we send blind letters asking for copies of the documents from purchasers. The response is very good but there are many catalogues we never see, and the Database is enabling us to reach many owners who would otherwise never know of the project. It is indeed performing a very valuable service to the scholarly community.[8]

Though an item might be signed by one of the great men or women in our historic past and may have been responsible for signaling a great event, it is very often the letter or statement by a common citizen of the day that lets us know how is life was shaped by an event over which he had little control.

In these cases, a researcher might want to look for a subject area, and the Civil War is a good example. We will find a small collection of letters written by a woman in Marion, Indiana to her father: "You must not think hard of

MANUSCRIPT SOCIETY
Information Exchange Database

ASU

Department of Archives & Manuscripts

Hayden Library

Tempe, Arizona 85287-1006

1. Doc. type	2. Author		
TLS	Mussolini, Benito, 1883-1945		
3. # of pages	4. Year	5. Month	6. Day
2	1927	10	28
7. Recipient		8. Place of origin	
Cavazzoni, Stephano		Rome	
9. First phrase of text			
Caro Cavazzoni: ho preso visione ...			
10. Description of contents			
The letter thanks him and approves of his work within the conference on Opium which is			
one part in the limitation of the international trade in narcotics. The conference was part			
of the League of Nations.			
11. Language note			
Italian			
12. Security #		13. Accession (office use only)	
0092		90A-37	
14. Subjects (office use only)			
Fascists - Italy / Politicians - Italy / Opium Trade / League of Nations			
15. Photocopy	16. Restrictions		
yes	none		

Figure 1. Database Entry Form

me if I do not write much this time for if our dear husband was in the army and you get word that he had started home and then here that he was surrounded by the rebels and could not get home you woul[d] feel very bad and you may ju[d]ge my feelings now it may be that I will never see him any more...if John ever lives to get home I think I will try and keep him."[9]

The variety of topics that can be searched is almost endless. There are preachers, paleontologists, Indians, and prime ministers. The arts are well represented, including poets and musicians, authors, and singers. One can find information on slavery, train robberies, the Dallas Cowboys, oysters, love letters, phrenology, and more. In short, a scholar will find material on almost any topic. We suggest that searchers repeat their search from time to time because new material is entered daily.

Because anything that happened yesterday is history today, many items in the Manuscript Society Collection can be quite current. George Bush appears in the database, for example. Readers might be interested in some of the older records in the collection. One is dated 1566, Moulin, France. It is a curious letter from Catherine de Medicis, Consort of Henry II, King of France. She writes to the French Ambassador to Spain, recommending baptism in Spain of a Jewish physician to the Christian religion.[10]

The database has been designed to provide a number of access points and to extract the most information from the various documents. We use *Marcon* software (Interactive Support Systems, New York), and it has worked very well for us. Field size is not limited. We sometimes take advantage of this in the subject field if a large number of names appear in the document. We mainly use Library of Congress subject headings to assist those who are interested in a subject research. Figure 1 shows a completed form. Data entry is made in the order shown in the 16 fields described below.

1. *Document Type.* The Manuscript Society describes the various types of documents with a two to three letter acronymn, their GMD (general material description), if you will. Some examples are: ACS (autograph card, signed); ADS (autograph document, signed); ALS (autograph letter, signed); DS (document signed); TLS (typed letter, signed), or MS (manuscript). The field is searchable. A patron, for example, might not want to see any letters that an individual wrote. Instead, he may want to know of any documents or deeds in existence that bear the subject's name.

2. *Author.* We use name authority from our online catalog and add it to the database. We only have to do this one time. A nice feature about the data base is that a repeated name just needs to be "popped in." We can also call up windows to view the frequency of various names entered in the database.

3. *# of Pages.* It is obvious that this tells how long the document is, but it also could be important to identifying a particular item.

4. *Year.* In addition to its research value, we can also search the database for letters written by an individual in a stated year. We learned from a patron that documents authored by William Henry Harrison between 1800 and 1815 are extremely rare. Thus, he ordered a search for documents that Harrison might have authored in those years.

5, 6. *Month, Day.*   The information is included when available for its research value. Of course, a search can also be made for a specific day, month, and year.

7. *Recipient.*   Again, we use library authority from our online catalog if available. In cases where we cannot identify the recipient, we repeat what is there: "Dear Aunt," or "Your Lordships," or "Sir," and "Darling," each giving us a clue as to the type of letter we might expect to find and the individual's relationship to the author. The field is searchable.

8. *Place of Origin.*   We do not use any authority for this field, simply adding what the author wrote: "Hermitage," "On Board the *Tasso,*" and so forth. If the author did include a city or town we will add the state.

9. *First Phrase of Text.*   This is a very important field for the collector because it is mainly used to identify the uniqueness of a document. It is also useful to us when we search for a filed document.

10. *Description of Contents.*   We include a short annotation on the subject of the document. Any names contained in the document are added to the subject field below. We have not made this a searchable field because there is no controlled vocabulary to help us locate such a varied group of material.

11. *Language Note.*   English is the main language represented, but we also have documents in German, Italian, French, Russian, Arabic, and so on.

12. *Security #.*   Every document that is received is marked with the special identification code of the owner of the material. All collections receive a unique code number. Their identities are known only to a member of the society who is responsible for interface with ASU.

13. *Accession #.*   Each group of accession numbers identifies the year in which the material was received: 1989—89-1, 89A-2; 1990—90A-1, 90A-2, and so forth. This number is written on each piece of material in the accession alongside the security number.

14. *Subjects.*   We use library of Congress Subject Headings and for the most part, are able to retrieve them from our general catalog on the CARL system. We also add proper names mentioned in the material, or names of organizations, places, and so on.

16. *Photocopy.*   This field contains a note regarding existence of a photocopy of the material.

17. Restrictions.   We prefer not to list material that could not be released because our intention is to make information available. There could be a restriction on making a photocopy of a document. In this instance, the patron would receive a printout of the entered data and the collector would be asked to contact him.

Librarians might ask, "Why is this not set up in AMC-MARC format?" There are several reasons. Our intent is to enter documents at the item level for quick retrieval of information. Because the process is closer to indexing than cataloging, the record does not lend itself to the MARC format. Additionally, this is a proprietary database which will not appear in the public online catalog.

The reader might be curious to know how we evaluate material to add to the database. Generally, the collectors send what they consider to be the best from their collection. They look at rarity, demand, and the content of the document. Of course, the library is more concerned with research value. For that reason, we do not as a rule enter autographs or signatures. We could make an exception in the case of First Ladies Martha Jefferson, Elizabeth Monroe, Hannah Van Buren, or Margaret Taylor because theirs are among the rarest of autographs.[11] Another exception has been made with a Soviet banknote bearing the signatures of Franklin Delano Roosevelt, Sir Winston Churchill, and Joseph Stalin, mainly because its provenance is so interesting. On February 5, 1945, Harry L. Hopkins obtained the leaders' signatures at the Yalta Conference. Hopkins believes that aside from the official communique issued at the end of the conference, this was the only document bearing the signatures of all three men. In addition, Hopkins noted that Marshal Stalin balked at the request, but Roosevelt fabricated a story about membership in a "Short Snorter Club." The Soviet leader fell for it and added his signature to the note.[12]

There is another common category that I like to call the "thank you for the nice..." letter category. These may have value to a collector because of rarity, but again, there would be little of interest here for the researcher unless the item was rather unusual thus giving additional insight to the personality of the recipient. We kept the 1908 letter of Helen Taft thanking Alice Chipman Dewey for the good luck charm in the shape of a swastika.[13]

For the most part, however, we receive material that is unique and important historically. Therefore, we believe it deserves to be processed on an item-by-item basis. As mentioned we have processed a group of letters as a collection, creating one entry in the database. But we have scanned the letters for important subjects and names of people mentioned in them. For example, Bvt. Lt. Col. Albert Hartsuff, surgeon at the Pine Ridge Indian Agency before and after the Battle of Wounded Knee, wrote a number of letters during his sojourn there. Quickly scanning the letters we find names like Sara Barton, Red Cloud, Crazy Horse, Sitting Bull, and George Armstrong Custer.[14]

The future is enormously promising. We have close to 3,000 entries in the database and hope to reach 5,000 entries in the next year or so. A long range goal is 20,000 entries and we believe this is entirely realistic given the amount of extant material that is tucked away in private collections. Nor is it unrealistic to predict that the database could list hundreds of thousands of pieces of material over the next ten years.

When the database contains a large enough sample, we might be able to derive some useful statistics that could determine trends in manuscript collecting. At the same time, it would be possible to determine trends in research and try to correlate the two.

The materials represented in the database to this time belong to members of the Manuscript Society. Membership in the society is not a criterion for listing in the database, however. For example, there are hundreds of small historical societies and libraries that have no outlet for listing historic documents they might own. At some future date, we might want to consider indexing material belonging to nonmembers of the society. We could also think about including important one-of-a-kind items from a processed collection held in any library. There is no charge for listing in the database, by the way.

Listing an item in the Manuscript Society database can be beneficial for the collector because it can verity ownership at the time the manuscript was submitted for inclusion. This provenance could be important at some time in the future, especially if documents change hands. More importantly, Philip H. Jones, past-president of the society, has written to say that the content of the thousands of documents he holds was literally lost without the database. As a result, the printouts of the material have been extremely useful for him.[15]

Thousands of individuals keep family papers and memorabilia, and for personal reasons will not entrust the material to a library or archive. This is unfortunate for many reasons. First, most individuals are not aware of conservation procedures that must be taken to preserve delicate material. Very often owners die without having made arrangements for disposal of historic records. And sometimes, family members throw all those "old papers" out. Maybe they sell them to a buyer who breaks up the collection and sells it in bits and pieces, thus losing all provenance. Dealers have even found old papers being sold at Flea Markets and garage sales. Ideally, of course, we would like to see this material safely housed in a library or archive. But we can only aim toward the "ideal." In the meantime, the Manuscript Society Information Exchange Database provides a terrific service by preserving the information, if not the document, right here in the library, and it is available to scholars over the world.

Ed Oetting has also suggested that by making chronological searches or searches specifying location that we might obtain some useful information on patterns in thought, literary style, gramatical usage, and so on.[16] We could also sample a group of letters from varying locations in the United States every ten years and compare and contrast change and thought in communities over time. The possibilities are endless.

There is no doubt that the Manuscript Society Information Exchange Database and other indexes to scholarly material will have some impact on scholarly research. Computers are able to provide access to library holdings all over the world. There are hundreds of automated indexes and catalogs to books, journals, statistics, and collections on every topic imaginable thus making it possible for a scholar to have more information at his/her fingertips than ever before. The proliferation of information and the ease with which it can be obtained should be a boon to scholars because it could shorten the amount of time spent on research and allow for earlier publication of results. At the same time, because information is more easily available, we should be able to expect more of a scholar because there would be a greater variety of sources and points of view to work with.

Ultimately, we would like to know that the Manuscript Society Information Exchange Database is one of the first research tools a scholar consults when embarking on a new project. The database has already provided the scholarly community with some rare and relatively unknown documents. And as we have seen, there is a new opportunity for interface between the scholar and the collector. This is a unique and exciting opportunity for all who seek information and for those of us who provide it. We have said it before: "all a scholar need do is to sit home and wait for the mail."

(Appendix follows)

APPENDIX

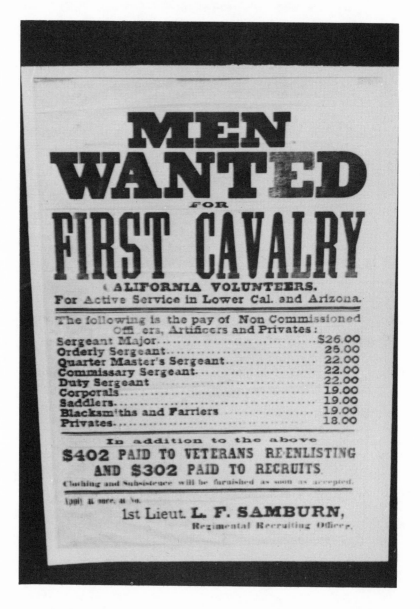

This is advertising for volunteers for active duty in Lower California and Arizona during the Civil War. (Manuscript Society Information Exchange Database, Collector 1801, 89A-12.)

Head Quarters Armies of the United States,
Appomattox C.H. Va. Apl 9th 1865

Gen R. E. Lee
Comdg C.S.A.
General.

In accordance with the substance of my letter to you of the 8th inst., I propose to receive the surrender of the Army of N. Va. on the following terms, to wit:

Rolls of all the officers and men to be made in duplicate, one copy to be given to an officer to be designated by me, the other to be retained by such officer or officers as you may designate. The officers to give their individual paroles not to take up arms against the Government of the United States until properly exchanged, and each Company or Regimental Commander to sign a like parole for the men of their commands.

The arms, artillery and public property to be parked and stacked and turned over to the officers appointed by me to receive them. This will not embrace the side arms of the officers nor their private horses or baggage. This done each officer and man will be allowed to return to their homes, not to be disturbed by United States authority as long as they observe their paroles and the laws in force where they may reside.

Very Respectfully
U. S. Grant
Lt Gen

General Ulysses S. Grant writes terms of surrender to General Robert E. Lee from Appomattox Court House at the end of the Civil War.

Courtesy Jessie Ball duPont Memorial Library, Stratford Hall Plantation, Virginia.

General Ulysses S. Grant writes terms of surrender to General Robert E. Lee from Appomattox Court House at the end of the Civil War. (Courtesy of Jessie Ball duPont Memorial Library, Stratford Hall Plantation, Virginia.)

NOTES

1. Personal interview, July 16, 1990.
2. Donald E. Riggs. Letter to Manuscript Society Participants, September 1988.
3. Edward C. Oetting. "The Information Exchange Data Base: The Future is Now." *Manuscripts* XLII (Winter 1990): 13-14.
4. *Barret* v. *Alton and Sangamon Railroad Company,* Springfield, IL: The Lincoln Legal Papers, 1989, preface.
5. Benjamin Harrison, November 10, 1889 (0001 89A-01), *Manuscript Society Information Exchange Database Collection,* Department of Archives and Manuscripts, Hayden Library, Arizona State University, Tempe, AZ.
6. Sam Houston, September 7, 1836 (1010 89A-24), *Manuscript Society Information Exchange Data Base Collection,* Department of Archives and Manuscripts, Hayden Library, Arizona State University, Tempe, AZ.
7. Ernest Joyce, April 7, 1930 (0059 89A-21), *Manuscript Society Information Exchange Data Base Collection,* Department of Archives and Manuscripts, Hayden Library, Arizona State University, Tempe, AZ.
8. Dorothy Twohig. Personal communication, October 30, 1990.
9. Martha Grant, September 11, 1864 (0002 89A-32), *Manuscript Society Information Exchange Data Base Collection,* Department of Archives and Manuscripts, Hayden Library, Arizona State University, Tempe, AZ.
10. Catherine de Medicis, Consort of Henry II, King of France, May 26, 1566 (1600 88A-26), *Manuscript Society Information Exchange Data Base Collection,* Department of Archives and Manuscripts, Hayden Library, Arizona State University, Tempe, AZ.
11. Walter A. Ostromecki, Jr. *The First Ladies of the United States.* Encino, CA: Privately printed, 1989.
12. Harry L. Hopkins, February 1970 (0070 89A-19), *Manuscript Society Information Exchange Data Base Collection,* Department of Archives and Manuscripts, Hayden Library, Arizona State University, Tempe, AZ.
13. Helen H. Taft, July 7, 1908 (0026 90A-32), *Manuscript Society Information Exchange Data Base Collection,* Department of Archives and Manuscripts, Hayden Library, Arizona State University, Tempe, AZ.
14. Albert Hartsuff Collection of letters, 1870 and 1893 (0002 90A-01), *Manuscript Society Information Exchange Data Base Collection,* Department of Archives and Manuscripts, Hayden Library, Arizona State University, Tempe, AZ.
15. Philip H. Jones. Personal communication.
16. Edward C. Oetting, op. Cit., p. 16.

BIBLIOGRAHIC INSTRUCTION:
EXAMINING THE PERSONAL CONTEXT

James R. Coffey and Theodora T. Haynes

INTRODUCTION

Concern with how the library user learns to locate and make use of information is an area of librarianship that seems to occupy the attention of most public service librarians on a continual basis. A great deal is written in the professional literature but much of it seems to give evidence more of anxiety over what is not happening in the learning process than with what has been successful. Most people who write on the subject seem to think that library instruction is important and the present authors agree that it is. Often what is valued by professionals in giving library instruction is both the relief it can afford the reference librarian who can thereby avoid repetitive and time-consuming questions and the opportunity to get the user oriented to using information tools. Even these modest goals, however, seem to result in frustration rather than satisfaction to the librarian, and one has a sense of giving personal instruction sessions a second time for people who were not reached the first time in a formal instruction session. Librarians are trying to achieve with users

Advances in Library Administration and Organization,
Volume 10, pages 67-96.
Copyright © 1992 by JAI Press Inc.
All rights of reproduction in any form reserved.
ISBN: 1-55938-460-3

a goal that seems elusive and yet increasingly more urgent: how to make the user competent in searching for information available through libraries.

Our experience with instructional services to users suggests to us that it is appropriate to examine the mental context of the instructional session and to reflect on what appears to be happening between the librarian and the user. The librarian/user dialogue is a complex process of communication and interaction and perhaps the many psychological and mental variables involved prevent effective communication. Recognizing these barriers may help librarians to be successful in training the user to be information literate.

While attempting to keep the personal perceptions of the user in mind, we will examine here the context of bibliographic instruction (BI) and suggest some strategies for teaching. It is hoped, in this way, to give the process clarity and to suggest techniques for practical action. A user-focused approach, we think, is more likely to make our efforts effective. We recognize that a great deal has happened in the last five years to make information available more quickly, but the advent of new technological means to information has highlighted user limitations and increased librarians' awareness of the need for users to learn a more judicious approach to information finding. We know there are people out there who want the information we have to provide. We see the ones not sufficiently versed in information-gathering techniques leaving a library with only part of what they could use. There are also people who need the information skills but have not been reached. It is obvious that the librarian cannot make the user learn; but one can market the service we have to offer in a way to make it more attractive to the user and thus of perceived value to the individual.

Understood in the context of the personally useful, bibliographic instruction can be meaningful to both the library user and to the librarian and will achieve its purpose with most library users. Library instruction seems often, from personal observations, to focus more on the library and the things in it than on the person receiving the instruction. Librarians seem to take for granted that the user will have at least a rudimentary concept of why he or she is in the library and what purpose or value it has; but partly because it requires effort to understand the value of information and partly because library users do not seem to connect their presence in libraries with any overall purpose in their lives, this assumption is not always valid.

In a world in which information plays so significant a role, it is useful for our purpose to consider the role of information as it affects the life of the individual. We are approaching it this way because we deal with people on a personal basis and because the interpersonal contact can be exploited to advertise the need for information and what the library can do to meet that need. Additionally, few library users are likely to take an interest in our information serving capabilities unless they see that "there is something in it for me."

Why are instructional sessions so difficult to conduct successfully? We think the reason is that information acquisition is so complex and that personal attitudes are at variance with each other in instructional sessions. This paper will examine the complexity and attempt to show why there is such difficulty. We are going to look at bibliographic instruction in the somewhat larger context of the individual and the mental requirements he or she needs to bring to the search for information. We see BI as a means to being functional in an information age. In discussing its conceptual basis, we will look at how information plays a role in the contemporary world, at the role of the librarian in facilitating the user's skill in acquiring information, at how the user seems to perceive information and its availability, at the complexity of the learning process and how different people learn, and at what might be useful to incorporate into a plan of action in a library which sees instruction as part of its service obligation.

A final word of introduction: we think the goal of instructional services is information literacy. Anything short of this will not be good enough. The user needs to be information-literate to hold a place in an information-based world, and the librarian needs to foster literacy in order to hold a secure position in an information-based world.

THE INFORMATION SOCIETY

Three areas of an individual's daily life are affected by information: the personal quality of life, the job one performs, and the way government operates to influence our behavior. The nuclear accident at Chernobyl can illustrate how the rulers of an information-restricted society can affect the daily life of an individual. In business, the fact that people who know more or who are "better-educated" rise faster and are paid more than those who are knowledge have-nots should illustrate the value of information to the individual. The quality of one's personal existence can be enhanced greatly by how competently one is able to find information ranging from health care to transcendental meditation. Ignorance of the means to change and to control one's life is often reflected in personal suffering and poverty.

Why is information so vital to the individual? On a daily basis, information about the time and weather is used to decide on a course of action. Schedules are used for public transportation. Good health is dependent on the information one can get regarding nutrition, exercise, medication, and developments in understanding disease, whether physical or psychological. Information acquired through news services influences what one will do either immediately or over a course of time. Information about money can be used to acquire more of it or to decide how to spend it to the best advantage. Consumer services provide information used to make decisions about purchasing. Information available on travel and vacations helps people decide how to get the most out of their leisure time. People read newspapers or periodicals to acquire information about products or people that are of interest to them personally and which can affect their own goals and personal self-esteem. Information is available to the information seeker when there is a need to repair a car, paint a house, raise a child, deal with legal problems, grow vegetables, or to engage in any other activity one views as conducive to personal satisfaction. Through personal subscriptions, people are willing to pay for information but it is all free if the person is aware that there are alternative ways to getting it. Whatever the method of acquisition, it is clear that people can and do use information to affect the way they live their lives—and a great deal of effort spent in our societies is expended for the purpose of generating this information because people will pay for it and because they feel the need to acquire and use it.

Information and Business

What relevance does information have for the individual who is going to provide an income either to oneself or to dependents by means of salaried employment? Most people hope to get jobs and to provide some measure of discretionary control over their own lives. If anyone expects both to get a job and to acquire income, then it will not be done without access to information.

In the first place, information is necessary to any commercial enterprise. Why? It is necessary because successful competition for the largest share of a market depends on how much one company knows about changes and new developments and how they can be used to provide a product more attractive to the consumer. Businesses collect data, analyze it, interpret it, and transform it into a competitive edge for their products. To do this effectively, it is important to be "in the know": to be able to collect the mass of information that is out there and to know what is useful and what is not, to know where the new information is coming from and who is likely to have it, even to anticipate its origination. Whoever is first on board with the know how can be the one to make it turn a profit. In addition, information processing systems help a business to make faster, more comprehensive decisions and they do so at a lower cost than the requisite human effort. What a business venture will value most is the employee who can contribute to gathering and recognizing the import of information and who can harness the efforts of likeminded people into an effective product to be marketed and sold. This in turn brings in capital to be used for further investment and for paying the workforce.

How does the individual fit into this view of the workforce? The security of being employed by a firm with a future is probably a basic consideration. Knowledge competence at any given point in time is also a valuable personal resource. Even more valuable is the ability to have one's personal knowledge evolve; and this requires active involvement in the information gathering and the self-education processes. The percentage of people employed in agriculture and industry (who also need to be informed to work well) is shrinking because more can be done with fewer people. The growth of knowledge-based business has required a greater number of people with skills to use or process information. In addition, as economic demands alter and the work scene changes, a worker's expertise becomes obsolete and he or she has to develop new specialities in order to adapt and to continue in employment. While many companies have the facilities for retraining and many provide support for further education, the individual is often on his or her own to become competent in the new skills required to keep working and providing a personal income. The knowledge-based employee therefore needs the services of information-based businesses such as publishing to "keep up with what is going on" and to educate oneself. Not all training is going to take place in a formal environment such as the classroom. Many companies exist to generate information for the consumer: publishing companies of all kinds rely on the need or the desire of the public to be informed on subjects ranging from leisure to professional development.

Further up the corporate ladder there is need for people who are informed enough about the overall picture to be able to pull together the efforts of teams of specialists as well as the efforts of the "production workers" who in turn will probably be only a small part of the industrial whole. So information ability does have import for the individual in the business world: whoever has it is employable and promotable. Whoever does not or does not have enough of it becomes a marginal factor in the economy.

Information in Government

Either by mandate or through the need to function, a government collects information and expends a great deal of effort and money to do so. Most of the information thus gathered is available free to whomever wants it and it is used to affect the daily life of people both inside and outside the jurisdiction of the government agencies collecting it. While the individual may be concerned more immediately with the work and income related aspect of information, there are personal dimensions to the gathering and making available of information collected by governments. To begin with, much of the information that can make the employed person knowledge-competent is available only through government agencies. So this information has value to people who want to be actively involved in their own career development. More fundamental, however, are the purposes of government in acquiring information about individuals and how that information may be used for them or against them. Domhoff (1967, 1983) has demonstrated that small elites of wealth and power determine a great deal of what happens in the United States and they do so by access to information and knowledge that is not available to most of the people.

A brief discussion of some of the information gathering activities of government illustrates how the individual can be affected by information. The census is used to determine representation and can be used to determine federal funding for localities. It can be used by market researchers to scan a geographical area for potential sales efforts. It can be used to determine an area's relative wealth in agricultural land or natural resources or to determine residential growth patterns. The IRS gathers information about income so a government can pay the bills and maintain the power that control over disbursements gives. Taxation is based on the earning power of people as reported to the IRS and decided upon by the legislature. The government maintains information on the wealthiest companies and their relative potential to be taxed. Legislators can and do use this information to make decisions that affect the daily lives of individuals: the 1986 tax law enacted in the United States is one case in point. Governments compile statistics on health and provide information to a variety of interested users. Education is another area for which a government is sometimes the only source of information. The government sponsors research and pays for consultation with specialized groups who provide an informed background to decisionmakers who use the information to make and implement policies that the average citizen usually has no say in formulating. For the legislative body to deliberate and make enactments for the regulation of its citizens' activities, much information is gathered and disseminated.

As long as the individual has access to the information available through the government, he or she can keep informed of what programs and policies are being considered, whether they have a bearing on an individual's activity, and what needs to be done to voice an opinion or affect an action. Even more important, one should know whether information paid for by the citizen is withheld from some people and shared or sold to others to the detriment of the excluded.

Private citizens or interest groups do not have the financial resources to gather and process information to the extent necessary for informed activity in the political process. Therefore, they have to rely on the same information and sources of information that government agencies use. The access to and analysis of government information is necessary to ensure both participation in the legislative process and informed consultation with those affected by the decisions made. If the average citizen does not keep aware of what those in power are doing and why, then his or her interest will not be consulted when legislation is passed.

The Informed Individual

Society has a stake also in the informed individual. If by being informed the individual gains personally in both wealth and control over one's environment, society also gains by a minimum investment in social services to its citizenry. The informed citizen pays for him- or herself; the uninformed or undereducated cannot contribute a productive share of the work effort and are often dependent for personal survival on the funding available from government sources. This does not ever seem to be effective in moving the recipient to independence of activity and control over one's future. There is a decreasing number of jobs available to people who do not have information skills or who are undereducated, and those jobs that are available are not always high-paying or sufficiently numerous to ensure employment to those competing for them. The new technologies, on the other hand, are constantly generating jobs for the right people. While industrial automation might be reducing the portion of the work force needed for manufacturing or the handling of raw materials, and while developments in agricultural production have reduced food producing to a fraction of the workforce engaged in it at the beginning of this century, the information workplace is generating new jobs. But the people in them have to bring certain competencies to the workplace and have to be able to grow into and out of these jobs. Now we may anticipate constant self-retraining as one of the educational skills we bring with us into adult life. One author (Cleveland, 1985, p. 190) put it this way:

> But to two predictions I would assign a high probability value. People who do not educate themselves, and keep reeducating themselves, to participate in the new knowledge environment will be the peasants of the information society. And societies that do not give all their people a chance at a relevant education, and also periodic opportunities to tune up their knowledge and their insights, will be left in the jetstream of those that do.

Whatever the aspirations of the individual may be, the opportunity for work, wealth, leisure, power, and control will go in varying degrees to those who possess the requisite knowledge and ability to acquire, shape, and create information.

In a competitive world it may well be viewed as the responsibility of the individual to acquire the education, knowledge, and information competence to achieve one's personal goals. Schools and libraries exist, however, to see that these goals are achieved, to guide the un- or underinitiated toward competence and independence. Their services are available to everyone and are the only means that everyone can resort to in order to realize whatever expectations one may have.

INFORMATION LITERACY

Having observed the relevance of information to the individual, the next factor we want to look at is how one acquires the skill and how to know when one has attained facility with it. We think it would be helpful to state the description of the information literate person from the 1989 final report of the American Library Association (ALA) Committee on Information Literacy.

> a person must be able to recognize when information is needed and have the ability to locate, evaluate, and use effectively the needed information ... Ultimately, information-literature people are those who have learned how to learn. They know how to learn because they know how knowledge is organized, how to find information, and how to use information in a way that others can learn from them. They are people prepared for lifelong learning, because they can always find the information needed for any task or decision (Ridgeway, 1990, p. 645).

At the outset it should be recognized that, as librarians, we know it is not easy to acquire a sense of ease in finding information. One does not just fiddle with a card catalog and come up with the answer, even though some library users see information acquisition in such simplistic terms. We can recognize also that, at the other extreme, online searchers who work for specialized information services tend to become thoroughly conversant with using certain data bases (whether printed or online) and can provide quick and accurate information to their client group. An example might be an online searcher in a pharmaceutical research library. Another would be a library pre-order searcher who may become an expert on bibliographic databases and who could readily provide information which someone experienced in an academic discipline might struggle to obtain unaided. We know how much time it takes to acquire such expertise with single databases so when we look at the universe of information sources, it becomes apparent that information literacy and the effort needed to acquire it are complex operations and require more than simple approaches.

It seems safe to say that information service librarians generally are familiar with a small number of their user public who know where relevant information in their areas of expertise is to be found. They know how to look for it and where to get it. Outside of this group of people, the only one adequately prepared to cope with information seeking is the professional librarian. On a daily basis librarians acquire knowledge of the sources and experience with information needs. Sometimes these needs are recurring and sometimes they are unique. Almost universally the librarian plays a role in facilitating the acquisition of information. This is done by making the search shorter for the individual in terms of time and by identifying the set of sources available to the user. If often involves a discussion of the relative merits of particular information sources and skill as a teacher. Librarians do not learn how to do this quickly; intensive concentration, exposure, and practice go into the development of a good reference librarian. What we know of the process from experience suggests to us that training the user to do the same thing is going to be difficult for us.

The library profession recognizes the need and has experience with the way information is obtained. Along with the schools, libraries can make real the potential to achieve information literacy. The elementary and secondary schools, however, lack the resources in their media centers to accomplish more than the introductory part of this process. In addition, it seems as if their primary goal is to impart the intellectual skills needed to deal with information. Once the user is trained by the schools (learning to read, write, think critically, and to evaluate), the library is the logical place to take over and to carry through the learning process to its completion. It should be noted that the schools are also teaching library skills to the students. The essential difference between the library and the school is in the degree of independence achieved by the user. The school library tends to guide the student, initiate the learning process, and to give elementary exposure through predetermined exercises. As one moves up through the system, independence and responsibility become the essential feature of the process. Ideally, the librarian deals with a user who has come to recognize a pattern in the process of acquiring information and only needs direction and focus. The reality of interfacing with users is other than the ideal. Whatever the preparedness of the user, librarians still hold the key to information access and are limited only by the extent of their knowledge of the sources and their ability to teach the user.

Efforts are under way in schools to introduce an information component to the curricula (Rader, 1990). While this does signify a recognition of the importance of altering the student to the need for developing competence in the handling of information, it is not clear what concrete format the programs will take. What seems to be happening so far is the statement of objectives and the implementation of experimental programs. How it will take form finally and how the faculty and the librarians will play parts in this remains to be seen. One thing that should be considered, however, is that the faculty will still be the ones responsible for being educators in a way more similar to school teachers than to librarians. Faculty will still expose the student to the world through their particular disciplines and stimulate a response to it. Faculty will still see information seeking as a means to an end while librarians will view information seeking as an end in itself. What each values the most and what each has the most experience of will influence the essence of the contribution to the learning process. The student will need both. It seems to us that only the rare individual can teach both approaches. In nonacademic libraries, the relationships will not be so clearly intertwined; but the competently educated user is still going to have the advantage in terms of learning from the librarian to be information literate.

The User

Library users cannot be categorized easily from any perspective. While information can have a significant influence on one's life and can enable one to take control of it, the realization of this is not universal. To those who, in varying degrees, are aware of value in information, there are many ways besides resorting to libraries in which one can get the information wanted, especially if the want is limited to the easily accessible. To those who are alert and aware, the limits of information available through libraries are often apparent. Part of our professional obligation is to shape the user's recognition of what are both the potential and the barriers to information.

The average user brings to the library an outlook which affects the chances of acquiring information and knowledge. Librarians may be at home in libraries and they may be at relative ease in interpreting the configurations of printed materials, electronic gear, departments, rules, and people; but the user is often out of his or her element. It may not occur to the librarian that anyone would be ill at ease in the library. Many people are, however, and effective learning and information seeking will not take place until this problem is resolved (Mellon, 1986).

Some of the factors influencing the individual are personal and some societal. On a personal level, the user may have a sense of inadequacy about how to proceed and may be afraid to appear stupid to anyone on the library staff. Sometimes an information need is felt vaguely but is difficult to articulate. Often the individual is subconsciously aware of the gap between his or her intellectual capabilities and the knowledge needed to satisfy the information need. The magnitude of the effort required is daunting to such people. Not having an idea of how information sources are differentiated in a library, or why, makes users feel as if they have to deal with the totality of things in the library all at once. That too can be daunting and may be viewed as too tedious to be worth the effort. Librarians recognize readily that only a small part of the whole is needed to connect the user to the information; to users this is not always apparent. What is satisfying and enjoyable to the reference librarian about information mediation is seldom grasped by the user. In the user's mind, it is sometimes apparent, the need to "get information about" entails the concommittant goal of getting out of the library as quickly as possible. Library encounters are not as satisfying personally to the user as librarians might assume and there are consequences for the teaching of information literacy. In addition, instructional services are wanted by librarians but seldom does the user ask for them (George, 1990, p. 107).

On another level and for those who do not bring such concerns with them, library users perceive information gathering as peripheral to their interests. Many of them, students particularly, have short-term goals in a library. Their information seeking is not related to future activity on their part. Using a library is viewed as a one-time only or infrequent happening. Such a user is not usually ready for the investment in time required for significant information acquisition. Libraries are also viewed as places to spend leisure-time or as places to do other work.

The popular image of the library and of librarians helps to create a sense of being out of place on the part of the user. Having knowledge or information, having an interest in intellectual pursuits, showing overt evidence of thinking things through are not qualities valued in the popular imagination. One reason that advertising is so effective is that it takes these attitudes into account. Advertisers recognize that intellectual effort is generally mistrusted; that how the thing advertised makes a person feel is the important factor in selling. The activity of spending for consumer items is motivated more readily by how they are presented than by how good they are. Even though real-life librarians often belie their popular image, the picture projected, from Sesame Street to Norman Rockwell, is often one of people who are slightly ridiculous. Whatever validity the images may have, it is probable that they engender attitudes that may not be either strong or conscious but which seem to play a role in shaping an individual user's attitude toward libraries and consequently to their perceptions of the role of information in their lives. Another popular misconception of users is that the service is free and, if so, it cannot be worth much.

A final consideration for the user is that there is usually not much time in people's lives for getting a healthy perspective on one's need for information. However, finding the time is a necessity; it takes time to acquire knowledge and to use it competently, to gather information, to interpret it, and to use it creatively. There are usually too many demands made on people for this to get a high priority, and when time does become available there are too many things to divert attention from it. Free time is often seen as an opportunity to relax and enjoy life and not to take responsibility for one more thing.

In light of the factors just mentioned, what is the probability that consciousness can be raised to make people aware of their opportunity to benefit personally from the availability of information? Business and government do not need such reminders and where the institutional library does not meed the needs, there is investment in specialized information centers or search services that get the desired data to where it is wanted. The aforementioned considerations should not be taken to be sure tokens of defeat for the information professional—but they are factors to be taken into account when the attempt is made to match people up to their information needs and to teach them how to do it for themselves. We are going to have a better chance of success if we keep ourselves conscious of what militates against success.

Acquiring the Skill

To librarians, who are usually highly literate, getting information does not seem to demand more than familiarity with the sources and a sensible judgment about what to look for first. Without knowing it many of them started training as information professionals early in childhood, and they bring to the job an array of mental capabilities that they use unconsciously to gather and present information. If often does not look as if it takes much but there is a complexity to the process which few people are ready to apply when they first become aware that they need to acquire their own facility with it.

It is ironic that the historical occurrence of a resource directly tied to wealth is accessible to everyone but is harder to acquire than oil or gold. The main reason for this is that the complex intellectual processes which must be brought to bear on the acquisition of information rarely mature in most individuals. This is partly due to the absence of recognition on the part of people as to how their intellectual capabilities can be responsible for their own advancement. The politics of getting along in a career may deter some people from achieving their goals. Another reason is that it takes a long period of time to become educated to the point of being able to use information as a resource. The intellectually gifted may arrive at the top faster but the top is also accessible to the less gifted but perseverant. The more gifted may also track themselves into specialization with the potential danger of having their knowledge base become obsolete. Adult learners who have tried to full in the gaps in their learning are often struck by the monumental effort it takes. Whatever the cause, reaching the full potential of one's learning abilities depends on a variety of factors going right over a long period of time. We venture to suggest that not one bibliographic instruction librarian who has ever given a class would say he or she has not encountered a student who lacked some one or other intellectual skill necessary to find information in a library.

To be information literate one's education has to have proceeded along a path of ever-widening competence from grade to grade. This often starts when children are not yet walking. Certainly by the time formal schooling starts or when the child is ready, the process should operate in such a way that learning takes place in stages of growth, each one building on and expanding the level reached before. By the time a student reaches college or university, the educational skills should have been acquired to the point at which the first moves toward specialization can be taken. In reality many students reach college with less than the mental equipment necessary. Many people never achieve competence in elementary school. Most librarians, however, are academically competent and have been able to develop the educational and informational skills necessary to find out whatever they want to. This may make it difficult for them, as is often the case for teachers, to imagine the mind set of the user to whom dealing with a library is a difficult task.

In order to understand what kind of preparation we think an ideal user would bring to the process and why the people librarians encounter on a daily basis have difficulty in libraries, some examination of the intellectual baggage necessary is called for. What exactly does it take for a person to become independent in locating information? Putting aside the cost of acquiring some kinds of information (current financial disclosures, for example), all the tools one needs to acquire and manipulate information are there at birth. All of them need to be trained and disciplined and, initially, this is what the educational systems do, aided and abetted by the families of children who go to school.

Reading Ability

The first skill is the ability to read. It takes years for children to master this skill so that it can be used to advantage. It takes place gradually and requires the person involved to feel psychologically comfortable with one stage of the process before going on to the next. Children learn first the sounds associated with letters and then the combination of sounds to represent words. Words are then strung together to show that ideas can be presented in print and used to communicate. After a couple of years of this, reading for comprehension is introduced and over a period of several years the mental discipline of reading for understanding the import of another's ideas is acquired. In the meanwhile children are learning, from exposure to other disciplines, what they can learn about other aspects of a complex world. In other words, they are acquiring information about how the world they live in is structured and how it functions. On the elementary level, children get a grasp of the rudimentary facts about a variety of subjects deemed necessary for functioning comfortably in their societies. Their perceptions of the world they live in are expanded and they learn to recognize basic differences between their personal world and the world around them. Hopefully, many of them learn to react reflectively to what they are taught. The end result of learning to read is the ability to interpret data, to recognize information, and to use it. Librarians who introduce users to the library tend to take the acquisition of this skill for granted; but it is not a capability that many people have and the lack of it limits their ability to take advantage of what a library has to offer. For bibliographic instruction what is important is what is missing from the interpersonal transaction when both the librarian and the user make false assumptions about the ability to read. The difference in perspective between the two is a block to any effective activity.

Communication Skills

Communicating well is the next skill necessary to the information-literate. What has meaning to the principals involved in a dialogue is often intriguing to a third party observer. People often try to use words, expressions, or indistinctly formulated phrases to convey meaning to each other, and unless the listener can make shrewd guesses as to the content of the message, communication does not take place. Informational transactions can get bogged down in the failure to make sense of the words or concepts a librarian is using. The assumption that the listener understands what is being said is not safe. Library jargon is the worst example of this kind of dialogue: MESH, LCSH, OPAC, OCLC, CD-ROM, and so forth. As soon as the first unfamiliar term comes out the listener is lost and is usually reluctant to stop a librarian and ask for an explanation. Granted that communication is a two-way process, the point is still that poor communication is another barrier to effective bibliographic instruction.

Formulating the Information Need

A user has to be able next to conceptualize and articulate the information need and may have to work with the librarian on this formulation. The librarian's experience with asking questions, paraphrasing, and using examples is useful at this point. Sometimes the librarian can construct the information need verbally but, whether it is correctly stated or not, the user will not know what the words mean. Librarians usually do not have trouble coming up with a verbal formulation for an information need and often do not recognize the sudden comprehension gap on the part of the user. While individual situations requiring information can be handled successfully by the librarian, the person needing information will not be able to do this without help until the intellectual skill of using words to express precise meaning is attained. Information literacy involves being able to do this if one intends to acquire independence in the process; it is part of the "learning how to learn." Hand-in-hand with precise verbal formulation goes the skill of mental analysis. One has to think through the elements involved in stating a question to be sure a sufficiently comprehensive understanding of the information need is arrived at.

Critical Thinking

Interacting mentally with data or information so that it can be made part of one's mental outlook is also a prerequisite. A great deal of stress is placed on critical thinking during the educational process from elementary school on. In giving library instruction, it becomes obvious that one needs to continue stressing the ability to think actively and critically about what a user is doing and what one has to do to get the desired information. Students especially often seem surprised by the notion that they can and should judge what they read and should use their own knowledge base as a frame of reference for making decisions about what someone else has written. A user acquires the habit of participating actively in the process when it becomes obvious that information is not just there to be incorporated into a position statement, that it becomes another clue in a widening perspective. Critical thinking about the process enables the user to acquire control over what is happening; it shifts the focus from the "book with the answer" to the person reacting and using what is being learned or used. But getting the user to realize that he or she needs to be using what is available and making it serve one's purposes rather than being driven by the goal of "getting the answer" is a difficult thing to do. Some people learn this in school; some learn to apply it in different situations; but most people seem to leave it aside when they are in a library. For librarians this part of the process of working with people can be frustrating. It does not come easily to some people and others are determined to avoid it. In any case, without the ability to reflect on information and to question its value and relevance, the user cannot progress very far in learning information skills.

Another aspect of critical thinking is the ability to evaluate information sources and the relative merit of the information contained in them. This requires a competent basic grasp of the subject, of course, but it also requires the habit of making comparisons and looking for what may be lacking. If the user has been trained to think logically as well, then evaluation can be more productive for interpreting useful information. Often, the only logic applied to the information source a user acquires is that if something is in a reference book which somebody wrote, then it must be true. The inability to question the validity or truth of something written or spoken by a supposed authority is socially dangerous as well as personally harmful.

When the searcher has gathered together whatever data is available, it is necessary to know how to synthesize it into something meaningful and comprehensive. The final step is to reduce the complex to the simple. This often opens up a whole new area of interest but at least the person looking has gained an important part of the whole and can grow with it. This is the "learning how to learn" process that BI librarians and people concerned with the role of information in society grope with. Unless people can do this, there is no growth in the learning process. For many people, the first time they realize they need to know how to use all the skills required is when they are in a library looking for something; and it is the librarian who gets the formidable job of making the process work.

How much can the librarian do? Practically speaking, the more critical we can train users to be, the less likely they are to want spoonfeeding. Reference librarians can often get bogged down in the attempt to help uncritical people get what they need. Unfortunately, there is not much time available for this. More people want more of our time and we seem to be more aware of how much less quality is going into the service. On the other hand, we may be able to raise consciousness about the need to be interactive; but the user has to make the decision to take over the process. We cannot force people to recognize when they have a good thing available to take advantage of; but we can be there when they are ready for it.

Mental Attitudes

With the first set of prerequisites out of the way (reading ability, communication skill, precision of expression, critical thinking, the ability to evaluate, logical thinking, synthesis, and reduction), the user brings into play the mental attitudes that motivate or drive the gathering process. Among these are: curiosity, determination, and the ability to do detective work. Initially, this process should be slow and careful because the user or researcher is looking for clues that give meaning to the search. Once the initial relevant data is identified, the rest of the process will probably flow through a mental channel of similar information.

Curiosity is something that can and should be cultivated for this process. One knows that the information needed is probably out there somewhere or has a way of being generated if it is not actually in some book. One's curiosity will stimulate the searcher to find out how it got there and how he or she is going to find out where it is. The mental exploration that is going to take place for the searcher to get to the desired goal takes on, for some, an aspect of the adventurous. In real library situations, users often become involved this way in getting the information they want. Librarians exhibit this attitude too and should pass it on to anyone they are helping. The user can learn attitudes toward information seeking by association with people who demonstrate a sense of satisfaction in doing so. The process does not appear so dry to the user who can observe positive attitudes in action and in fact the activity is a satisfying one and should appear to be to any observer.

Determination is another mental attitude that is rewarded eventually. Prospecting for gold or drilling for oil takes determination. Achieving almost any goal does. Learning to learn, learning to locate information involves the recognition that the end result requires the pursuit sometimes of false or irrelevant leads. It may take painstaking effort to gather small amounts of data or facts; it may take trial and error approaches. Librarians take these approaches themselves when ferreting out information, and while sometimes it is done because of a failure to plan an effective strategy, sometimes it is because the strategy requires following one's instinct.

Finding information requires the habits of a detective in formulating, testing, and proving or disproving hypotheses. Positive experiences in acquiring knowledge or information by shrewdly planned strategies give the individual a sense of power and control over information seeking. This feeling is important to giving one a sense of self-confidence. It makes it possible for a person to see that getting the desired information depends more on the ability to formulate and carry through on a plan of attack than on an instantaneous recognition of the right answer. The confidence that the answer is probably there and the facility of knowing how the plan can work strengthens a mental attitude that has to be present in competent information seeking. Because this attitude is so common to the experience of librarians and because they sometimes assume it of the user, it tends to be overlooked in the course of assisting or teaching people to search for information.

Motivation

Teachers and personnel managers pay a great deal of attention to motivation in getting something accomplished by others. Whoever, in the future, will train society to acquire meaningful information will have to take ways of motivating into consideration. Training people to become self-sufficient entails some idea of the motivation of the individual. If, as in most BI classes, a user "just has to be here," then the main goal is usually to get away as soon as possible. If that goal cannot be changed or modified by the librarian, then instruction will probably not accomplish much. Perhaps it is beyond the scope of bibliographic instruction to deal with the theories and practice of motivation. But if librarians can judge what is motivating their users at the time an information need is being negotiated or a desired skill is being taught, then the interpersonal transaction can be made more meaningful and effective. If there is no motivation, then the strategy may be not to try. Classroom teachers often know when it is appropriate not to start teaching a new lesson because sometimes students are not receptive to trying something new.

Some people simplify the information gathering process in their own minds and are not prepared to discuss how to go about conducting a somewhat complex search. It may be best to let that kind of situation go and not address the need. For others, however, who think they want to tackle the process, librarians have to be prepared to recognize when people are ready and know how to kindle their interest in going as far as necessary. This is an ability that some say can be learned or demonstrated. If it can, all well and good; if it cannot, then it is reasonable to assume that the user has to bring his or her own active and eager motivation to the situation. Whatever the circumstances, some value to be derived has to be a part of the mental outlook of the user in order for instruction to have positive results.

Recognizing Resources

Now the user who has not yet been eliminated from the competition is ready to consider the resources at his or her disposal. First, this takes a recognition that someone may have collected the data in printed or electronic form. One also has to recognize that the information center at hand may not have all the pertinent resources. Anyone browsing through a bookmobile and conducting serious research on AIDS has to become aware that statistical information on the subject is likely to be located elsewhere. Another requirement of the searcher is recognizing hierarchies of value in the sources that are potentially useful. If one's knowledge of a subject is nonexistent or rudimentary, then what has value at first is what is only introductory to the field of inquiry. As the knowledge becomes more sophisticated, there is a corresponding need to differentiate the sources into the useful and the irrelevant. Eventually, all the sources become useless as the researcher becomes more informed and comes to the point of creating information. Users and librarians who help them have to determine their awareness level before the right resources can be selected and exploited purposefully.

Problem Solving

Having ascertained the appropriate level of sources to use, the searcher has to decide how the goal is to be reached. Specific sources have to be identified and an array of problem-solving techniques need to be used to make effective use of time and to avoid inappropriate strategies. Part of the problem solving process involves knowing when to get help and when to work alone. A preliminary plan should be constructed and a sense of how to proceed should be articulated. The searcher should have a sense of why the first step is a reasonable one to take and what is expected of it. The searcher should be able to reason to the next step once the first one is taken and to be flexible in changing the plan as new material develops and directs the strategy. Some users come back to the librarian at this point to discuss the strategy; if the librarian has something to add, fine; otherwise just the opportunity to sound out the theory of the approach is valuable to the searcher. A librarian can make suggestions at this point; but it might be better to let someone who has come this far in the process learn by trial and error. It might be advisable for the librarian to be available for direction and consultation. In addition, the librarian may want to refer to the existence of other sources to be introduced later when the user is ready for them. At any rate, what is important to the user is to develop the habit of the problem-solving approach with its gradual recognition that the usable materials for one's purposes is really a subset of all the materials a library holds. This makes it possible psychologically for an individual to deal with the mass of library resources and not feel overwhelmed by them. It gives a person more of a feeling of comfort and control over the process.

THE INFORMATION THRESHOLD

Having come so far the user is now in a position to recognize new and meaningful information when it appears. Up to this point the user has gathered facts and data that are already meaningful and part of the mental experience brought to bear on the search. After this point the librarian may be able to point out bibliographies for locating more specialized sources of information but usually does not need to know about the subject. It is important to know when the absence of information or data is meaningful and the experienced user will recognize this when it happens. It may be that the absence of data means that the library's resources have been exhausted but it could mean also that the searcher has reached the limit of readily available information. The searcher is still at the point of dealing with known information—unknown to him or her perhaps but known to somebody else (compilers, other researchers, experts in the field, etc.). Librarians in most information centers can apply their own skills to facilitating the process up to this point and some librarians are in a position to make knowledgeable suggestions for further research activity. The user however now has to determine the course of action in creating or locating new information. Ideally bibliographic instruction has played a role in guiding but not in controlling this process. The librarian has a crucial role to play in the same way he or she has traditionally: in knowing the sources, responding comprehensive to inquiries, and in instructing in the use of the library. While reference librarians have probably all had some experience of the process as just described, most information mediation encounters require a great deal more effort.

Getting to the Facts

While it might be reasonable (though not realistic maybe) to expect that the information seeker will come to the library with all the aforementioned mental skills, it is not reasonable to expect someone to know where information in a given discipline comes from. Becoming independent means that the user must understand who provides information, how it is organized, and how it is disseminated. Once a person is competent in a discipline and aware of the channels for supplying data and information, it is possible to sort out the important and the trivial, that is, to "keep up" with what's going on and to know when something is new and what is its relative importance. The result is the ability to recognize the difference between known facts and uninterpreted data and to create information out of what is already known. It probably takes a special talent to do this; but the talent cannot be exercised without all of the other well-disciplined abilities already mentioned.

The librarian is usually the only one available to make clear to the user how knowledge and information becomes available and how to go about searching for it. This is a professional skill which, in a broad area of subjects, only the librarian has taken the time to cultivate. Trial and error on the user's part is usually a wasted effort and people who know what they are doing usually ask up front for a description of the ways and means to gather information in an area not familiar to them.

Justifying Bibliographic Instruction

The question of why librarians should provide instructional services ought to get some consideration. If we give so much time and attention to this activity, there ought to be a good reason for it and there are several of them. To begin with, we recognize the gap between the information people ask for and their ability to get it without help. Second, we recognize that their need for information goes beyond the basic and the simplistic. The fact that some people use libraries just to get facts to put into a school report does not obscure the fact that they need power over information in order to be in control of their lives. We know also that people who are information-independent are economically viable and not dependent on others. We know also that they can be informed active participants who can influence the course of events in the political process. They can improve the quality of their lives and enhance their personal satisfaction. They can improve their chances of mobility in their jobs. They can acquire expertise that will enable them to move into new kinds of work. We know too that they are not going to do any of this without help. After people leave school, the only expense-free recourse for self-development is the library; and the only one who is going to give the advice is the librarian. In addition the only ones who have the experience and knowledge to impart are the librarians. We know that libraries can supply all the published information available. We know how important that information is for the quality of life and for economic viability, and we know how important information is as a check on the political power of governing elites. Pragmatically, as information services librarians, we will never be able to do anything else but show people where things are if we do not get library users functioning independently. We want to avoid endless repetition.

In view of the fact that the need is there and that the ability to fill that need is also there, instructional services are an important part of what a library has to offer. Developing an effective approach becomes a worthwhile goal for the librarian.

Information has been called a fluid resource because, unlike natural resources, it cannot be kept from going to the recipient; it is free and must be shared in order to benefit the processor. If information is a source of wealth, then who is going to be able to hoard it and use it for the benefit of a small group? The answer is that it does not have to be safeguarded against everyone because the effort required to get it may be more than most people want to expend. If one is kept safely unaware of the value of information and if one is never motivated to become functionally literate, then one is removed effectively from the competition. There is the element of freedom and personal choice to be reckoned with. Librarians and other educators are faced with the task of imparting a talent which some people will not want to acquire. If, for the sake of comparison, we consider what it would be like if a violin teacher suddenly realized that in order to survive economically everyone had to learn to play the violin, we might have an idea of what we are up against. Some people would not want to do it, some would avoid it, and the few who are talented and have the ambition would acquire the control and the power. That is what has happened historically—elites control the wealth and power as long as they have the perspective on what is going on and the ambition to rule. Nevertheless, an informed citizenry needs to acquire information skills in order to provide an income and to influence the process of government. We cannot set for ourselves the social goal of saving people from the consequences of their own choice. We can make them aware, however, and we can be ready with our own program to provide the learning environment when the time comes that the individual is ready for it.

Electronic Phenomena

No one who works in a library can fail to be aware of the presence and impact of developments in technology. There is a great deal of excitement over it and its possibilities seem endless. There is a great deal of anxiety over it too—on the part of timid or reluctant users. In addition, there is much ignorance over what it can do and how it can be used. Most people can learn to handle "computers" as they are referred to and, in the final analysis, will probably become comfortable with them. At some point in the future, people will see the new technological advances as just other conveniences to use. For librarians, it seems as if there are two extreme attitudes to deal with at the present moment: people who are confident that they know what they are doing and who miss much of what an electronic data base can offer, and people who are afraid to touch a terminal for fear they will cause it blow up. There are people who fit in between the extremes but there do not seem to be many of them. A further complication to the picture is that remote access will become more prevalent (as long as dial-in access does not become costly). This means that untried users can perpetuate ineffective search habits and not get information that is available. As reference librarians we think this is a major concern for the profession. Information is valuable. Frustration in finding it may lead to the failure to appreciate its value; it can lead to alienation of the "information deprived;" it can encourage manipulation by the "information wealthy."

Reference librarians who work with people using electronic information sources recognize that there is a need to guide people in their use: both in the manipulation of the software and in the formulation of search strategy. Many people who use these data bases are deceived in thinking they are easy to use. They are not easy to use. They take thought and planning and require determined critical thinking to get the most out of them. For college students writing term papers, they serve the immediate purpose of developing a bibliography—but students often have no idea of why it is worthwhile to know how to develop a bibliography. Not only is the reference librarian aware of the complexity of these sources, but also of the time it takes to familiarize the user with manipulating them. Instead of spending our time running from one computer or terminal to another and repeating the same lesson to new and infrequent users, one would like to hope there is a method of instruction that can be employed to avoid the investment in time. The idea is to free the librarian to be available for consultation with increasing numbers of users.

The Self-Confident Electronic User

Many people using libraries come in with computer skills that enable them to deal confidently with the electronic data bases available. These people have little need for direction in using a CD-ROM or a computer terminal. They understand the gadgetry and the wizardry and are ready to search. Because these databases are new forms of the printed sources, they are conceived and organized in the same way that they always have been and in a way that librarians are familiar with. What they offer is more access points and simultaneous use of all the access points being used. The danger is that the unguided user may stop at the first satisfactory response. The user may never refine the search and thus locate more pertinent and useful information. This type of information seeker may lose sight of the fact that the important thing for him or her is not so much to locate one useful answer but to acquire familiarity with techniques for searching. This is the same threshold that the unfamiliar user encounters. It is still a matter of not recognizing the need to learn how to go about competently finding information on one's own. It might be a relief to the librarian to deal with users who can handle the machinery but there is till the concern that left to their own devices, these users will be cut off from access to important information (Charles and Clark, 1990).

The Anxious Electronic User

At the other end of this continuum are the people who are lacking in self-confidence with any sort of automated device. They think something will "go wrong" if they use them and they often bring other library anxieties to the search process. Like the self-confident, they too do not seem to be aware that the important thing is to learn the skill of information seeking. For librarians it is sometimes difficult to recognize and to sympathize with this mental scenario. We do not usually have this kind of problem, we do not always view ourselves as counsellors, and we may not appreciate the library perspective of the worried user. There are often aids to the user but the language employed is not always clear and it varies from one data base to another. With library specific data bases such as an online catalog, jargon often confuses the uninitiated. Librarians who help these users find themselves devoting time to getting them past the anxiety stage. It is also obvious that getting such people on to the self-sufficiency stage is going to take a lot of work. Again the librarian is caught between giving time to people who need help and recognizing that there is not enough time to do everything.

Remote Access

   With remote access, the user is being taken out of the library and left to his or her own devices. In some cases this may be good but it may fill the librarian with information anxiety. If studies suggest that, in the library environment, some unguided users obtain inadequate information (Charles and Clark, 1990), then what are the implications for the totally unguided user? Whatever the approach to information, whether automated or printed, remote or proximate, the reference librarian is still more likely to be the one with the knowledge of the sources and sufficient experience to maximize their potential for the user. Because it takes so long to become proficient and because it takes experience to know the limitations of a given source, we know that the librarian's expertise is not replaceable. It may not be recognized but it cannot be duplicated easily over a broad range of subjects. Nor can there be a substitute for the constant practice the librarian gets. Without users who have competent access skills, remote access will be of benefit to only a few people and could become an expensive waste of time. The assumption that, if the technology is there, people will use it wisely is probably not a safe one. It seems probable, then, that to get the most out of information available through electronic technology, librarians will need to devote time to instructing the user. Like any craft or art, information seeking needs to be disciplined and understood to be employed effectively. If there are people out there who are reachable, then the librarian will be the one to provide the service.

Training the User

   If, as part of their professional obligation, librarians still want to consider teaching people how to use the library, then it is important to keep in mind that different people learn effectively by using one or another mode of learning. Often people who give library instruction do not reach the audience and it is because of a failure to make the effort. What can happen is that the audience, or certain people in the audience, fail to make sense of what is being said because one or another of their personal mental requirements for learning is missing. For example, some people need background to understand what is being taught. Other people need a clear reason in the form of a personal benefit to pay attention to what is being said. Some people need simpler language or a more elementary approach. Others need to go off on their own, try things, and then come back for guidance when they know what they do not know. Readiness is an important concept for the librarian to keep in mind, and at the same time the learner has to feel as if he or she is in control of the process.

Admittedly, it is not always easy to determine who is ready nor do we meet people at the point of readiness. But no one who is in the library for instruction will get anything out of it if he or she has not focused attention on what is happening or is not prepared mentally for the process. Anyone who has taught in a classroom has experienced that. Fortunately for teachers they can rearrange their schedules and get the students when they are ready. Librarians do not have that option. We have outlined what we think is required of people to be prepared mentally for the process and we will discuss ideas for focusing attention in the instructional situation. We would like to turn attention for a moment to various methods of teaching and learning (U.S. Department of the Treasury, Internal Revenue Service, 1989). Some basic recognition of what they are may be useful to the reader who needs to be ready with a fresh approach when the standard presentation is not working.

A good guide to assessing the library awareness of the user is the *Taxonomy of Library Skills and Errors* (Jakobovits and Nahl-Jakobovits, 1990). Using this, the instructional services librarian can figure out the starting point for the user and build from there. It appears to assume, however, that the individual brings an adequately developed fund of educational skills to be learning session. If the instructional session is not formal, the librarian would have to use his or her familiarity with this tool to make an informed guess as to where an individual may fit in the scheme.

An awareness of cognitive task analysis, which examines a mental process as applied to a problem by an expert, can be used to track the progress of a user as he or she goes through the task of getting information on a particular topic. Many of us are aware of people who ask how to get some item or other of information and who go off leaving us with the feeling that something is missing in their approach but we do not know what. If we analyze the ways we go about finding certain kinds of information, we will be able to keep alert to recognizing when the user is not yet prepared to handle the search adequately.

When users become more practiced in the use of libraries, the librarian can have ready guides that show how the expert finds information in a particular field. One often finds in libraries bibliographical guides to sources available. We need to go a step further and provide guides to how we found information and how we would solve problems in information finding.

Any librarian who has trained either a co-worker or a user has encountered the problem of teaching so that the other person learns. We may tend at first to impose our own learning style on the object of our efforts, but it soon becomes clear that the person learns when the teaching adjusts to the learning style. Metacognition is the individual's conscious employment of thinking to learn something. We can benefit from a thorough understanding of metacognition, but practically speaking we are more likely to be in a position of observing and getting information about a person's learning style while we are in the process of a reference interview. If we keep alert to the user, we can make use of his or her interactions to decide how best to communicate the training or information required.

After the right training techniques have been applied, one can always hope that a transfer across disciplines will take place. That often does not happen because people sometimes find themselves at a loss when the information need is different. Our experience with law students is curious; they undergo some rigorous exercises in legal research and may ask for help when they have to find business information. If the librarian has trained a user successfully in learning how to locate information, then a final step would be to steer that person into doing the same thing for another type of information search. At least we need to underscore the fact that if it can be done one way for their most recent question, it probably can be done the same way for the next one. We may think this is obvious but it is not necessarily so to the user.

It is intriguing to explore the idea of using computer programs to train users. We think they have possibilities once the face-to-face interaction has taken place satisfactorily (Bramm Dunn, 1988).

One of the things that can discourage the library user in learning to become self-sufficient in the library is the amount of information he or she gets at one time from the librarian. Not only do we dispense jargon sometimes, we also give out too much for one person to absorb at one time. If the person is ready to learn, then it is important to sequence the material so that it goes from the general idea to the increasingly more detailed application or practice. This is another reason why the whole process will not take place over a brief session: there is usually too much for the user to learn. We have to catch them at the right point and instruct from there.

We need finally to recognize that the user's knowledge base grows and alters as he or she becomes more proficient. The way an initiate is prepared to receive instruction and to relate it to what is already known and understood is different from the way the expert assimilates and organizes it. This requires flexibility on our part and when we recognize the degree of understanding evidenced by the individual, we have to adjust to it and discard the irrelevant.

Techniques

One thing that may be apparent at this point is that there is a wide gap between the librarian's perspective and that of the library user. Most users are not scholars and have no desire to get mixed up in what they consider "intellectual pursuits." There are quite a few of them, however, who get a sense of satisfaction out of knowing that important information is available to them and they can control their own access. People who are setting up their own businesses are among the most satisfying for a librarian to work with. They need to be independent; they need unmediated access to a variety of sources;

and they are motivated to do things right. They learn quickly how to take advantage of a library's resources.

How does one infuse the instructional group setting with the same sense of directedness? It may require something of a theatrical touch on the part of the instructor. It requires an assessment of where the people in the audience are on the learning continuum. In our experience one thing that can be of help is consciousness raising. People have to be told how important information is to them. It has to be demonstrated with real situations. The danger of not being in control of important information has to be made clear. Health hazards get a lot of attention in the media and people have become aware of them to the point at which they can and will do something about them. The value of information in one's career and in one's personal life can be made clear also. If information gathering skills are not perceived as personally helpful or self-affirming, then users will view librarians trying to instruct as preachers with an ulterior motive if there is any motive ascribed at all. By focusing the attention on the personal value of information, librarians shift the emphasis from themselves and the proprietary library to the individual who now may not feel so alienated and who may start seeing the library as a means to an end.

Involvement in the learning experience has more value, we find, than does lecturing or discussion although any "personal encounter" approach seems to be more effective as oposed to the printed guide approach alone (George, 1990, pp. 123-124). CD-ROMS especially lend themselves to this technique. If the group is receiving instruction as part of a class requirement, then ask the teacher to be the one to try out the idea being presented. It helps to have one or more students suggest search strategies and to demonstrate them themselves. If they do not volunteer, then call on them. It is important to be sensitive and fair to the students but the involvement approach shows people that an information search on a database (printed or otherwise) can be productive and satisfying— and that one can escape unscathed. In the end there is a sense of empowerment for the individual even though most people do not like being asked to perform before a group.

Making eye contact with everyone at least once makes a difference in the response on the part of the user. Good public relations has a part to play in marketing the information services product. Again the focus is on the user. As long as one is made to feel that he or she is more important than the product and that the product has definite personal value, there will be more of an inclination to listen, learn, and make it part of one's personal outlook.

Librarians could keep handy a store of examples of how information made a significant difference. When Frances Kelsey kept thalidomide off the shelves in the 1960s, she made a difference that could have been felt by almost anyone who could walk into a library today. The career of Ralph Nader is also useful as an example. Tax laws might be written differently if more people have access to information about the process as it is in progress. Lack of information about

Chernobyl had disasterous consequences for people. What we know or do not know about radon can make a difference to us. Information available from the Consumers' Union makes a difference to many people who read their publications. It is most important to tailor the example to what would matter to the person or persons getting instruction; but the aim is to make them conscious of the fact that they can control their own access to information and that there is a good reason to do so. If people do not hear this from librarians, they are not likely to hear it from anyone else. Politicians have no compelling reasons for keeping the public informed, nor do businesses. All that is necessary from the people is that they work, vote, and buy.

Instruction could benefit from advertising. The user public should know what is available to them and that they can get help to make use of it. The exhortatory signage that one finds in libraries does not seem to be of much help. Good advertising can be developed. As long as it catches the attention, makes clear the benefit, and makes a realistic claim about what it is and does, it can be used effectively to market the library's services and to make people aware of their need. The idea is to change the scenario from librarians wanting to give instruction to users wanting to get it. But people will not ask for it unless we first get them thinking about it.

Once the user's attention is focused on the need for information gathering skills, the business of instruction can proceed. Students, the younger they are, tend to be more receptive to directed learning and to sit back and let themselves be taught. If that works, and if the end result is that they can function on their own, then that is the way to proceed with instructional services. Adult learners bring their life experience to the instructional setting and seem to prefer relating the instruction to that life experience. It becomes necessary then to take the ideas presented and indicate first why they are valuable to the individual and where they fit in to their mental picture. Once that relationship is established, then it is necessary to let the person control the pace of learning and to be the principal participant. The instructor acts as a guide and facilitator and it is here that his or her knowledge of the sources is most valuable to the learning environment.

CONCLUSION

It seems clear that library instruction is an exceedingly complex process that is handicapped by the short period of time that can be devoted to it. What can be accomplished by the instructor in so short a time? The literature proliferates but the sense of satisfaction does not seem to be present. Nobody seems to be writing about successful BI; and everybody seems to be worrying over unsuccessful BI. To serve the receptive user's need in an instructional setting is not going to be a simple matter of one short class on BI. Because the opportunity to reach people in an instructional setting is limited, the librarian has to take advantage of other techniques such as advertising and consciousness to convey the message and to turn the need into a want. In the instructional session, the message that information is vital to the interests of the participants can be delivered clearly and effectively.

Librarians can separate the process into constituent parts once the person is motivated. One step will be learning how to use the tools: indexes, card catalog, online catalog, CD-ROMS, fiche, film, and so on. Another step will be developing search strategies and accessing the information. We can provide staff accordingly. Professional staff can work on the second step; with limited guidance, nonprofessional staff can work on the first step. Once the initial person-to-person session is finished, a user can be presented with procedures to be utilized on one's own. When the finding skills are refined and practiced, then the person can be directed to developing ideas about the specific sources available in the desired discipline. Finally the user can be taught to evaluate sources in terms of their potential usefulness.

Of course, this takes time and does not happen in the course of one learning session. Effective BI needs to be spread out over a period of sessions with assessment and reinforcement becoming a part of the whole. It should take on the atmosphere of a classroom with the idea that it is training and not learning in the formal sense. It does not need to take as long as a course of study but it should last longer than one class session—and some device for measuring the acquisition of skills will be needed. Let us recognize that we are dealing not only with possibly reluctant learners but also with possibly reluctant teachers. Many librarians will admit that they became librarians after discovering that teaching was not satisfactory. While the user has to be both ready to learn and prepared to absorb the skills, the librarian has to be ready and prepared also. As with the business of book acquisitions, many librarians seem to feel that they have learned to give instructional services on the job and on the fly.

Librarians need to be aware that it is not their failure to make the effort that is the problem with instructional services, it is the complexity of the process and the attitudes of the people involved. Only when we take the full picture into account can we make some progress toward workable instructional programs. Teaching faculty often experience the same frustration with school or college students as librarians do. However, the importance of information to the individual can be a powerful motivating force for people to want instruction and to be willing to profit by it.

REFERENCES

Bramm Dunn, Elizabeth. "The Challenges of Automation and the Library Instruction Program." *North Carolina Libraries* 46(Winter 1988): 219-222.

Charles, Susan K. and Katharine E. Clark. "Enhancing CD-ROM Searches with Online Updates: An Examination of End-User Needs, Strategies, and Problems." *College and Research Libraries* 51(July 1990): 321-328.

Cleveland, Harlan. *The Knowledge Executive: Leadership in an Information Society.* New York: Truman Talley Books, 1985.

Domhoff, G. William. *Who Rules America?* Englewood Cliffs, NJ: Prentice-Hall, 1967.

_____. *Who Rules America Now?* Englewood Cliffs, NJ: Prentice-Hall, 1983.

George, Mary W. "Instructional Services." In *Academic Libraries: Research Perspectives,* ed. Mary Jo Lynch. Chicago: American Library Association, 1990.

Jakobovits, Leon A. and Diane Nahl-Jakobovits. "Measuring Information Searching Competence." *College and Research Libraries* 51(September 1990): 448-462.

Mellon, Constance. "Library Anxiety: A Grounded Theory and Its Development." *College and Research Libraries News* 47(March 1986): 160-165.

Rader, Hannelore. "Bringing Information Literacy into the Academic Curriculum." *College and Research Libraries News* 51(October 1990): 879-880.

Ridgeway, Trish. "Information Literacy: An Introductory Reading List." *College and Research Libraries News* 51(July/August 1990): 645-648.

U.S. Department of the Treasury, Internal Revenue Service. "Educational Theories and Methodologies." *Training 2000.* [Publication 1480 (11-89). T22.44/2:1480/989: pp. 77-86.] Washington, DC: Government Printing Office, 1989.

BIBLIOGRAPHY

Allen, Gillian. "CD-ROM Training: What do the Patrons Want?" *RQ* 30 (Fall 1990): 88-93.

Allen, Mary Beth. "Focusing the One-shot Lecture." *Research Strategies* 7 (Summer 1989): 100-105.

Batt, Fred. "Bibliographic Instruction (BI): Examination of Changing Emphasis." In Advances in Library Administration and Organization, eds. Gerard B. McCabe and Bernard Kreissman. Greenwich, CT: JAI Press, 1986.

Drucker, Peter F. *The New Realities.* New York: Harper & Row, 1989.

Fink, Deborah. *Process and Politics in Library Research: A Model for Course Design.* Chicago: American Library Association, 1989.

Gilder, George. *Microcosm: The Quantum Revolution in Economics and Technology.* New York: Simon and Schuster, 1989.

Hopkins, Frances L. "A Century of Bibliographic Instruction: The Historical Claim to Professional and Academic Legitimacy." *College and Research Libraries* 43 (May 1982): 192-198.

Huston, Mary M. "Extending Information Universes through Systems Thinking." *College and Research Libraries News* 51 (September 1990): 692-695.

Joyce, Bruce and Beverly Showers. "Improving Inservice Training: The Messages of Research." *Educational Leadership* (February 1980): 379-385.

Kohl, David F. "Library Instruction." *Reference Services and Library Instruction: A Handbook for Library Management.* Santa Barbara: ABC-CLIO, 1985.

Lewis, David W. "Inventing the Electronic University." *College and Research Libraries* 49 (July 1988): 291-304.

Love, Barbara. "The 19th Annual Workshop on Instruction in Library Use: The Challenge of the 90s." *College and Research Libraries News* 51 (September 1990); 734-736.

MacAdam, Barbara. "Information Literacy: Models for the Curriculum." *College and Research Libraries News* 51 (November 1990): 948-951.

Mandernack, Scott B. "An Assessment of Education and Training Needs for Bibliographic Instruction Librarians.' *Journal of Education for Library and Information Science* 30 (Winter 1990): 193-205.

Moholt, Pat. "The Future of Reference III: A Paradigm Shift for Information Services." *College and Research Libraries News* 51 (December 1990): 1045-1052.

Moran, Barbara B. "Library/Classroom Partnerships for the 1990s." *College and Research Libraries News* 51 (June 1990): 511-514.

Reichel, Mary. "Library Literacy." *RQ* 30 (Fall 1990): 46-49.

Sheridan, Jean. "The Reflective Librarian: Some Observations on Bibliographic Instruction in the Academic Library." *The Journal of Academic Librarianship* 16 (March 1990): 22-26.

Slamecka, Vladimir. "Information Processing and Information Systems." *The New Encyclopedia Britannica: Macropedia,* 1990.

Wurman, Richard Saul. *Information Anxiety.* New York: Doubleday, 1989.

Zand, Dale E. *Information, Organization, and Power.* New York: McGraw-Hill, 1981.

THE ROLE OF CITATION ANALYSIS IN EVALUATING CHEMISTRY JOURNALS:
A PILOT STUDY

Sandra E. Goldstein

INTRODUCTION

Many studies have investigated techniques for serials management and evaluation. Common techniques include examination of interlibrary loan requests, circulation statistics, use studies, user studies, and citation analysis. A number of other journal evaluation studies have explored techniques for evaluating science journals as a whole ((Rice, 1979; Stankus and Rice, 1982) or concentrated on journals in specific scientific disciplines, such as biochemistry (Marton, 1983), the health sciences (Bourne and Gregor, 1975; Usdin, 1979), and physics (Singleton, 1976). However, a review of the literature revealed only one article (Rice, 1983) that examined serials management issues specifically for chemical literature and no articles that assessed the viability of using the process in a small chemistry library setting. In order to determine

Advances in Library Administration and Organization,
Volume 10, pages 97-112.
ISBN: 1-55938-460-3

whether citation analysis can be used effectively as a serials evaluation technique for chemistry journals and as a predictor of local use patterns in small library settings, this pilot study was conducted.

Citation analysis can be used to determine a journal's value and importance in a field. Serial literature plays an important role in chemistry research, even more than in most other fields. In fact, Heinzkill (1980) reports that 93.6 percent of chemists' citations are to journals, as compared to 91.8 percent by physicists, 80.8 percent by zoologists, 76.8 percent by mathematicians, 41.9 percent by sociologists, and 23.3 percent by historians (Heinzkill, 1980, p. 352). Because serial literature is critical to chemistry research and citation analysis is a commonly used technique for determining the importance of journals, citation analysis was chosen as the collection management tool to be evaluated for its usefulness in this pilot study. According to Garfield, citation measures are most reliable when examining homogeneous (i.e., similar) fields (Garfield, 1979, pp. 248-249). Therefore, the chemistry discipline was broken down into three important subfields (analytical, organic, and physical chemistry) and the results of the citation analysis conducted in this pilot study were used to examine the applicability of Garfield's conclusions.

This paper addresses two basic research questions:

1. Can citation analysis be used as an effective journal evaluation technique for chemistry serials, particularly in a small library setting?
2. Does the effectiveness of citation analysis as a collection management tool increase when it is used to measure homogeneous subfields of a discipline rather than the literature of the discipline as a whole?

LITERATURE REVIEW

Many studies of journal evaluation techniques can be found in library literature. Two of the main methods are citation analysis and use or user studies. Some of the advantages and disadvantages of these methods, as discussed in the literature, are detailed here.

Broadus' (1985) article provides the best overview to the subject, particularly in his defense of Institute for Scientific Information (ISI) *Journal Citation Reports (JCR)* as a valid method of journal evaluation. One of the advantages of citation measures is that they offer a way to evaluate collections "unobtrusively, providing numerical data that can be analyzed" (Singleton, 1976, p. 270). In addition, citation analysis can be implemented by one person and is not dependent on direct input from the users (McCain and Bobick, 1981, p. 258). Finally, according to Garfield, the father of *Science Citation Index* and *Journal Citation Reports,* high citation rates correlate with peer judgment about scientific excellence and the importance of contribution (Garfield, 1979, p. 250).

However, others criticize citation measures for several reasons. First, Skolnik argues that citation measures are biased toward review journals (Skolnik, 1982, p. 136). Second, citation studies do not reflect all kinds of use, because some journals that are widely read are not frequently cited (Wiberley, 1982, p. 357). Third, Garfield notes that 25 percent of the scientific papers published are never cited even once (Garfield, 1979, p. 240). Finally, some argue that citation rates are not a valid indicator of local use because the citation rankings are based on national citation patterns.

Use and user studies, on the other hand, are dependent on the "good will, objectivity, and cooperation of the users" (McCain and Bobick, 1981, p. 258). In addition, there is not an accepted definition of what constitutes "use" (Rice, 1979, p. 36). Definition of use becomes even more problematic when trying to measure in-house use. Rice points out that use studies are time consuming and only indicate what is being used, not what may be needed (Rice, 1983, p. 58). However, use and user studies are effective in indicating the local use patterns of a library's collection.

Many authors argue that there is no single evaluation method that will provide the "magic" list of core or "fringe" titles and that more than one method should be used (Pravdic and Oluic-Vukovic, 1987; Garfield, 1979; Dombrowski, 1988). In fact, Garfield urges that citation analysis methods are not intended to be used alone or indiscriminately but should be viewed as objective information to be used in concert with other objective and subjective considerations (Garfield, 1979, p. 243).

PROBLEM STATEMENT

To test if citation analysis can serve as a predictor of local use of chemistry serials, particularly in a small library setting, a shelving use study was conducted at the University of Michigan Chemistry Library. The subfields (analytical, physical, and organic chemistry) were selected for the study because they are natural divisions for the field. The results of this study should suggest the value of (1) employing citation measures as predictors of local use patterns and (2) analyzing disciplines by subfields in the collection management process.

The University of Michigan Chemistry Library is a small departmental library serving 50 faculty members and 160 graduate students. The library has over 50,000 volumes and approximately 400 current journal subscriptions. The departmental strengths are in organic, physical, analytical, and inorganic chemistry, and the library's collection supports the research interests of the faculty and the curriculum for upper-division/graduate-level courses in chemistry. The Chemistry Department is growing in stature and recently moved into a new chemistry building with state-of-the-art laboratory and research facilities. Similarly, the chemistry library has been enhancing its serials collection, with the addition of over 30 new chemistry journal subscriptions and backorders in the 1990 fiscal year. Shelf space is limited, however, and serials have already outgrown the space generated from the last storage project, implemented in 1987 (30 percent of the Chemistry Library's collection is in storage).

At the time of the 1987 storage project, many of the established methods of identifying storage candidates were implemented. Titles sent to storage included those not currently received (due to cancellation or ceased publications), earlier years of long-running titles, less-used foreign language titles, and titles duplicated elsewhere within the library system. Consequently, further collection evaluation techniques were needed to examine the chemistry serials collection, a problem commonly faced by other libraries. After reviewing the literature, citation analysis was selected as the technique to use to evaluate this specialized serials collection.

RESEARCH METHODOLOGY

Definition of the Population

The first step in the research process was to determine the population of journal titles to be studied. Three subfields of chemistry were selected: analytical, organic, and physical chemistry. These areas were chosen because they are major subfields of the chemistry discipline.

The Institute for Scientific Information's *Journal Citation Reports* was used as the citation analysis tool in this study. *JCR* is based on national citation patterns and some criticize the source for not reflecting local citation/use patterns. This is refuted by Wiberley, who found that national data bases of citations are almost as good as local data in predicting future citations of journals by local authors and that the compilation of local citation data is extremely time consuming and labor intensive (Wiberley, 1982, p. 358). Consequently, for the purposes of this study, *JCR* was used to determine the citation data for the journals studied.

JCR includes a section in which all titles are subdivided by subject categories and so these subdivisions were used to determine the initial population. These were then weeded of titles that were monographic series not owned by the Chemistry Library and titles already in storage. New journals added to the collection since 1988 were not considered in this study for these reasons: (1) there were not enough volumes available to evaluate use adequately; (2) they do not yet present a shelf space problem; and (3) citation analysis measures have not proved effective for new titles (Stankus and Rice, 1982, p. 97). Once the weeding was completed, a final population of 67 titles was identified: 18 in analytical chemistry, 23 in organic chemistry, and 26 in physical chemistry (see Appendix for a complete listing of titles studied).

Journal Citation Reports Data Collection

Once the final population of journal titles was determined, the following data were collected for each title.

1. *Call number.*
2. *Holdings information.* The beginning volume and year of what is physically kept in the Chemistry Library was noted for each title.
3. *Impact factor.* This is the average citation rate of a journal's articles, calculated by dividing the number of citable articles the journal published within the two preceding calendar years by the number of times the articles were cited. This figure is used as an indicator of the journal's value within its field.
4. *Actual JCR ranking.* Rankings are assigned to each subject area according to impact factors. The journal with the highest impact factor receives a *JCR* ranking of "'1."
5. *Relative JCR ranking.* This is a renumbering of *JCR* rankings to reflect the relative position of a title among the population of journals in the study.

Data from the 1988 *JCR* were used for this study because the 1989 *JCR* was not yet available.

Description of the Methodology

The purpose of this pilot study was to examine the viability of *JCR* as a collection evaluation technique and as a predictor of local use. To test this, a shelving use study of chemistry journals was conducted at the University of Michigan Chemistry Library over a six-week period in 1990.

The Chemistry Library's periodicals collection does not circulate. In addition, the Chemistry Department's faculty and graduate students have keys to the library. Because no circulation statistics could be gathered, a different approach had to be used to collect data on usage. The cooperation of the patrons was solicited; they were asked to not reshelve their materials during the six-week study period (April and May 1990). The Chemistry Library patrons generally had not been reshelving their materials, and this did not require a major change in their behavior. Use, for the purposes of this study, was then defined as the reshelving of a volume left near the photocopiers or on library tables.

A tally sheet was created for each title in the population, and titles were arranged in call number order to facilitate the recording process. Each title entry had the following information: title, subject area, actual *JCR* rank, call number, beginning holdings date, and space for tally marks to be made. For six weeks, Chemistry Library student shelvers recorded on the tally sheet each time they reshelved a journal volume. Data collection occurred, on average, two or three times per day during the six-week study period. During the spring term (May 1990), the Chemistry Library had no weekend hours and so no weekend shelving statistics were gathered then.

Statistical Analysis Techniques

A statistical package, STATVIEW 512+, was used to analyze the data. Three types of examinations were conducted: reliability, assessments, correlations, and simple regression.

Reliability Assessments

The use study data were examined in two ways to determine reliability. First, titles with greater than 20 overall uses were examined to see if their weekly use patterns remained constant or varied by week during the study. Area charts were produced to provide a visual display of the results. Second, the use data were tested to see if they conformed to Bradford's Law (that a few core journals constitute the majority of use within any given field).

Correlations

Tests of correlations were performed to test the strength of relationships between the following variables for each subject area and for the entire data set:

1. impact factor (the average citation rate of a journal's articles);
2. relative *JCR* rankings (the relative position of each title based on an ordered list of impact factors);
3. use sum (the total number of times each journal title was used); and
4. use rankings (the position of each title based on an ordered list of use sums).

Simple Regression

Regression analysis was performed to test if impact factors and *JCR* rankings could be used to predict local use patterns for each subject area and for the entire data set.

RESULTS AND DISCUSSION

Reliability Assessment

Titles from each subject area that were used at least 20 times were selected for analysis to determine if the usage was constant throughout the study period. In general, the analysis showed that use was low during week three (April 27-May 3, 1990) of the study. This can be explained by the fact that week three of the use study coincided with winter term finals week, when both students and faculty were involved with testing rather than research. Use also appeared to drop off a little in the sixth week (May 18-24, 1990) for several titles; however, this cannot be explained by the data. Overall, use was constant during each week of the study, except during finals week.

The data were checked to verify if overall use patterns conformed to Bradford's contention that a very small group of journals could predominate in a given field (Fang, 1989, p. 207). As it turned out, 11 titles (16.4 percent of the population) accounted for more than 80 percent of the overall use in this study. This was also true for each of the subfields of chemistry. For analytical chemistry, three titles out of the 18 total accounted for 80 percent of the use (225 out of 281 uses). Out of 23 organic chemistry titles, four titles accounted for nearly 80 percent of the use (486 out of 630 uses). Finally, out of the 26 physical chemistry titles, five titles accounted for nearly 80 percent of the overall use (104 out of 141 uses). Thus, the use data collected appeared to be constant from week to week (except for finals week) and to fit known usage patterns (Bradford's Law).

Correlations

Correlations measure the degree or strength of relationship between two variables. Overall, a moderate correlation was calculated between the selected variables (see Table 1). For the correlations between impact factor and use sum, analytical chemistry was found to have a very strong correlation ($r =$ .901). The other subject areas had moderate correlations with organic chemistry at .427 and physical chemistry at .44. The correlation for the entire data set was .501. In general, the correlations between use sums and impact factors were higher than those between JCR rank and use rank. For example, the correlation for JCR rank and use rank for analytical chemistry was .603 and organic chemistry .394. However, physical chemistry had a higher correlation ($r =$ .526) between JCR rank and use rank than between its impact factor and use sum ($r =$ .44). Because the subject area of analytical chemistry had a much higher correlation between impact factor and use sum than the other subject areas, this variable was investigated further, using regression analysis and scatter plots.

Table 1. Correlations for Selected Variables by Subject

Subject	Impact and Use Sum	JCR Rank and Use Rank
Analytical	.901	.603
Organic	.427	.394
Physical	.44	.526
All Subjects	.501	*

Note: * Rankings were not assigned to the entire data set, only to subject areas.

Simple Regression

Simple regression techniques were used to determine whether *JCR* impact factors and/or rankings could serve as predictors of local use of chemistry titles. Regression analysis was performed on two different sets of variables:

1. impact factors and use sums, and
2. *JCR* relative rankings and use rankings.

Regression statistics were calculated for each subject (analytical, organic, and physical) and for the entire data set. In nearly all cases, the regression line (the line that best fits the data) is a valid line and can be used for predictive purposes (see Tables 2 and 3).

Table 2 shows that impact factors are significant as predictors of use frequencies (1) at the .001 level for analytical chemistry and for all subjects, and (2) at the .05 level for physical and organic chemistry. This means that impact factors can be used as predictors of local use of chemistry titles for each subject area.

Table 3 shows that *JCR* rankings are significant as predictors of use rankings at the .01 level for both analytical and physical chemistry. Interestingly, the *JCR* rankings are not significant as predictors of use rank at the .05 level for the area of organic chemistry. This could be explained by the fact that, for

Table 2. Regression Data for Using Impact Factors as Predictors of Use Sums by Subject

Subject	r	r^2	t-value	p	sig.
Analytical ($n = 18$)	.901	.811	8.299	.0001	**
Physical ($n = 26$)	.44	.194	2.4	.0245	*
Organic ($n = 23$)	.427	.183	2.165	.042	*
All Subjects ($n = 67$)	.501	.251	11.563	.0001	**

Notes: * $p < .05$
          ** $p < .001$

Table 3. Regression Data for Using *JCR* Relative Rankings as
Predictors of Use Rankings by Subject

Subject	r	r²	t-value	p	sig.
Analytical (n = 18)	.603	.363	3.02	.0081	*
Physical (n = 26)	.526	.277	3.30	.0058	*
Organic (n = 23)	.394	.155	1.962	.0632	—

Note: $* p < .01$

this subfield, the degree of difference between each *JCR* rank is small (the impact factors, on which *JCR* rankings are based, are very close together) while the local use data indicated titles that clearly dominated the field of organic chemistry.

As noted earlier, the subject area of analytical chemistry had a significantly higher correlation ($r = .901$ for impact factors and use names) than the other subject areas. After inspecting a scatter plot, it became apparent that these data were being distorted by an extreme outlier. The outlier is the title *Analytical Chemistry,* which has an impact factor of 12.25 and use of 150. The next highest impact factor among the analytical chemistry titles is 3.818 and the next highest use count is 56 uses. By removing this outlier from the data set and testing the regression relationship again, the results are dramatically different (see Table 4).

These results indicate that the title *Analytical Chemistry* distorted the results and without it, there would be a very low correlation between the variables and no statistical significance to impact factors as predictors of use sum for the subject area of analytical chemistry. One explanation for why a single title can have such a strong impact on the data is the small population size. The subject analytical chemistry has the least number of titles (only 18 total). In addition, in this particular case, it appears that this branch of chemistry is truly dominated by one title.

Interestingly, *JCR* rank is significant as a predictor of use rank for analytical chemistry without *Analytical Chemistry* at the .001 level and the correlation

Table 4. Regression Data With and Without the Title *Analytical Chemistry*
for the Subject Area of Analytical Chemistry Using Impact Factors
as Predictors of Use Sums

Subject	r	r²	t-value	p	sig.
Analytical (n = 18)	.901	.811	8.299	.0001	*
Analytical (n = 17)	.15	.023	1.519	.1319	—

Note: $* p < .001$

between these variables is moderate ($r = .526$). This is probably because the rankings are on the same ordered scale and so the difference is less acute when a single title is removed than when the actual impact factors and use data are used. Because *JCR* relative rankings and use rankings are based on actual use sums and impact factors, the rankings data are less precise and the differences in the actual contradicts the findings of Pan (1978), who reported that *JCR* rankings and use rankings had statistically significant correlations ($r = .47$), while the impact factors and use frequencies did not. Both types of comparisons in this study were found to be statistically significant according to Pan's definition for most subject areas, but impact factors and use frequencies were found to be more reflective of the actual data. Therefore, the remainder of this discussion will focus on the relationship between impact factors and use sums.

The slope of the regression line was found to be an indicator of how heavily used the journals were within a discipline and its subfields. For example, the subject area of organic chemistry, which is the University of Michigan's primary strength, had a regression line with a slope of 30.541, which is much larger than any of the other subject areas included in this study. The slope of the regression line for physical chemistry was 4.91 and for analytical chemistry was 12.022 (but only 2.451 without the title *Analytical Chemistry*). These slopes represent substantially lower usages than the area of organic chemistry. The overall use of the chemistry collection, as represented by the complete data set, had a regression line with a slope of 11.99. This means that with each additional impact factor point, on average, use of the chemistry journal collection can be expected to increase by 11.99 uses.

Finally, after reviewing the scatter plots for the data under examination, it was discovered that titles with low impact factors (below 1.0) did not receive high use. However, several titles with high impact factors were found to have low or no usage (e.g., *Organometallics, Organic Mass Spectrometry,* and *Catalysis Reviews*). These data indicate that journals with low impact factors may be good candidates for storage or cancellation projects. On the other hand, journals with high impact factors may have little or no use and therefore my require further examination before making collection management decisions.

CONCLUSIONS

As previous studies have found (Pravdic and Oluic-Vukovic, 1987; Garfield, 1979; Dombrowski, 1988), it is unlikely that any one journal evaluation method or mechanistic approach to selection and deselection will ever be effective in all libraries. Collection usage will vary from place to place and time to time, depending on patron research strengths and interests. This study was conducted to test whether citation measures (*JCR* impact factors and rankings) can be used to predict local use patterns—in this case, in a collection of chemistry serials in a small academic library. This study also examined whether the evaluation of chemistry journals by subfields of chemistry (i.e., analytical, organic, and physical) is a more accurate collection management technique than the examination of chemistry journals as a whole.

Use Study Reliability

While the subfield population sizes were small and the use study was conducted over a brief period of time, in general the use data appears to be consistent. The main deviation in the use study data occurred during the third week, which was finals week. The use data conforms with Bradford's Law, which states that a few core titles dominate a field. Eleven titles (out of 67) accounted for over 80 percent of the overall use in this study.

Moderate Correlations

The correlations between impact factors and use sums, as well as those between *JCR* ranks and use ranks, were found to be moderate. As a next step, the data were submitted to further analysis, using simple regression techniques.

Citation Data as Predictors

Both impact factors and *JCR* rankings were found to be statistically significant predictors of local journal use (.05 level for all subjects and subfields) at the University of Michigan Chemistry Library. The exceptions were the use of *JCR* rankings as predictors for organic chemistry and the use of impact factors as predictors for analytical chemistry without the journal *Analytical Chemistry*.

Slopes as Indicators of Use

The slopes of the regression lines were found to be an indicator of how much a subfield is being used. The field of organic chemistry was found to have the highest average usage, with a slope of 30.451 (this corresponds to the fact that organic chemistry is the primary strength of the Chemistry Department). The other subfields had much lower use totals: 12.022 (2.451 without *Analytical Chemistry*) and 4.91 for the areas of analytical and physical chemistry respectively.

Low versus High Impact Factors

The scatter plots generated for the study data showed, as expected, that journals with low impact factors (less than one) did not get highly used. This would indicate that librarians can use low impact factors as criteria for storage or cancellation projects. However, it should be noted that several titles with high impact factors got little or no use during the course of this investigation. This is a surprising result and should be explored in another study.

Outliers in Subfields

The title *Analytical Chemistry* was found to be a significant outlier in the data set for analytical chemistry. As a result, it was removed from some calculations. Without it, there was no statistical significance to impact factors as predictors of actual use in analytical chemistry. This is an argument for examining an entire discipline rather than focusing on its subfields. By breaking the field of chemistry down into subfields, the population sizes become so small that they are extremely affected by variations in the data.

Impact Factors versus Rankings

Partially because of the above outlier, it was found that it is more meaningful to examine the relationships between impact factors and use frequencies than *JCR* and use rankings, because the rankings are merely an ordered set based on the original data. Rankings appear to obscure the differences in the data. However, unlike Pan's findings, both techniques in this study were found to be statistically significant as predictors of use patterns.

Subfields versus Disciplines

One of the primary research questions explored in this paper was whether it is meaningful to analyze chemistry journals by major subfields in the journal evaluation process. The conclusions drawn from this study are that if the researcher is interested in finding out the specific strengths, weaknesses, and use patterns of a subfield, then analyzing the discipline by subject areas provides useful information. However, if the researcher is interested in doing a large-scale evaluation of the chemistry collection, then breaking the discipline down into smaller subfields is not necessary. The overall use and citation patterns in this study were found to be similar to the use and citation patterns of the subfields. Also, the larger the number of titles considered, the less affected by outliers the data are.

SUMMARY

This paper represents a first step in examining the utility of citation analysis as a tool for chemistry serials collection development/management in small library settings.

The pilot study investigated whether citation measures could serve as predictors of local use patterns for chemistry journals. The findings of this study indicate that citation data can be employed as a starting point in the collection management process for specific library collections. In addition, the study indicates that examination of journals by subfields is useful for an in-depth investigation of citation and usage patterns for specific subject areas in a library. However, a study of all journals in a field is more effective for large-scale journal evaluation.

The findings of this pilot study also suggest that *Journal Citation Reports* can be effectively and easily used as a citation analysis and collection evaluation technique in small library settings. This process is not as time consuming as other collection evaluation techniques (e.g., use studies). Furthermore, the Institute for Scientific Information is exploring the possibility of redesigning *JCR* to make it easier to use—perhaps even putting it in an electronic format. If this happens, *Journal Citation Reports* will become an even more important and heavily utilized collection management tool.

While further investigation of citation analysis as a tool for making collection management decisions is recommended before this process can be fully accepted, this pilot study suggests that citation analysis techniques may be used effectively and easily for chemistry serials management, particularly in small library settings.

APPENDIX: LIST OF JOURNAL TITLES BY SUBJECT

Analytical Chemistry (18 Titles)

Anales de Quimica-B
Analusis. Chemie Analytique
Analyst
Analytica Chimica Acta
Analytical Chemistry
Analytical Letters
Frensenius Zeitschrift fur Analytische Chemie
Journal of Chromatographic Science
Journal of Chromatography
Journal of Electroanalytical Chemistry and Interfacial Electrochemistry
Journal of Labelled Compounds and Radiopharmaceuticals
Journal of Liquid Chromatography
Journal of Thermal Analysis
Microchemical Journal
Selective Electrode Reviews
Talanta

Thermochimica Acta
TRAC: Trends in Analytical Chemistry

Organic Chemistry (23 Titles)

Acta Chemica Scandinavica B
Anales de Quimica, C
Bioorganic Chemistry
Bulletin de la Societe Chimique de France
Carbohydrate Research
Heterocycles
Journal of Heterocyclic Chemistry
Journal of Organic Chemistry
Journal of Organic Chemistry of the USSR (Translation)
Journal of Organometallic Chemistry
Journal of the Chemical Society, Perkin Transactions I
Journal of the Chemical Society, Perkin Transactions II
Magnetic Resonance in Chemistry
Natural Product Reports
Organic Mass Spectrometry
Organic Preparations and Procedures International
Organic Reactivity
Organometallics
Synthesis (Stuttgart)
Synthetic Communications
Tetrahedron
Tetrahedron Letters
Zeitschrift fur Naturforschung. Teil B

Physical Chemistry (26 Titles)

Acta Chemica Scandinavica
Anales de Quimica, Series A
Berichte der Bunsengesellschaft fur Physikalische Chemie
Catalysis Reviews
Faraday Discussions of the Chemical Society
High Energy Chemistry
International Journal of Chemical Kinetics
International Journal of Quantum Chemistry
International Journal of Thermophysics
Journal de Chimie Physique et de Physico-Chimie Biologique
Journal of Catalysis
Journal of Chemical Thermodynamics

Journal of Colloid and Interface Science
Journal of Dispersion Science and Technology
Journal of Molecular Catalysis
Journal of Molecular Structure/THEOCHEM
Journal of Photochemistry; A:Chemistry
Journal of Physical Chemistry (US)
Journal of Structural Chemistry
Journal of the Chemical Society, Faraday Transactions I
Langmuir
Physics and Chemistry of Liquids
Theoretica Chimica Acta
Zeitschrift fur Physikalische Chemie. Leipzig.
Zeitschrift fur Physikalische Chemie. Neue Folge.
Zhurnal Fizicheskoi Khimii

REFERENCES

Bourne, Charles P. and Dorothy Gregor. "Planning Serials Cancellations and Cooperative Collection Development in the Health Sciences: Methodology and Background Information." *Bulletin of the Medical Library Association* 63 (October 1975): 366-377.

Broadus, Robert N. "A Proposed Method for Eliminating Titles from Periodical Subscription Lists." *College & Research Libraries* 46 (January 1985): 30-35.

Dombrowski, Theresa. "Journal Evaluation Using *Journal Citation Reports* as a Collection Development Tool." *Collection Management* 10 (1988): 175-180.

Fang, Min-Lin Emily. "Journal Rankings by Citation Analysis in Health Sciences Librarianship." *Bulletin of the Medical Library Association* 77 (April 1989): 205-210.

Garfield, Eugene. *Citation Indexing: Its Theory and Application in Science, Technology, and Humanities.* Philadelphia: ISI Press, 1979.

Hartley, J., et al. "Readability and Prestige in Scientific Journals." *Journal of Information Science* 14 (1988): 69-75.

Heinzkill, Richard. "Characteristics of References in Selected Scholarly English Literary Journals." *Library Quarterly* 50 (July 1980): 352-365.

Marton, Janos. "Causes of Low and High Citation Potentials in Science: Citation Analysis of Biochemistry and Plant Physiology Journals." *Journal of the American Society for Information Science* 34 (1983): 244-246.

McCain, Katherine W. and James E. Bobick. "Patterns of Journal Use in a Departmental Library: A Citation Analysis." *Journal of the American Society for Information Science* 32 (July 1981): 257-267.

Pan, Elizabeth. "Journal Citation as a Predictor of Journal Usage in Libraries." *Collection Management* 2 (Spring 1978): 29-38.

Pravdic, Nevenka and Vesna Oluic-Vukovic. "Application of Overlapping Techniques in Selection of Scientific Journals for a Particular Discipline—Methodological Approach." *Information Processing & Management* 23 (1987): 25-32.

Rice, Barbara A. "Science Periodicals Use Study." *The Serials Librarian* (Fall 1979): 35-47.

——————. "Selection and Evaluation of Chemistry Periodicals." *Science & Technology Libraries* 4 (Fall 1983): 43-59.

Singleton, Alan. "Journal Ranking and Selection: A Review in Physics." *Journal of Documentation* 32 (December 1976): 258-289.

Skolnik, Herman. *The Literature Matrix of Chemistry.* New York: Wiley, 1982.

Stankus, Tony and Barbara Rice. "Handle with Care: Use and Citation Data for Science Journal Management." *Collection Management* 4 (Spring/Summer 1982): 95-110.

Usdin, B. Tommie. "Core Lists of Medical Journals: A Comparison." *Bulletin of the Medical Library Association* 67 (April 1979): 212-217.

Wiberley, Stephen E., Jr. "Journal Rankings from Citation Studies: A Comparison of National and Local Data from Social Work." *Library Quarterly* 52 (1982): 348-359.

THE PROCESS OF
COST JUSTIFICATION

Thomas J. Waldhart

INTRODUCTION

Two important responsibilities of library management are to define what it is that the library should seek to accomplish (i.e., the library's objectives), and bringing together the best combination of organizational resources to achieve those objectives. Whenever people organize to accomplish desired ends, justification becomes a central social process. It occurs in all kinds of organizations, at the top (when the chief executive officer is called on to justify the actions of the organization to its funding source, shareholders, clients, government, or the general public), in the middle (when the head of a department must justify a request for additional staff), and at the bottom (when a technician seeks to justify a change in departmental procedures). The players or stakeholders in the process change, and the organizational focus of the justification is altered, but the process itself remains essentially the same—*someone in the organization is seeking to persuade others that something is justified or warranted.* The process of justification is important to the effective management of all types of organizations because it provides a primary

Advances in Library Administration and Organization,
Volume 10, pages 113-127.
Copyright © 1992 by JAI Press Inc.
All rights of reproduction in any form reserved.
ISBN: 1-55938-460-3

Table 1. Justification Examples in Libraries

Focus of Justification Efforts	Examples
Policies	Limit library access to employees of the company.
Procedures	Send overdue notices to all faculty at the end of each semester rather than once a year.
Goals and Objectives	Expand the number of clients using the current awareness service provided by the library.
Facilities	Acquire 10,000 square feet of remote space to store little used library materials.
Equipment	Acquire three duplicating machines that are capable of enlarging and reducing images.
Information System	Introduce a CD-ROM mediated information retrieval system to chemistry library.
Collections	Discontinue subscriptions to 35 selected periodicals in the area of science and technology.
Services	Introduce outreach services for physically handicapped clients.
Programs	Develop an instructional services program for undergraduate students who are foreign nationals.
Library Performance	Reduce interlibrary loan response time by an average of 30 percent.
Budgets	Change current patterns of allocating the materials budget.
Staff	Increase staffing levels in Reference Department by two professional positions.

mechanism for securing the commitment, cooperation, and action of others which is so often necessary to accomplish personal or organizational goals.

In the library environment we are constantly faced with the need to justify things to others—a subordinate, a colleague, a superior, or perhaps a patron. Occasionally, we may even find that we need to justify things to ourselves. Not all of our attempts at justification succeed, nor do they all receive the amount of time or effort necessary. The strategy we adopt for justification purposes will vary depending on the nature of the situation in which we find ourselves. If we are attempting to justify something that is very important to the library's staff, its clients, or the institution that provides financial support to the library, the justification process may take place over a long period of time, require the contributions of many people, and consume significant library resources. For instance, justifying the construction of a new $30 million university library to various people, agencies, and organizations (e.g., members of the state legislature, the state agency that coordinates higher education programs, the institution's administrators, faculty members and students, the library's staff members, a federal agency or private donors, etc.) can represent an effort that extends over several years and involves the participation of many people, both inside and outside the library. In contrast, if there is general agreement that something needs to be done (e.g., a decision made, a policy changed, a procedure modified, a new system introduced, or an existing service expanded or discontinued), and the proposed action has low costs and high benefits that are apparent to all, the need to engage in a complicated justification effort is substantially reduced or eliminated.

Justification efforts are most common in libraries when one or more of the following conditions exist: (1) there is the expection of broad-based participation of staff in decision making within the library system; (2) other people have an important role to play in the implementation of a decision or the accomplishment of a goal; (3) the approval of someone is needed before a decision can be taken or a goal accomplished, or (4) the successful implementation of a decision requires additional resources that can only come from a source other than the decisionmaker. Some things that commonly provide the focus for justification efforts in libraries are described in Table 1.

In reality, any aspect of a library (including some which are not listed in Table 1) can require justification at one time or another. This paper examines the structure of a specific form of justification, commonly referred to as *cost justification,* and discusses how it can contribute to effective library management.

COST JUSTIFICATION

For years the library community has struggled with the problems of accurately measuring and comparing costs and benefits in the library setting. While some progress has been made in quantifying *economic costs* in libraries, less has been accomplished as regards measuring *economic benefits, noneconomic costs,* and *noneconomic benefits.* Finally, comparing different kinds of costs and benefits, in the traditional economic sense, has seen little progress. In sum, significant methodological problems continue to limit the profession's ability to accurately measure and compare costs and benefits. Indeed, the lack of progress in this area has caused some professionals to question the usefulness of the most popular cost analytic methods (especially classic cost-benefits analysis) in the library context (DeGennaro, 1983; White, 1985). Nevertheless, most librarians, and those who fund or use libraries, feel librarians, like managers in other organizations, should be required to justify their use of organizational resources in terms of value returned to the organization. While cost justification does not solve the problems inherent in measuring and comparing costs and benefits in libraries, it does offer libraries a systematic strategy for justifying the use of organizational resources in relation to the value returned to the organization and its clients or funding agency.

In this paper, cost justification is considered a fundamental organizational process by which someone seeks to persuade others that the negative effects of that which is being justified are warranted by its positive effects—that the costs of something are justified by its benefits. The *someone* developing or presenting the cost justification may be a single person, a group of people drawn from one or more administrative units within a library, or they may even originate from outside the library. The *something* being cost justified can be any identifiable aspect of the library that needs justification, for whatever reason. The *others* who are being persuaded by the cost justification can consist of one or more people originating from either inside or outside the library. In cost justification, the *negative effects* of that which is being cost justified are summarized as all perceived *costs,* while the *positive effects* are summarized as all perceived *benefits.*

Expressed this way, cost justification is a concept that is relatively easy to understand. In the real world, however, cost justification is considerably more complicated and involved than this definition would at first suggest. In part, this complexity is attributable to the nature of the process itself and to the nature of libraries and their services. While cost justification is a subject that is often mentioned in the library literature, there is little agreement regarding the details of the process itself. Indeed, in many cases, professionals are clearly confusing the process of cost justification with selected analytic methods that can be used in cost justification. One purpose of this paper is to clarify the distinction between the *means* of cost justification and its *ends,* and to develop a structural model for this complex and important organizational process which can be effectively used in managing libraries.

A general model of cost justification is presented in Figure 1. The type of library in which a cost justification occurs (e.g., public, college, university, special, school media center, etc.) has little effect on the structure of the process. The environmental setting of cost justification may, however, influence who develops the cost justification, what costs and benefits are considered most important, how the costs and benefits are assessed, and who is included in the audience or group of people at which the cost justification is directed.

In some situations involving justification, people seek to persuade others by making generally unsupported personal assertions regarding the costs and benefits of that which they are justifying. Usually these assertions tend to focus on the benefits to be realized with less attention given to relevant costs. As the old song says, accent the positive. For instance, the cost of a new system might be justified by an assertion that "The introduction of the new system will result in a significant increase in the productivity of the unit's professional staff, it will allow the library to greatly reduce its response time, and it will greatly enhance the patron's access to information." If the person claiming such

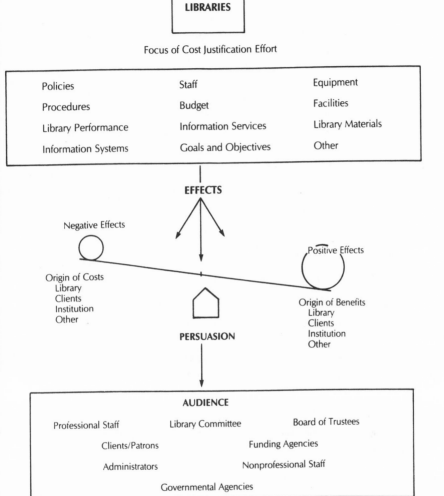

Figure 1. The Structure of Cost Justification

benefits has a high level of credibility among those he is seeking to persuade, simple assertion can be an effective persuasive strategy, and it requires only modest effort on the part of the persuader. However, when the persuader's assertions are not sufficiently persuasive, a more rational, reasoned, and systematic demonstration that benefits justify costs may be needed to affect persuasion. Such a demonstration often requires the acquisition and presentation of evidence that supports the justification argument.

When the members of a cost justification audience are similar (having essentially the same perceptions, beliefs, attitudes, values, and behaviors) the persuasive messages forming the basis of a cost justification can be reasonably simple and still be effective. However, when there is a wide variation in the audience's perceptions, beliefs, attitudes, values, and behaviors, the persuasive process increases in complexity, often requiring the development of persuasive strategies that are uniquely tailored to the different segments of the audience holding varying views.

Little of the published literature of library and information science considers the subject of cost justification in anything more than an indirect or superficial way, and none offers the professional much help in structuring the process itself. Nevertheless, much of the literature is relevant to cost justification. Hundreds of papers and books examine the process of budget preparation and presentation, cost analysis, efficiency, cost-effectiveness and cost-benefits analysis, value analysis, costing alternative information systems, utility analysis, decision making, communication, and a host of other topics that relate to cost justification. Some of the literature emphasizes specific analytical methods and techniques that can be used in cost justification (Plate, 1984; Williams, 1984); some focuses on the evaluation and comparison of alternative information systems, products and services (Bommer and Ford, 1974; Elchesen, 1978); and, some offers suggestions regarding strategies that might be effectively used in persuasion (Allen and Branson, 1982; Moore, 1985; Nameth, 1984; Roose, 1987). What is generally lacking in the existing literature is a clear understanding of the purpose of cost justification and how the process can be structured in libraries.

PERSUASION—THE KEY TO EFFECTIVE COST JUSTIFICATION

Some professionals might argue that the concept of cost justification offered here represents little that is new—that the use of cost justification as a basic persuasive strategy has been a part of libraries and library management for years. To some extent, this assertion may be true. However, the differences between cost justification as it is practiced in libraries and as it is proposed here are considerable. In practice, most cost justification efforts are fragmented, occur inconsistently, provide highly selected evidence relating to costs and benefits, and take place mainly on an informal level in libraries. Seldom is an attempt made to establish a formal structure for the process, to compare costs and benefits in any systematic way, or, more importantly to develop effective strategies of persuasion.

Too often in practice, the means and ends of cost justification are confused. Cost justification is taken to be the use of a variety of analytical methods and techniques (typically emphasizing economic-based quantitative methods such as efficiency, cost-effectiveness and cost-benefits analysis) to demonstrate that the costs of something are warranted by its benefits. In this view of cost justification, the methods and techniques of analyzing and comparing costs and benefits is cost justification.

As conceived here, the basic purpose of cost justification is not only to compare the negative effects (costs) of something with its positive effects (benefits), but rather to use this information as a means of persuasion. Cost justification is a broad organizational strategy that seeks to use any available method or technique of analysis that will provide credible evidence that can be combined with a purposeful strategy of persuasion to convince an audience that the negative effects of something are justified or warranted by its positive effects. The end of cost justification is persuasion, not the application of any specific analytical method or technique that may serve as a means of persuasion.

Collectively, people employ a variety of different strategies in persuasive situations. Sometimes a single strategy is used and other times multiple strategies are used in combination. Some persuasive strategies that are commonly used in libraries include: (1) analysis and reason (careful explanation frequently accompanied by detailed analysis which appeals to reason); (2) building coalitions (obtaining support of superiors, coworkers and subordinates); and (3) appealing to higher authority (formal or informal appeal for support from those higher in the organization); (4) bargaining (proposing an exchange of something valued for support of others); (5) appealing to friendship (seeking support of others by appealing to existing friendships); (6) intimidation (seeking to acquire support through threats, coercion, and confrontations); and (7) assertiveness (securing support through repeated assertations or reminders and face-to-face interactions). Effective persuaders tend to vary the persuasive strategies they use in a particular situation on the basis of the needs of the situation (Clark, 1984).

In this context, the term *persuasion* refers to any situation where one or more people seek to influence the behavior of others through symbolic transactions (messages) that are sometimes linked to coercive force, and that appeal to the reason and emotions of those being persuaded (Miller, 1980). In some cases, the impact of persuasion on behavior is direct and observable, while in other cases indirect and less observable (e.g., when the persuader first seeks to change the attitudes, beliefs, or values of others in order to then change their behavior). Miller (1987) indicates that persuasion seeks to change behavior in three possible ways: (1) by changing existing responses; (2) by reinforcing existing responses, or (3) by shaping new responses. For instance, the director of a library might seek to cost justify the library's materials budget

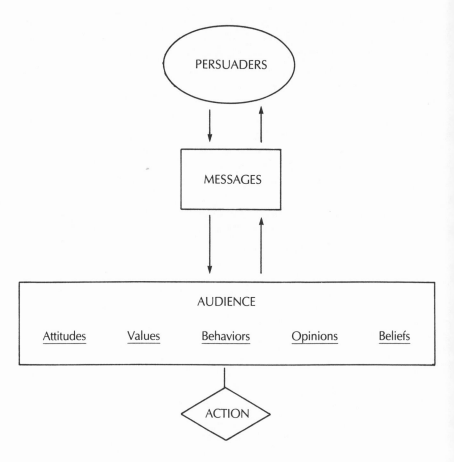

Figure 2.   The Persuasive Process

in order to persuade the funding agency that the materials budget for the library should be increased (initiation of a change in funding behavior), that current funding levels should be maintained (inhibition of a change in funding behavior), or that the needs of the library's clients warrant an increase in the library's materials budget sometime in the future.

In Figure 2, persuasion is characterized as a process that involves the preparation of one or more messages by those who hope to influence the attitudes, opinions, beliefs, values, or behaviors of others. Usually the persuader is not a part of the audience being persuaded, however, this need not necessarily be the case. In some instances, the role of the persuader may be assumed by one or more members of the audience (e.g., the head of the reference department taking responsibility for cost justifying a proposed new service to the staff of the reference department). In this case, the head of the reference department would seek out information regarding the positive and negative effects of the proposed service and then use that evidence to influence the staff members of the reference department. The initial desire to seek out information may originate within the audience, or someone outside the audience might encourage the members of the audience to seek the information—in effect, to persuade themselves. For instance, the director of a college library might ask his executive committee to examine the processes involved in sending overdue notices to faculty members, knowing that the information the committee collects will very likely persuade them that a change in library policy is badly needed. This form of persuasion is called self-persuasion, for obvious reason, and it has been shown to be a very effective persuasive strategy (Miller and Burgoon, 1973).

While some efforts at cost justification may begin with an attempt to influence the attitudes, opinions, beliefs, and values of the members of the audience, the underlying motive of most cost justification efforts in the library setting is behavioral in nature. That is, persuaders, through the process of cost justification, attempt to elicit some desired overt behavior from the members of the audience, even though the initial focus of the cost justification may be to change, maintain, or structure attitudes, beliefs, opinions, or values.

THE PROCESS OF COST JUSTIFICATION

According to *Webster's Third International Dictionary* (1966), a *process* can be thought of as "a particular method or system of doing something, producing something, or accomplishing a desired result." In cost justification, the process may be simple or complex; it may involve one person or many; it may represent a one time effort, or it may be an integral part of the organization's continuing effort to demonstrate accountability to its clients or funding source. The specific form that a given cost justification takes depends greatly on the individual circumstances surrounding the process itself. While the intended result of cost justification is persuasion, it may employ any strategy or form of persuasion *which is based on an assessment of the favorable and unfavorable effects of that which is being cost justified.*

As described here, the process of cost justification consists of five distinct elements or stages:

1. defining the problem underlying the cost justification and setting the objectives of the cost justification;
2. analyzing the intended audience of the cost justification;
3. assessing relevant costs and benefits;
4. presenting the cost justification to the audience; and
5. evaluating the results of the cost justification.

While the process begins conceptually with the definition of the underlying problem and ends with the evaluation of the justification effort, all of the elements of a cost justification are highly interrelated.

Defining Problems and Objectives

The first requirement of effective cost justification is to have a clear understanding of what constitutes the problem or problems giving rise to the cost justification. It is important that a justification effort begin with a formal statement of the problem. Once the problem(s) underlying the cost justification are suitably defined, a formal statement of the objective of the cost justification (not the objectives of that which is being cost justified) should be prepared. The statement of objective should clearly define what is to be accomplished by the cost justification. Confusion, or disagreement, regarding either the problem statement or state of objectives can lead to serious difficulties in defining the focus of the exercise, selecting appropriate evidence, defining the audience, selecting effective persuasive strategies, and evaluating the cost justification effort. If the organizational problem addressed by the cost justification, or the objective of the cost justification, cannot be adequately defined, it is highly unlikely that the cost justification will succeed in any meaningful way.

While the origin of most cost justification efforts in libraries is found in organizational problem solving and decision making, the focus of cost justification in libraries is generally provided by specific information systems, information products or information services, and the decisions which affect them: decisions to expand, maintain or contract existing systems, products, or services; decisions to add new systems, products, or services not previously offered by the library; and, decisions to change systems, products, or services in ways that will make them more efficient or effective.

Audience Analysis

The audience of a cost justification consists of all those people at whom the persuasive effort should be directed. It should include people who may be instrumental in the persuasive process, people who might initiate desired actions, and people who might be involved in the implementation phase of action-oriented cost justifications (Benveniste, 1977). At one extreme, the audience might consist of a single person who is seeking to persuade himself that the costs associated with a decision he is about to make are justified by the benefits which will result from that decision. At the other extreme, a number of people, holding varying views and possessing different values, may be attempting to cost justify a complex and expensive new system to a large audience consisting of (1) professional and nonprofessional staff members of the library who will be expected to implement the new system if it is funded; (2) executive and staff officers from a number of supported units who will be expected to provide the funds needed to acquire the new system; and (3) clients of varying persuasions, some of whom will benefit greatly from the system and others who will not. Effective cost justification depends on the persuader having a clear understanding of the opinions, beliefs, attitudes, values, and behaviors of the different members of the audience, in order that persuasive strategies used in justification can be adapted to the views of the audience members. Clark (1984, p. 17) emphasizes the vital role of audience analysis by noting that the "most fundamental requirement in constructing a persuasive message is to select arguments that are consistent with the beliefs and values of the audience."

Assessing Costs and Benefits

While it has been argued that the analysis of costs and benefits is only a part of cost justification, not cost justification itself, it is a very important part. The systematic assessment of costs and benefits, and their comparison, is what gives cost justification its unique strength. It provides the basic evidence on which much of the persuasive power of a cost justification rests (Reinnard, 1988; McCroskey, 1969). In developing an effective cost justification, one that has some reasonable change of persuading an audience to a particular point of view, the persuader needs to consider several different aspects of both costs and benefits.

- What costs and benefits are relevant to the cost justification?
- How can the identified costs and benefits be defined? Compared? Demonstrated?
- Who incurs the identified costs?
- Who realizes the identified benefits?

When asked about the costs of something, people tend to respond in terms of dollar expenditures. They define cost by personal or institutional dollars needed to implement a decision, achieve a desired result, or acquire something. When the concern is with the expenditure of personal resources (e.g., How much did the literature search cost you?), cost may be essentially the same as price. When concerned with the expenditure of organizational resources (e.g., How much did it cost the library to do the literature search?), cost may be expressed in terms of the sum of the institution's resources employed in providing the service, and this sum may or may not be the same as the price of the literature search. While organizational costs may initially be expressed in terms of manpower, facilities, equipment, supplies, service charges, communication charges, or other resource categories, in the end, organizational costs are normally defined by the dollar value of those resources.

The concept of cost as dollar expenditures is useful for many purposes in libraries, however, it is not sufficient for cost justification. In cost justification, an adequate assessment of costs must include elements of cost which go beyond those that can be narrowly expressed by dollar expenditures. Costs, in cost justification, are *all* the negative effects associated with that which is being cost justified, and which we would like to avoid or minimize if possible. Benefits, in contrast, are *all* the positive effects we seek to realize or maximize, not only those benefits which can be expressed as dollars saved.

Many costs and benefits occurring in libraries, which might be relevant to a cost justification presentation, cannot be adequately expressed in terms of dollar expenditures or dollar savings. Consequently, librarians preparing a cost justification need to seek other methods of expressing costs and benefits in meaningful ways.

To ensure that a study of costs is as comprehensive and systematic as possible, Quade (1982) recommends that costs be categorized in several different ways:

- as dollar expenditures;
- as costs that can be measured in dollars;
- as costs that can be quantified but not measured in dollars; and
- as costs that cannot be quantified.

The analytic categories used by Quade to describe costs can be used equally well to describe benefits (i.e., as dollar savings, as benefits that can be measured in dollars, as benefits that can be quantified but not measured in dollars, and benefits that cannot be quantified). Costs and benefits that can be expressed in dollars are usually considered economic costs and benefits, while those that cannot be expressed in dollars are considered noneconomic costs and benefits.

When costs and benefits cannot be expressed in economic terms, an effort should be made to quantify them in some way so as to indicate the magnitude or scale of an effect. When effects cannot be expressed in either economic terms or quantified, an expression of effects in a verbal form can often ensure that an important effect is not ignored or disregarded in a cost justification.

Presenting the Case

Cost justification is essentially a strategy of persuasion that emphasizes the systematic analysis of costs and benefits in a persuasive situation. It relies heavily on analysis and reason as the primary persuasive strategy; however, a cost justification can also include the use of other persuasive strategies as well, including the formation of coalitions, appealing to higher authority, bargaining, appealing to friendships, assertiveness, and perhaps even intimidation.

In discussing the introduction of online information services in public libraries, Roose (1987, p. 60) offers some answers to her question "How do you persuade either your board or your administration to begin online search?" She argues that you can tell those you are trying to persuade about the benefits of online searching (e.g., more, faster, and better service; access to information not available in print sources; cost effectiveness; access to more complete, current, and accurate information; and enhancement of the image of the library and librarians). In addition, Roose recommends that personalized searches be performed for individual members of the group being persuaded in order to demonstrate the benefits of online searching in the most personal terms. While she encourages librarians to tell the audience about the benefits of online searching, in order to persuade them, she makes no mention of telling them about the costs or negative effects of online searching. Neither does she suggest that we should define the benefits of online searching in anything but the most general terms (i.e., telling them about the benefits). Roose's persuasive strategy may be effective but it is not cost justification as described here. To change Roose's general persuasive strategy into a cost justification of online searching would require that much greater attention be given to documenting and comparing both *costs* and *benefits* of online searching in public libraries.

One might ask "Why should anyone want to point out the negative effects of something that we are trying to 'sell' to an audience?" The answer to that question lies very much in the nature of the persuasive situation. The use of cost justification in libraries is most appropriate *when it is felt that a systematic and reasoned argument is either required or would be more persuasive.* The choice of cost justification, over other methods or strategies of persuasion, then, is determined by a professional judgment regarding which persuasive strategy would be most effective, which is required because of the situation or circumstance, or which is expected by the audience.

Presenting the cost justification case to the audience involves more than the selection of a persuasive strategy. The persuader must also select or develop an effective method of presentation which considers the mode of communication that will be used (e.g., oral, written, or a combination), the structure and content of the persuasive messages that will be used, and how the messages will be delivered (e.g., in small groups, individually, etc.).

Evaluating the Effort

To ensure the effective use of scarce organizational resources (e.g., people, facilities, etc.), cost justification needs to include an evaluative component. Cost justification, as an organizational activity, is not without its own costs and benefits, and evaluation can contribute to effective cost justification in a number of ways by: (1) providing some measure of how effective the cost justification has been; (2) providing an indication of the extent to which the objectives of the cost justification has been achieved; (3) providing help in determining if the cost justification should be continued, expanded, or terminated; (4) helping to determine how the cost justification might be changed in order to improve its chances of success; and (5) guiding the development of future cost justification efforts.

CONCLUSION

Justification is an important social mechanism for accomplishing desired goals in any organization, including libraries. Cost justification has considerable potential for improving the management of libraries, and almost assuredly it will become more important in the future as competition for resources increases. Nevertheless, the extent to which cost justification is widely adopted by the profession depends on satisfying a number of conditions: Librarians will need to be convinced that the use of cost justification can result in improved library management, and that the time given to the process is well worth the effort. They will need to become familiar with the structure and process of cost justification and they will need to familiarize themselves with the various analytical methods and techniques, including their capabilities and limitations, which can be used to assess and compare costs and benefits in libraries. Finally, they will need to acquire a better understanding of the process of persuasion, including what methods, techniques, and persuasive strategies contribute to effective persuasion in given circumstances.

As a profession, we must move beyond our understanding of cost justification as some predefined set of analytical methods or techniques, to a view of cost justification as a persuasive strategy designed to demonstrate that the negative effects of that which is being cost justified are warranted by its positive effects. When library managers, at all levels, begin to require subordinates to provide systematic cost justifications for requests, proposals, or recommendations as a matter of course, the process of cost justification will become an integral part of the library environment. Library managers have a clear responsibility to understand the costs and benefits associated with decisions they make, and cost justification offers the profession a vehicle for fulfilling that responsibility.

REFERENCES

Allen, Chris W. and J.R. Branson. "OCLC for the Hospital Library: The Justification Plan for Hospital Administration." *Bulletin of the Medical Library Association* 70 (July 1982): 293-297.
Beneveniste, Guy. *The Politics of Expertise,* 2nd edition. San Francisco, CA: Boyd and Fraser, 1977.

Bommer, Michael R.W. and Bernard Ford. "Cost-Benefit Analysis for Determining the Value of an Electronic Security System." *College and Research Libraries* 35 (July 1974): 270-279.

Clark, Ruth A. *Persuasive Messages.* New York: Harper & Row, 1984.

DeGennaro, Richard. "Theory vs. Practice in Library Management." *Library Journal* 108 (July 1983): 1318-1321.

Elchesen, Dennis R. "Cost-Effectiveness Comparison of Manual and Online Retrospective Bibliographic Search." *Journal of the American Society for Information Science* 29 (March 1978): 56-66.

McCroskey, James C. "A Summary of Experimental Research on the Effects of Evidence in Persuasive Communication." *The Quarterly Journal of Speech* 55 (April 1969): 169-176.

Miller, Gerald R. "On Being Persuaded: Some Basic Distinctions." In *Persuasion: New Directions in Theory and Research,* eds. M.E. Roloff and G.R. Miller. Newbury Park, CA: Sage, 1980.

————. "Persuasion." In *Handbook of Communication Science,* eds. C.R. Berger and S.H. Chaffee. Newbury Park, CA: Sage, 1987.

Miller, Gerald R. and Michael Burgoon. *New Techniques of Persuasion.* New York: Harper & Row, 1973.

Moore, Barbara A. "Underhanded Strategies: How to Get Staff Agreement on the Operation of an Automated Circulation System." *Library Journal* 110 (February 1, 1985): 62-63.

Nameth, Nardina L. "Justifying an Automated Library Network: Concept and Process." *Medical Reference Services Quarterly* 3 (Winter 1984): 57-62.

Plate, Kenneth H. *Cost Justification of Information Services.* Studio City, CA: Pacific Information, 1984.

Quade, E.S. *Analysis for Public Decisions,* 2nd edition. New York: North Holland, 1982.

Reinnard, John C. "The Empirical Study of the Persuasive Effects of Evidence: The Status After Fifty Years of Research." *Human Communication Research* 15 (Fall 1988): 3-59.

Roose, Tina. "Persuading Your Board, Promoting Your Service." *Library Journal* 112 (April 15, 1987): 60-61.

Webster's Third New International Dictionary of the English Language. Ed. P.B. Gove. Springfield, MA: C.C. Merriam, 1966.

White, Herbert S. "Cost Benefit Analysis & Other Fun & Games." *Library Journal* 110 (February 15, 1985): 118-121.

Williams, Sally F. "Budget Justification Closing the Gap Between Request and Result." *Library Resources and Technical Services* 28 (April/June 1984): 129-135.

THE DEVELOPMENT OF
LIBRARY LIGHTING:
THE EVOLUTION OF THE LIGHTING
PROBLEMS WE ARE FACING TODAY

Ellsworth Mason

All of us are creatures of light; the human organism craves light in its deepest being. For the earliest people, darkness was a time of terror, a time of the monster Grendel in "Beowulf" rising from the swamp to feast on men, of frigid night air laden with pestilence and fearsome invisible creatures. Darkness lulls us to sleep; daylight brings us to life again. Light grows us food, greens the grass, leafs out the trees. Such age-old experiences convinced early man that light was the source of all life, and sun-worship was the earliest religion. Ancient Jewish prophets describe the ultimate desolation of man like this, "the sun will be darkened and the moon will not give her light." In the New Testament, St. John, near the end of his life, foretells the celestial city which "does not need the sun or the moon to shine on it, for the glory of God gives it light."

Advances in Library Administration and Organization,
Volume 10, pages 129-144.
ISBN: 1-55938-460-3

We read Pliny the Younger's magnificent letter to the Roman historian Tacitus describing the great eruption of Mount Vesuvius that completely obliterated the cities of Pompeii and Herculaneum on the 24th of August 79 A.D., and hear him describe the vigil he kept with his mother on their front lawn, 30 miles down the coast, awaiting word of his uncle, Pliny the Elder, who had gone to investigate this phenomenon and died there. In a cloud of volcanic ash so heavy they had to shake its weight continually off their covering cloths, so thick that it totally excluded daylight, they waited with an oil lantern beside them to give them comfort. This yearning for the comfort and security of light still lurks as a primitive necessity in all of us, even today when in cities there is no night, and it enters into our response to illumination, and conditions it.

From a very early time, this fact has been used in the design of buildings. Listen to a prominent art critic, Aline Saarinen, daughter of the great architect Eero Saarinen:

> Light is a magic element. The great builders of the past used it masterfully to manipulate mood. The Egyptians cut the Temple at Deir el Bahri from rocks on the west bank of the Nile so the morning sun would stain it an awesome purplish-bloody red. The Byzantine architects covered their domes with glistening mosaics, so that light would reflect dizzyingly and dazzlingly back and forth, obscuring form with mystery. The Gothic builders filtered light through colored glass, to set it dappling and dancing on the gray stone. And the baroque masters, in their churches, focussed the sun like a spotlight to heighten the drama of their designs, and in their palaces let it in against a wall of mirrors, to flood the room with brilliance.

Or listen to one of my literature students, Larry Richman, in a poem entitled "In the Sun Room":

> There must be a way
> to get loose from history,
>   that gaping mouth with the broken teeth.
> Here,
> in this room of the sun,
> luminous planes intersect and reflect,
> shades and shadows
> play hide and seek with the spirit of shine,
> mirrors throw and catch light,
> and time, dragging its horrors,
> confused by the magic of glass, disappears...

But to subdue light completely and mold it to our purposes in every way, we first had to make it, and that took a very long time in human history.

Some of the earliest recorded stories in many cultures tell of attempts to set traps to catch the sun, but the sun always proves too clever and too strong to be caught. One day, in man's marvelous ingenuity, someone did catch the counterpart of the sun, and with the coming of fire, in addition to its other benefits, came for the first time the power to hold back the darkness, to extend the day, and to explore lightless areas, such as underground caves. The earliest library lighting must have been the torches used to illuminate caves like those at Lascaux, where artists recorded on the walls their impression and interpretations of life around them in a form that would last, the earliest counterpart of the book.

Advances in ways of making light were among man's earliest technology and, as in all technology, his ingenuity and variety were infinite and his memory very finite. Devices invented were lost, only to be reinvented 1,500 years later. For about 4,000 years fuel sources were woody vegetation, solidified fats, and oils. Devices to improve the burning of oil were invented beyond number. Every fuel source and every burning device had problems. Tallow candles, made of solidified animal fat, would melt in hot climates, and although they were useful for lubricating wagon axles, and were so used on our overland journeys of the 1840s, they also could be eaten up by hungry servants. Wick oil lamps tended to drip, and lamp wicks had to be trimmed continually to produce steady light. Despite all efforts, there was little progress in illumination between the early dynastic period at Ur, on the Euphrates River in the Mesopotamia valley before 2,500 B.C., and the late eighteenth century. Pre-Christian Greeks and Romans knew almost as much about lighting as eighteenth and early nineteenth century Europeans.

The first striking advance in illuminating power did not come until 1784, with the invention of an oil lamp that combined air flow inside and outside of a tubular wick—which greatly increased the amount of light produced. It exceeded in brilliance the gas illumination of the time, which was first used in 1765 by a man who piped coal gas from a mine to illuminate his office. Not until the beginning of the nineteenth century was gas used for illumination in cotton mills, and the success of the Industrial Revolution depended heavily on advances in lighting, to provide safety and accuracy of work in those "dark Satanic mills," whose intrusion into "England's green and pleasant land" the poet William Blake decried in the early 1800s. For nearly a century gas illumination guttered along very unsatisfactorily, until the invention of the gas mantle in 1893, at which time gas and electricity began to compete neck and neck for some years.

Electricity had been long in coming. As a source of illumination it is only 110 years old, and as a generally available source only 50 years old. In 1922, my family moved into a house without access to electric lines in a Connecticut village on the edge of a city of 100,000 people. The following year I remember watching as a child with great awe an electric lineman, who was bringing us electricity, go up a pole with climbing spurs before the earth had been tamped down around the base of the pole. At about the same time, I remember climbing

up on a dining room table and poking my finger through the mantle of the
gas light above it to find out why it was not glowing in East Orange, New
Jersey, then a pretty and sophisticated city within stone's throw of New York.
In 1933 I remember watching men jack up the rear wheel of a Model-T Ford
to use the tire rim as a pulley to drive a portable generator, to feed a string
of unfrosted light bulbs that greatly enlivened an outdoor party, in another
village at the edge of that city of 100,000 people. In the fall of 1964 my wife
and I spent our honeymoon on Monhegan Island, nine miles offshore from
Port Clyde, Maine, where one-half of the houses on the island were without
electricity. So, as you may one day tell your unbelieving grandchildren, you
see standing before you a relict (that lovely word) of the pre-electric age, an
age that still exists in spots in this country, and generally throughout the world.
That grim contrast, indeed, contradiction, is marked most vividly in a story
told by Walford Erickson, former Librarian of the University of Minnesota,
about the ceremony to celebrate the installation of the first electric generator
in a small village in India, where he was working about 1960. The highlight
of the ceremony was the sacrifice of a live goat on the generator, to endow
it by its blood with unusual power.

Billions of people around the world are still without electricity. But as early
as 1810 Sir Humphrey Davy had demonstrated in public a successful carbon
arc light, fueled by Voltaic batteries, and shortly after mid-century an English
lighthouse was equipped with a 1,000 candlepower arc lamp. For the next
twenty years arc lighting, which is of dramatic intensity, aroused great
excitement and was used for the lighting of streets, theaters, and large factories.
But the great heat and intensity of these lamps kept them from becoming a
source of general illumination. The long-delayed electric lighting waited upon
large factors, such as the development of adequate generating sources and
distribution systems, and upon as small a factor as the development of a
practical filament, with reasonable life expectancy, for the electric light bulb.
This was finally achieved in 1879, and electricity took off with great fanfare.
Just two years after the invention of the filament lamp, the Savoy Theatre in
London was gayly lit with 1,200 bulbs in the auditorium and 715 clear bulbs
and 100 blue-tinted bulbs (for night scenes) on stage.

While the filament lamp held unchallenged ascendancy for general
illumination until the late 1930s, discharge lamps, which in a different form
would later give them severe competition, were developed shortly after them
in the form of low-pressure mercury vapor lamps. These were too hot, too
noisy, and of the wrong color to compete with filament lamps at that time,
but the low input of electricity they required for a high output of illumination
made them suitable for large outdoor installations. One of the earliest was in
nearby Austin, Texas, as my trusty Triple-A travel book tells me. I quote,
"Regardless of the weather Austin appears to be bathed in moonlight 365 nights
a year, from mercury vapor lamps atop 165-foot towers that have cast artificial

moonbeams over Austin every night since May 6, 1895." Twenty-one of the original 31 towers still are standing.

One more step was required to give us the potential for illumination that we have today—the development of the fluorescent tube. Luminescent materials go back as far as 980 A.D., when Japanese artists used pigments that were undetectable in daylight, but luminescent in the dark. By 1937 we had learned to coat the insides of short-length glass tubes with luminescent materials that were activated by ultra-violet light emitted by ingredients inside the tube. This light source produced about three times the illumination per watt as filament bulbs, in an acceptable color range, and with much less heat. In the 1930s the low heat factor was not of great consequence, because air conditioning was not yet available, but today fluorescents are often chosen to minimize the heat load on air conditioners.

The impact of this development on libraries can be seen in what happened at the University of Colorado's Norlin Library during its construction in 1938, due to a remarkable man named Waldo Brockway. Brockway was Treasurer and Business Manager of the university, but he had been Superintendent of the Construction Department of the School of Engineering and had supervised the construction of the university's first library building. While Norlin Library was under construction, fluorescent lighting was first made commercially available, and Brockway immediately launched a meticulous study into the value of fluorescent versus incandescent lighting systems. He concluded that fluorescents provided better quality lighting at a much lower power consumption, which in his mind more than offset the risk of using a product as yet untried. Because the plans for the building's electrical system were nearly completed, they had to be completely redesigned to reduce the capacities and sizes of switchboards, transformers, lighting cabinets, and feeders to accommodate less power. This cut the costs of the electrical system between 25 and 50 percent.

Because the architect would not hear of the use of bare tubes (good for him), he designed a tubular cover for them, 6" in diameter, pierced by a classical fret design that matched the trim in the building. These covers concealed aluminum reflectors and the 4-foot tubes used in continuous troffers. The architects set up experimental installations to determine how high to hang the fixtures and how wide to space them for adequate illumination. They were stem-dropped to a height of 10′ 3″ and spaced on 9′ and 11′ centers, depending on the size of the rooms. The original equipment was activated by crude thermal-magnetic switches, but by great good luck, while the fixtures were in the process of being manufactured, replaceable glow-switch starters (like those today) were developed and used in Norlin Library. A few weeks after installation, the lighting developed an annoying hum, and the Physics Department was set to work to remedy it. They traced the hum to the ballast coils, and eliminated it by shielding the ballasts with sheet-iron sleeves, which became standard manufacturing items for future fluorescent fixtures.

These fixtures cost twice as much as comparable incandescent fixtures, but they cost 44 percent less to maintain because they used less power. Therefore, the new system paid off its additional installation costs within four years. In use, they proved to cost less to keep clean, and produced much less heat per watt and less glare than incandescent lights. Six months after installation, the following lighting intensities were maintained:

10-12 footcandles on the face of wall bookstacks.
On 9' centers: 25 footcandles directly below fixtures; 28 footcandles halfway between fixtures.
On 11' centers: 22 footcandles directly below fixtures; 26 footcandles halfway between fixtures.

These were high lighting intensities for 1938, and this library became noted as a leader in the field of public building illumination.

All the major aspects of planning for this first large-scale installation of fluorescent light in libraries were done well. The university carefully investigated a new product, and when assured of better lighting and lower costs in the long run, they scrapped their current planning and bought the more expensive fixtures. The architects then took over and improved the system, esthetically by enclosing the fixtures in an ornamental cover, and functionally by making that cover large enough to contain reflectors. Without the kind of technical data we get for fixtures today, much of which is undependable, the architects determined by real, not mathematical, experience how they could be used effectively, by observing a large mock-up. After installation, the university solved a difficult hum problem by using its academic technical experts, and passed on its knowledge to the manufacturers. They then precisely measured and recorded the maintained lighting intensities, and the benefits of the new system. Everything was done right. These procedures were governed by intelligence, foresight, common sense, and three-dimensional experience— the best possible experience in planning buildings. We began almost at the top. By 1938 we had in our hands technology and demonstrated methods of planning to give us controlled and predetermined illumination at the proper level on the working plane and its surroundings for any library activity, the fruit of more than 4,000 years of development.

So, we lived happily ever after? All the libraries built in the last 50 years have good lighting? Probably less than one-half of the 600 library buildings I have examined had good lighting. What went wrong? There have been multiple barriers on the way to the promised land, and when one was overcome another seemed to loom ahead. All of the problems had the effect of making readers feel uncomfortable enough to leave the library sooner than they would have done otherwise.

The first barrier was the difficulty of obtaining the right intensity. In 1879 when the electric filament lamp was invented, most libraries were not open at night, especially not to ladies. During the daytime, all right-thinking people read books near windows. Let me describe Coburn Library at Colorado College, built in 1894. When I joined its staff in 1954 it was pretty much unchanged, even to the furniture, except for a modern tierstack on the back of it. It had very high and large windows to provide reading light. On the east south, and west sides of the library these windows let in direct sunlight which, in Colorado, is intense enough to knock your eyes out. So, shades had to be pulled down, which, strangely, kept the light out. They also let in heat, so in summer, to supply a little ventilation, the windows were opened a foot at the bottom. This let in birds, who immediately soared to the twenty-foot ceiling and never could find their way out again at the bottom of the windows. After days of disconcerting flitting about, dispensing their favors everywhere, they would tire and slip behind the window shades low enough for me to catch them and release them a block away. The students thought the white spots on the spines of periodicals were paint. But the uncontrollable condition of the light was a bigger problem than the birds. In the basement rooms, bare light bulbs screwed into a socket at the end of eight-foot long light cords swung from the ceiling. Because the bookstacks climbed twelve feet high, you reached them on a ladder, carrying the light bulb up with you if you wanted to see everything. When, as time wore on, the library kept open at night, the windows in the reading room were black, as all windows are at night, and the few bulbs mounted on the high ceilings did not give enough light for reading comfort. That library's use quickly doubled when we moved into a new very well lit building. The condition I have described was not unusual for libraries at the turn of the century.

Over the next 30 years, improvements in library lighting consisted mostly in using more incandescent light bulbs than formerly, and in 1934 I encountered in the Yale University Library, then only four years old, the typical condition of library illumination just before the advent of fluorescent lighting. The Yale library is a monumental building that resembles a Gothic cathedral, which seemed to attempt to achieve within a medieval gloom. Windows were to a large extent deep-set arrow slits. The main entry was lit by artificial torches mounted on great stone columns, and the main reference reading room was lit by large chandeliers, but the ceilings above them both were so high they swallowed up light. I once saw a light meter placed on a table directly below a chandelier containing about 30 light bulbs, pointed upward, of course, instead of downward, and it registered five footcandles. Stack aisles were lit by bulbs on the ceiling inside of a white enameled grilled cage that diffused the light poorly. Stack carrels, assigned only to faculty and doctoral students writing theses, and therefore the locus of long and intensive study, were lit by highly inadequate single light bulbs. Everywhere in the building, including offices, lighting was of very inadequate intensity, except in the fiction browsing room, where bridge lamps were installed beside lounge chairs.

This condition was typical of prefluorescent lighting, and the advent of cool lighting that produced much higher illumination at much lower cost was a giant step forward. Before World War II, 20 footcandles intensity was more or less accepted as a standard of illumination in libraries. That is why the University of Colorado's 22 to 28 footcandles loomed large in 1938.

Air conditioning, which came in during the 1950s, made it possible to build much larger floors with much lower ceilings, because the last reasons for high ceilings—to provide breathing space and relieve the smells of humanity—disappeared. With low ceilings and interior spaces far from windows, we began to use general lighting for the first time in the form of fluorescent fixtures. From the beginning, they gave enough light, and the practice in all except research library stacks of keeping the lights on all the time made libraries brighter and more appealing. Large increases in lighting bills were absorbed in the expanding prosperity of the 1950s and the fact that more students were required to read more books more often. Libraries were becoming more important, and while their lighting was not always good, it almost always was of adequate intensity, about 50 to 55 footcandles.

Americans never get enough of a good thing, especially if they do not know anything about it. So, having essentially solved the problem of lighting intensity, we asked for more. During the 1960s, when government money flowed over us like Niagara Falls, the lighting levels specified for many libraries were hard to believe—from 150 to 250 footcandles. Electric companies, which love to sell generators, pricked up their ears and began to plump for 300 footcandles. To prove their point, they led the way. The architect Pietro Belluschi consulted for two power companies at about this time, one of which lit an entire 30-story building at 300 footcandles intensity, and the other lit its own office at 600 footcandles. So we began to get overlit libraries, many of them with bad lighting, because under the wrong conditions, the higher the intensity the worse the light. The result of this confusion was that by the 1970s, many new libraries were lit at 150 to 250 footcandles of illumination, a 10-fold leap from the 20 footcandles of the 1940s, and quite unnecessary.

In the early 1970s, the financial support of much of the intellectual world collapsed. From 1965 on, radical students burned or blew up academic buildings all over the land, or occupied them with armed students. Even more discouraging, the most violent confrontations had taken place in what was considered the upper crust of education—Harvard, Yale, Columbia, Cornell, Stanford, and the universities of California, Michigan, and Wisconsin. The public grew sick of it and cut the funding of higher education. The costs of the Vietnam War swallowed the grand surpluses of money the federal government had been showering on us. Severe inflation, which at one point exceeded 20 percent a year, destroyed the usefulness of what money we could get, and severe retrenchment was the order of the day.

In libraries, building maintenance was the easiest budget to cut, and this included the costs of illumination. The easiest way to cut lighting was to remove the tubes from fixtures, sometimes cutting their numbers in half. In many libraries, this cut the intensity considerably below 50 footcandles and greatly impaired the feeling of the building. In the University of Toronto Library, which I examined in 1976, many of their triangular lighting fixtures, which had been mounted in a pattern both esthetically pleasing and designed to distribute light in a balanced way, were randomly unlit. To understand that lighting pattern, you have to see pictures of it in my book on library buildings, which were taken shortly after the building opened. Even worse, in many libraries, cool white tubes were mixed with warm white tubes, sometimes in the same fixture, and the color combination was nauseating. The result of all this scramble, which was usually placed in the hands of the maintenance department, was ghastly esthetics in the lighting and undesirably low levels.

In the 1980s, some geniuses realized that if we were going to light libraries, we should agree in advance what kind of tubes we would use, and how many of them our budget would allow us to keep lit. The rise in oil prices and air pollution made us aware of the need to economize our resources for generating electricity, and the result has been a more sensible view of the lighting intensity in libraries. Over the past five years, buildings I have examined or consulted on have tended toward 70 footcandles in most of the building.

But what is all this about intensity? After all, the eye is a marvelous instrument. In fact, its complexity and adaptability caused Charles Darwin to have serious doubts about his theory of evolution by natural selection. The eye can read a book in 10,000 footcandles illumination of bright sunlight, yet one-hundredth of one footcandle is enough for a walker to make his way along a road securely, and indeed, in 1931 that was a British standard for illuminating class H roads. Let me make that fact starkly clear. Sunlight is one million times brighter than the British standard for class H roads, but the eye can adjust itself to that enormous difference. Bright moonlight measures only four-hundredths of a footcandle on the ground, and we know how easy it is to move around in moonlight. In the pre-Christian era, Greek dramas were often presented in the amphitheaters on moonlit nights with no supplementary illumination. The Davy lamp, developed in 1850 to mine underground coal, gave less than half a footcandle of illumination, and experts have conjectured that the lowest level of visual response may be as low as one ten-thousandth of a footcandle.

Although the pupil of the eye can open wide enough to permit seeing at these very low light levels, it can also close almost completely if it is irritated. The eye does not permit the retina to become sunburned. Just as the mind is the greatest barrier to learning, because it easily convinces itself it is overloaded, so too the eye is the greatest barrier to seeing, in the presence of glare. Glare is produced by any light source intense enough to cause the eye discomfort or annoyance. This causes the pupil of the eye to contract and decreases our ability to see. In 1964, I gave a ceremonial address on James Joyce to open the summer session at Colorado College, on a stage flooded with light prepared for a dramatic presentation to follow my speech. One spotlight was aimed directly at my face, and it was almost impossible to see the text of my speech, though the light intensity must have been more than 500 footcandles.

When I was a college student, our dormitory desks were equipped with an incandescent lamp containing two bulbs. The stem of the lamp was unusually high and I was unusually short, a perfect combination for exposing my eye maximally to the full glare of those bulbs, and I remember to this day how tired I used to get studying at that desk at any time of the day. I now know that the glare fatigued my eye, as it does to all eyes when it occurs in libraries, and it makes students leave.

The glare problem has been with us from the earliest times. I can imagine that artist in the Lascaux caves saying to his torch bearer, "Don't stand there; hold the torch over to the side." The open flame of oil lamps produces glare. Open gas flames used for illumination were full of glare. Electric arc lamps were of such intense glare they could hardly be looked at. Ironically, just about at the time the electric filament lamp was invented, the invention of the gas mantle made gas illumination, for the first time, bright and very comfortable to the eye, as those of you who use Coleman lanterns will know. But the advantages of the electric bulb won out, and electric bulbs had very high glare, because the light was concentrated into a very small ball, and the glow of the filament was bright. Their glare problem was reduced somewhat when it became possible to make frosted bulbs, and then enclose them in frosted globes.

Even before electricity, natural light was a very great glare problem in libraries on three sides of the building. When the first separate library building came to the University of Colorado in 1904, it handled the glare from natural light highly effectively. The outer walls of the reading room had few windows. The east and west faces of the roof pitch were equipped with skylights, and below the pitch of the roof was a clerestory around most of the roof support. Inside the building, where the large reading room and stacks occupied most of the main floor, the ceiling was composed entirely of glass diffusing panels, located low enough so they were not struck by sunlight at any time of the day. The result must have been as glare-free natural light as you can get. But, on the whole, glare from natural light was controlled in libraries by pulling down the shades.

You recall that one advantage Waldo Brockway found in the 1938 fluorescent lighting at the University of Colorado was that it produced less glare than incandescent bulbs. To a certain extent this was due to the fact that fluorescent tubes distribute their light over a longer area than incandescent lights, which concentrate their intensity into a small ball. No matter whether you use incandescent or fluorescent lighting, properly designed fixtures strategically located will provide light of sufficient intensity to make reading easy and comfortable and make the environment around the reader feel pleasant. But this is not usually done.

Libraries have had very few successful installations of incandescent lighting in recent years, but one notable exception is the library area of I.M. Pei's East Wing addition to the National Gallery of Art in the District of Columbia, on which I consulted. Pei is probably our greatest architectural designer at the present time, and this building is a great one, designed with two unusual requirements. For the art works, sunlight had to be excluded as much as possible while still making the interior humanly attractive. Second, because of the personal preference of Paul Mellon, no fluorescent lighting was to be used in any part of the building. Because Mellon was giving the money to build the addition, no one argued with him. By giving up incandescent downlights in the high ceiling coffers of the reading room, which were originally proposed, and substituting table lamps for readers, and by carefully controlling the glare of fixtures in the work room, this library provides excellent lighting.

The greater output of illumination from fluorescent tubes, which will be our main concern for some time to come, makes its glare difficult to cope with. How can this be done? Direct glare comes directly from the fixture itself to the eye. The closer it is to the line of sight, the less bright it has to be to cause glare problems. It is most acute at a 45 degree angle to the eye, and it can be controlled by placing the fixtures out of sight. The Colorado College Library, completed in 1962, had exposed concrete ceilings with 4' × 4' coffers 18" deep provided especially to hold the fixtures. Although the architects, Skidmore, Owings, and Merrill had different ideas, all of them bad, we finally sent them home, and Professor John Kraehenbuehl selected and improved the design of a 2' × 4' fluorescent fixture to be placed up into each coffer. Most of them were out of the line of sight from any angle to the reader, and the direct glare problem largely disappeared.

The best possible lighting was in Professor Kraehenbuehl's student drafting room, where drafting was done in pencil on linen sheets. Fluorescent tubes were mounted above a frame that held continuous strips of translucent corrugated fiberglass, run at right angles to the tubes. There was no glare of any kind, and the strands in the fiberglass plus the effect of the corrugation produced interreflection within the room so great that the light was almost completely shadowless.

The cover below the tubes eliminated the second kind of glare we have to minimize, reflected glare, caused by reflection of the lighting fixture off the reading task directly below it. Without a cover below fluorescent tubes it is impossible to control reflected glare, which is at its worst when reading pages of coated paper—science books, periodicals, and other books. The cover, or lens, of the fixture must prevent the tubes from being seen through it or reflected glare, although less intense, will still be a problem. The corrugated fiberglass did this.

This installation was very pleasant and bright to work in, but it was esthetically dull, and would never have gotten past an architect. But the necessity of placing bulbs out of sight, of diffusing the light well, and of preventing bulbs from showing through the cover was made clear, and these are the principles for obtaining glare free, or as it is referred to, high quality illumination. For many reasons, it is not always possible to get all three factors at their most effective level. But it is always possible, with knowledge, mock-up installations, and sensitive observation of the results, to minimize glare to an acceptable level while still providing adequate lighting intensity. We have known how to do this since about 1950; why do we not do it all the time? What has evolved in the conditions that determine the planning of lighting in libraries?

One of the most perceptive experts interviewed by Keyes Metcalf, former director of the Harvard University Library, for his book *Library Lighting* (Washington, DC: Association of Research Libraries, 1970), made this comment, "At present very few institutions, architects, or electrical engineers are competent in the area of specifying lighting or are likely to become competent in the near future" (p. 29). How right he was is marked by the fact that lighting installations are less successful today, 20 years later, then they were in 1967. How can this be so?

Since 1965 there has been a decline in most of the learned professions, which have become more self-serving and far less interested in serving people than at any time in my life. This is painfully true in librarianship, and possibly least true in the field of architecture, which I find on the whole still to be dedicated and responsive to its clients, if they know what they want. At the same time, the great expansion of current knowledge and the multiplication of specialities has generated the practice in many fields of proceeding on designated tasks without assembling all of the knowledge pertinent to their performance. Such is the case in engineering education. Thirty years ago, when I met John Kraehenbuehl, two subjects were already being dropped from the engineering schools—illumination and power—because of the new importance of electronics in technology. By 1967 when, at Professor Kraehenbuehl's advice, we hired Professor George Pierce of the University of Illinois to review lighting proposals for the Fieldston School Library, he had already retired from teaching illumination and that subject had completely disappeared from their curriculum, even as a concern in larger courses, although the University of Illinois has a large College of Electrical Engineering. Obviously, new specialists in this field of engineering were not being generated. To prepare for this paper, I talked with the College of Engineering at the University of Kentucky in Lexington, where I live, and was told that, because of the large number of fields that compete to be taught in a 4-year engineering program, no aspect of illumination was being taught by anyone, but that there was a course in the Department of Architecture. We are talking about a chunk being yanked out of the academic curriculum as important as the removal of English history from the history department, with no active authorities left in the demolished field.

Obviously, no one can learn much from an architect about the engineering aspects of illumination, which include appraisal of the technological design of lighting fixtures, specifying them for solutions to different needs, and calculating from spectromatic data the comparative desirability of different fixtures. Nevertheless, I contacted the professor of architecture who, yes, indeed, taught illumination. He told me that this subject is taught in the school of architecture at most universities that bother with it at all, and his attitude was summed up in a single sentence, which I wrote down verbatim: "[Illumination] is not an engineering problem; it is an architectural and psychological problem." Indeed it is an architectural and psychological problem, but it is also profoundly an engineering problem. Five years from now, will Illumination be taught in the psychology department? I hope that you are horrified by all of this. This scientific field of major importance to the entire world is being emptied of expertise. In such a knowledge gap, two fields have reached out to fill it—first, architecture.

Light fixtures in libraries have always placed demands on architects that they would like to avoid. After all, have they not reconciled themselves to those gruesome objects called bookstacks, which used to be decently hidden in the closed center of the buildings, but since 1950 have been pulled out into reading rooms? That was like placing the toilet stool out in the living room. Now, with general lighting, they not only have to cope with great numbers of light fixtures, which to architects are pieces of furniture that call attention to themselves, but whereas they used to be round and symmetrical and placed on walls or tables, now they are square or rectangular and they march in rows on the ceiling where everyone can see them. My sympathies are with the architects; lighting fixtures are very difficult to handle esthetically, and if handled badly they can devastate the feeling of the interior. Architects tend to favor downlights, a single high-power incandescent bulb in a tubular container, with an open bottom that produces no diffusion of light and creates the worst possible reflected glare. Except in corridors, I have been fighting them in my consultant work since 1963, winning only about half of the battles. Let us not, colleagues, turn illumination over to the architects.

The other field moving to fill this knowledge gap is manufacturing. Manufacturers have changed in my lifetime from enterprises that respond to well-defined needs, to enterprises that control and manipulate markets through advertising. I mentioned earlier the electric companies' attempt to hook us on 300 footcandles illumination. They had a gimmick in the 1960s in an experimental laboratory near Rochester, where they placed you in a chair in a lighted room, gave you a book, and put in your hand a rheostat control you would adjust until you thought the light was good for reading. Then they would tell you how many footcandles of illumination you had chosen, which often was 250 footcandles or more. What they did not tell you was that your eye was in the presence of such intense glare that its pupil was nearly closed, and very little of that light was getting in. The great demand for lighting in our world today is for dramatic and display lighting, which has very little to do`with libraries. So we cannot expect much from manufacturing.

But then, if the planning does not develop well, there is the institutional review of the plans before they are accepted. Metcalf's expert named institutions among the incompetents. Second only to faculty meetings, institutional review is the best argument against education. I am awed at most universities' ability to ignore their own academic expertise, often world renowned, while hiring consultants from off campus. Professor Stanley McCandless of Yale's school of drama was a noted appraiser of quality lighting in his time. For 20 years he designed lighting fixtures for manufacturers, and complex lighting consoles for sophisticated stage lighting, but Yale never spoke to him about the lighting in six buildings by big-name architects they built in the 1950s and 1960s. The library in their school of architecture, located half a block from McCandless's office, is lit by bare bulbs, screwed into bare sockets, attached to bare wiring conduits, located barely above head height. No lighting could be worse. My book on library buildings analyzes in detail the lighting in Yale's Beinecke Rare Book Library, where, across the corridor from one of the finest lighting installations I know, in its reading room, is one of the worst that I know, in its technical processing room, both by the same lighting designer. But Professor McCandless was never asked to review any lighting. In most places, we cannot count on high quality institutional review of lighting plans.

But suppose that we can find a competent reviewer of lighting somewhere, maybe we can dig one up. Then we face the quirks of the planning and the bidding process. The electrical engineer should be called in at the very beginning of the planning process, because, as we saw at Colorado College, the basic structural system of the building can be used to achieve good quality lighting. The electrical engineers are usually not part of the architect's firm, and they usually do not see floor plans before the design development stage. While developing their electrical plans, they often are using a set of floor plans one or two versions behind the current plans. I describe the accident-prone nature of planning in my book. The electrical engineers should know immediately of any change in architectural drawings, and especially of changes in finishes and coverings in the building. The interior designer also should be in on the earliest planning of the building and kept totally current with changes. But these things are seldom done, although interaction of these three specialists is of critical importance to the success of lighting.

But suppose, by some miracle, all of the things that are generally done badly have been done right. Then we are faced with two words in the bidding specifications that can totally destroy what has been planned well, the words, "or equal." In any industry handling as much money as construction does, there is a great deal of chicanery and corruption of various kinds. For this reason, except for specialized items that are almost unique, most items in the library building specifications are designated by the exact manufacturer and model number of a known item, with the words added, "or equal." This is to insure against connivance with a supplier or against a manufacturer hammering you with a high bid price if only he can supply what you want—common sense precaution. But, while a desk quoted "as equal" can be quite like a desk specified, no lighting fixture is even approximately equal to another. Especially in the case of $1' \times 4'$ or $2' \times 4'$ fluorescent fixtures, which are often used, two fixtures that may look alike and cost about the same can be, and usually are, radically different in the quality and intensity of the light they produce.

We got caught in this bind in planning the Hofstra University Library, which ultimately won four architectural awards. We had specified a totally satisfactory fixture, which we had chosen after arguing the architects out of their original proposal, intensive shopping in the New York area, and carefully examining a mock-up of eight fixtures under conditions typical of their use in the new library. The successful bidder included a subcontractor who submitted a so-called "equal." When we mounted it for inspection it was a turkey, a perfect producer of intense glare. So we had to hammer the subcontractor to consider a whole range of other fixtures, and to modify the lenses on those that seemed possible. The one finally accepted was not nearly as good as the one specified.

So, what is this about the evolution of library lighting, my assigned topic, when conditions seem to be leading us back to the cave? I have rather been talking about devolution, which means, "falling, with a rolling motion." In the complex confusions produced by the enormous energy and variety of our technological and commercial world since 1950, we went from a high plateau of library lighting to dropping over the edge of the cliff in the high intensities of the 1960s. Somewhat battered, we have slowly climbed back up the rock face, painfully driving piton after piton all the way, to a level of sanity again. Our knowledge of controlling glare is still up on the plateau, but few ever go up to look at it.

Our times have lost, to a great extent, the ability to distinguish permanently important things from the transitory, and have lost a view of the critical necessity of retaining the permanently important. In a way, any library planner pursuing good lighting today is like the Pilgrim in John Bunyan's *Pilgrim's Progress*. To reach the heavenly city of high quality, well balanced, adequate intensity, lighting one must go through the Slough of Despond, the Valley of Humiliation, and the Dungeon of Despair. But a dedicated person, armed with knowledge of the hazards, a true eye, a stout heart, and abiding faith, can sometimes reach that goal.

ACKNOWLEDGMENT

The author wishes to acknowledge his indebtedness to *A Short History of Lighting* by William T. O'Dea, 1958.

WHAT DO LIBERAL ARTS COLLEGE DEANS THINK ABOUT THE LIBRARY?

Larry Hardesty

INTRODUCTION

"What do academic administrators think about the library?" Robert M. Munn (1968), librarian-turned-administrator, posed this question more than twenty years ago in his classic article, "The Bottomless Pit, or the Academic Library as Viewed from the Administration Building." The anwer to this question has important consequences for academic libraries because, as Munn wrote:

> It is the Administration which establishes the salaries and official status of the director and his staff, which sets at least the total library budget, which decides if and when a new library building shall be constructed and at what cost (1968, p. 51).

"In short," concluded Munn, "it is the Administration—not the faculty and still less the students—which determines the fate of the library and those who toil therein" (1968, p. 51).

Unfortunately, Munn found academic administrators not particularly well-informed nor supportive of academic libraries. He concluded, "The most

Advances in Library Administration and Organization,
Volume 10, pages 145-186.
Copyright © 1992 by JAI Press Inc.
All rights of reproduction in any form reserved.
ISBN: 1-55938-460-3

accurate answer to the question, 'what do academic administrators think about the library,' is that they don't think very much about it at all" (1968, p. 52).

William A. Moffett, former director of libraries at Oberlin College, echoed similar sentiments in a study he conducted in the early 1980s. Moffett "sought advice from academic librarians across the country from virtually every type of postsecondary institution" (1982a, p. 46). In response to his request of fellow librarians to identify the traits, practices, and attitudes and procedures of the administrative and teaching colleagues that had proved the most troublesome, Moffett "predictably" found:

> Stories of administrators who tend to see the library budget as a kind of reserve fund for meeting emergencies; of library facilities designed without the professional advice of the prospective occupants; of the assignment of building space to nonlibrary use without due consideration of the library's own needs; [and] of changes in library services mandated by faculty and administrators unable or unwilling to provide funds to meet the financial impact (1982b, pp. 13-14).

While most of the respondents did not cite horror stories, Moffett concluded, "Many of my fellow directors felt they had received considerably less support than they needed from their institutional colleagues" (1982b, p. 13).

Librarians, unfortunately, often know little about the attitudes of administrators toward the library. Administrators infrequently write about the library in professional journals. Also, as Munn correctly observed, few librarians are part of administrative inner circles. Consequently, librarians typically base their opinions about administrators on impressionistic and anecdotal information. Perhaps because of a penchant for bad news, examples of unsupportive administrators who neglect and misuse the library tend to obscure any reports of thoughtful administrators who have a genuine understanding of libraries and librarians.

Munn and Moffett are virtually alone in their careful examination of library-related attitudes of administrators. Recently, *College & Research Libraries* reprinted Munn's (1989) article as a "classic"—thereby reinforcing his perception of administrators in the minds of another generation of academic librarians as conventional wisdom. Our personal experiences, however, suggest that librarians should be cautious in projecting negative views of administrators, particularly at liberal arts colleges.

THE STUDY

In re-examining Munn's conclusions, we posed the question, "Are his observations, based upon his position at a major university during the 1960s, valid at selective liberal arts colleges in the 1990s?" We identified institutions defined as "competitive" to "most competitive" by the 16th edition of *Barron's*

Profiles of American Colleges. The National Center for Education Statistics, as reported in the March-April 1988 issue of *Academe,* classified most of the institutions as either IIA or IIB liberal arts colleges.

During the fall of 1988 we wrote the library directors of 50 of the 59 institutions that met our criteria. We explained the purpose of the project and requested help in arranging interviews with the chief academic officer (hereafter termed deans) of their institution. While we received a handful of negative responses and a few library directors did not respond at all, most directors responded positively. The responses enabled us to arrange 39 interviews at 36 institutions.[1] Because personal interviews required considerable travel, we had to consider logistics in making the final selections. Available time did not allow more interviews. In general, the institutions selected have small enrollments, strong libraries, and healthy endowments.[2] They are all institutions that could support active library involvement in the curriculum.

We decided to use personal interviews to explore in-depth the attitudes of the administrators (Katz and Kahn, 1966). We organized the interview questions into a moderately or semi-structured guide. This technique permitted us considerable flexibility (Stewart and Cash, 1974). We tape recorded 38 of the 39 interviews. Throughout this report we have relied heavily on the actual words of the deans so they could speak for themselves as much as possible.

The interviews lasted between 30 and 90 minutes, with most of them lasting 45 to 60 minutes. At three institutions we also interviewed the associate dean. We conducted the interviews from November 1988 through August 1989.

RESULTS

Support of Institutional Mission

Did the deans at these small liberal arts colleges think about the library? The answer is an emphatic "Yes!" Early in each interview we asked the dean to describe, "How does or should the library support the goals and mission of your institution?" The deans, of course, responded they supported the library, and we found many of the answers quite predictable.

The library is perceived as the intellectual center of the academic enterprise.

The library is obviously a complement to our academic curricular program.

The library is absolutely vital to one of the things we want to accomplish, that is, the independence of individual education.

The library is central to this whole endeavor, not simply as a depository for books that the students go and check out, but in a symbolic way as well. The library is absolutely fundamental to the instructional program of the college.

Obviously, we found, as Munn reported earlier, some deans supported the library because it is a "good thing." Some had not given a lot of thought about the specifics of how the library should support the institutional mission.

Many deans, however, spoke quite articulately about the role of the library. For example, a well-respected dean from a prestigious eastern college responded:

> I am very taken by what Earlham does; would very much like to see the library woven into the fabric of the institution in a very different way where students are not just using the library, but getting the instruction and information technology that supports their particular discipline very early in the courses.

Another dean responded:

> I have trouble when people use the library simply as a depository or place to hold reserve readings because then it is an adjunct to content. When you think of independent learning and lifelong learning, which I think of just as important as content and depth, then you have the library just absolutely crucial, rather than simply filling a more passive role and adjunct to content.

Other deans, while supportive of the library, responded more globally:

> The library has a very integral role to play. The library is a symbol. It sets a tone for the college and for the students. The library not only provides the materials, but also, in the intangible sense, sets a tone and sends a message representing the highest aspirations of the college.

We found no shortage of verbal support for the library, but the deans varied as to how informed and articulately they spoke of the library.

Throughout our interviews most deans expressed considerable satisfaction with the library. A few, however, had found themselves wanting the librarians to take more initiative. For example:

> I am not sure that the library itself has played an effective and proactive role and I may be wrong here and this is not an indictment, but I think there are some communications and some initiatives the library itself could be taking to encourage a more consistent pattern both of usage and of acquisitions.

Finally, we had a handful of deans who responded to this question with such remarks, as "There has not been a lot of thought about the library."

Undergraduate Library Skills

We next asked, "How would you characterize the effort needed to develop in undergraduates the skills needed to use the library to fulfill the role you want?" Most deans believed that teaching students how to use the library required considerable effort.

> We find a lot of students coming in ill-prepared to use the library, and I think, in fairness, some of our students, even by the time they graduate, are not as good as they ought to be on fundamental library research.

> I think students do need a lot of help. I think it is naive to assume that they can move into a college library and know how to make it useful for their educational purposes.

> I do not think you can approach this library informally. I do not think you can approach any library informally. It needs a formal introduction by the staff, it needs a formal introduction by the faculty.

> I do not think they will pick it up on their own. I think the best ones will if they are required to use the library. They will figure it our for themselves. But I think we have missed in the past. In general, in higher education we have missed and certainly we have missed here in not arranging things such that we are sure students get those skills.

Interestingly, we discovered no relationships between the wealth and prestige of the institution and the deans' response to this question.

While most deans recognized the need for formal instruction by librarians and classroom faculty, they often appeared either ambivalent or dissatisfied with current efforts. Typically they responded:

> I don't think they have enough opportunity or incentive. I think I have a real concern about the use of the library.

> It is really a mixed picture and I do not know how to quantify it or give you a better picture of it.

> We try a number of things that all colleges try at orientation time. As much as we think those things are important, I don't think we have had a lot of success because students don't have a specific particular interest at that time.

> There is no quantitative answer to that. What we are doing now is right. We have to do it more and better.

Some deans had given more thought to the problem and had specific ideas. For example:

> We have tried general introductions to the library where we send the students and the librarians try to introduce them. The attention span is not great. They do not see it connecting with anything they are actually doing in the classroom at that point and they do not learn much. When it links to a specific course-related assignment, it has a lot higher retention rate for them.

I think students learn how to use the library when they have a reason or need to know how to use the library and have a specific project to work on and then have people in the library who are skilled in picking up on that opportunity.

Nevertheless, some deans had given very little thought to student library skills. We found a few deans who responded, as one dean did, to our question, "This topic has not had a lot of discussion since I got here."

Responsibilities of Librarians and Classroom Faculty to Develop Student Library Skills

In probing this area further, we asked, "What is the responsibility of librarians and of classroom faculty to develop those skills? How might their responsibilities overlap and how might they differ?" Most deans answered that they viewed the responsibility as shared.

Obviously a partnership; librarians have a lot of responsibility to reach out to the faculty and to educate them as to their role in their partnership.

The responsibility for seeing students get skills falls on faculty, on librarians, and on students. It is a shared responsibility.

Ideally, it is a collaborate enterprise. I don't know if it always works out to be that way. There tends to be some faculty feeling of a separation of labor, which I think is undesirable, but is a reality. But ideally, I think it should be a collaborate venture in which the faculty member would assign work that would require students to make good use of the library, would meet with the librarians or appropriate members of the library staff, and say to them this is what I am going to assign. Is the library going to be able to handle this or is it equipped to deal with this sort of assignment? How can we make students profit from this better?

I would argue that both the faculty member and the librarians are responsible together. The librarians cannot do much if the faculty don't see to it that their students get there.

Another group of deans placed most of the responsibility on the classroom faculty.

I think this is largely the responsibility of faculty who need to take thought about how to be sure that they get students into the library and making use of the information base that is there.

Many also thought the classroom faculty should do more. Some deans commented on the limitations of the faculty approach toward student use of the library.

Classroom teachers, when they think about putting together a course, are trained in graduate school and, in their own unreflective approach, usually think about getting the information out.

I think that you ought to be able to expect your faculty in their courses and in their disciplines [to do] some of it. They cannot provide the kind of integrative task that often needs to be carried out when a student is doing an interdisciplinary piece of research.

Even those faculty who see their professional satisfaction being derived from teaching see teaching as a matter of delivering interesting, well-thought out lectures. The faculty is in the library doing the work and the research to pass information on to the students. We ought to begin to start thinking about our role as teachers, to how to get students to do the work.

I think the faculty basically have to take it. The faculty themselves have to be encouraged. My sense is that library skills are something that faculty in academic disciplines do not have ownership. They think it is someone else's responsibility that students should learn how to use the library.

The response of many deans to these questions revealed their interest in undergraduate education and the library. Many continued to teach part time and some planned to return to the classroom full time.

Many deans spoke highly of the role of librarians in getting undergraduates to use the library.

The logical answer is that the faculty are responsible for the education of the students. The practical answer is that the librarians really have to take that as their responsibility.

Librarians need to help teachers to figure out not just how to introduce the library, but why they ought to do so.

I really see librarians as part of the instructional staff. I could not feel more strongly about the importance and the value of the library playing an active part in providing students with kinds of guidance.

The classroom instructor obviously sets assignments that require use of the library. The library and the librarians make the students feel the library is helpful. I quite frankly feel that it is almost essential that the professional library staff be involved in educating students to the use of the library. I think that is true more today than any other time in my experience.

[Librarians] do remind you of resources that you have known about once, but kind of forgotten about. They just have a seriousness and a professionalism with the way they conduct those sessions that tell those students that this is important business.

From these interviews, we concluded that most deans had at least a general understanding of the importance of librarians in getting students to use the library. Perhaps the individuals who become deans have more a tendency to step back from their disciplinary training than do many faculty members who remain in teaching and view overall educational practices and issues.

Evaluating Student Use of the Library

We next probed further to determine how deans evaluated or judged the involvement of the library in undergraduate education. We asked, "Do you have a level of comfort or expectation regarding student use of the library?" We found most deans did not have specific expectations. Their answers seemed vague and sometimes even evasive.

> I have a sense, but I don't keep tabs.
>
> I don't have a clear sense of what it ought to be.
>
> I cannot think of any facet of the academic experience in which they are devoting as much time as I would want them to. That includes the library.

Only a few deans provided details or elaborated in their responses to this question.

We then asked, "What do you look at to determine if student library use is up to your expectation or level of comfort?" Through this question we tried to learn how deans evaluate the library. Seldom did any dean refer to statistics or reports on student library use.

> I do not have a measure. I am not very quantitatively oriented and it would not much occur to me in my annual review when I talk with [the library director] to go a great deal into measures.

We discovered most deans informally gathered much of their information about the library.

Often deans referred to conversations and information from the faculty.

> The measures I use are admittedly subjective, but I am rather closely tied to the issue of faculty satisfaction with the library.
>
> Talking to department chairs is where I get primarily that. I probably ought to do that more and more and be more self-conscious in a systematic way to include that in my discussions with department chairs.

Deans also referred to their own use of the library and information from students.

I am in our library a fair amount so I know how heavily it is used and used for more than a study hall. All one has to do is to listen to the amount of student complaints that goes on about something in the library to know that they are in there actively working away.

On a small college campus such informal information gathering techniques may work well. Deans, of course, have to determine between typical information and information that fits part of a larger pattern. Nevertheless, we suspect at these small colleges there is little information of importance that does not eventually reach the dean's office.

College Library Resources

In earlier research we found faculty members often had difficulty distinguishing between resources needed for undergraduates and those more appropriate for graduate purposes (Hardesty, 1986). We also asked the deans of these liberal arts colleges, "How would you characterize the type of library collections needed to support undergraduate education at this institution?" Most of them tried to make a distinction between undergraduate and graduate libraries.

We do not promise faculty here that they will be able to do very esoteric research in any part of the collection without substantial use of other libraries and interlibrary loan. In fact, if we find that we do have a collection substantial enough to allow esoteric research, I would see it as a danger because it means we are wasting money.

The library is a library for an undergraduate institution. We do not think of it in terms of supporting faculty research. That is a given.

The problem is what you will hear from your faculty, and it happens at every one of the campuses, is that any good institution worth its salt will have this in its collection. That logic will send us to bankruptcy. Then you go to the collection and find the item that any good institution will have and the binding has never been broken and no one has ever looked at it.

I came from a school where we were able to spend a lot of money on the library, so it was spent stupidly. In fact, we are better off not having quite too much to spend.

At first, we found such responses surprising. However, while college deans may be close to teaching, they may have moved away from research in their discipline. In addition, because deans deal with budgets and the fiscal demands of faculty research, they probably are more aware than individual faculty members of the cost of supporting a research-level library. We found deans who supported extensive growth of the library tended to be either new in the position or strongly research-oriented.

Responsibilities of Librarians and Classroom Faculty to Develop the Library Collections

We then asked, "What are the responsibilities of librarians and of classroom faculty to develop those collections? How might their responsibilities overlap and how might they differ?" As with the development of library skills, many deans emphasized collaborative efforts between classroom faculty and librarians.

> I find myself as an academic administrator always trying to encourage and to work for the overlapping so the library staff and the faculty are on the same wave length about collection development.

> I see each of them having their own responsibilities here, but being very important that they understand one another and that they have the same set of goals.

Typically, these deans viewed the faculty's role as critical to the materials the library actually acquired. The librarians served to help keep the faculty informed.

Some deans tended to more strongly view the faculty members as the primary developers of the library collection. For these deans, librarians served more as monitors to fill in gaps and to remind the faculty members of needs.

> I think the faculty should be primarily responsible for the development of the collection. I think the librarians have the responsibility of kind of being the monitors of that, and if the faculty have failed in their responsibility, then (a) [the librarians] let faculty know that they have failed and (b) [the librarians] become active in correcting the problem.

In the eyes of these deans, librarians play a more reactive role in collection development.

Other deans saw faculty members recommending the purchase of items but the librarians are responsible for overall development of the collection.

> The goal is trying to balance the degree of academic freedom faculty have about the selection of materials and the degree of structure and direction and organization when a relatively few minds look at the decisions being made and refer to some standard works of reference.

> The faculty is primarily going to worry about collection building of very focused materials on courses they are teaching and research they are doing. It is the job of the librarians to see where you got to have some cement in between these stones so you end up with a wall and not just a pile of rocks.

The librarians have the responsibility for keeping some kind of basic collection. They have to do that for at any given moment faculty interests will vary. So librarians have a terrific responsibility in a sense to keep smoothing out these peaks and valleys.

For these deans, librarians had responsibility for filling in the gaps created by faculty members' more specialized interests.

We found many deans quite outspoken about the dangers of too much faculty involvement in developing a college library's collection. These deans often argued for librarians having more responsibility for collection development.

It should be a collaborative effort because the faculty cannot be trusted to build the collection. The faculty can never be trusted to build the collection because they always will be biased toward building in their specific areas of expertise and self-interest. If left uncontrolled, they will not only build in their areas of expertise, but also at the graduate level.

There has to be a dialogue. I think in an undergraduate college, faculty come here tending to do and to duplicate and to replicate the things they learned both as undergraduate and graduate students. But very quickly they lose touch both with what is available [and] with different formats for what is available.

It seems to me that the departments get a larger share of the decision making and the budget for acquisitions than I would think should be the case. I would be more comfortable with a librarian being more responsible for acquisitions. I know enough about small colleges that it is a world of fiefdoms and treaties.

The librarian has to be the person who finally has the responsibility for the development of the collection. It finally has to rest with somebody. A faculty member in religion is going to know his field or perhaps only his specialty within religion. Somebody has to look at the overall collection and the broad perspective. The librarians obviously have got training in that area that others do not have.

I think that most of my colleagues on the faculty would disagree with me. I feel that professional library staff should have greater responsibility in developing the collection than is now the case at [institution]. I think they have an expertise that the faculty in general do not have. They have an objectivity that the faculty in general do not have.

In general, the deans' strong support for the librarians' role in collection development surprised us.

All the deans we interviewed had come from the faculty. They had Ph.D.s and had taught at the undergraduate level. Nevertheless, they frequently had a different perspective in this area than did the faculty members we interviewed in our earlier research (Hardesty, 1986). Perhaps they are more aware of budgetary constraints and overall undergraduate educational goals than are many faculty members. We did find a few deans who avoided this question almost altogether, "I am not very well informed about that."

Evaluation of Use of the Library Collections

We asked the deans how they evaluated the use of the library collection. We found they relied largely on subjective impressions to check the use of the library collections.

> It is quite a good library from what I have seen, in the areas I know well. I can check it out to see what it has that would be of interest.

> I think you have to listen to faculty who make assignments.

A few expressed concerns about the lack of use of the library.

> I think there are substantial amounts of materials that are purchased that are not used and that bothers me. I do not have a solution for that except for over the long term a regular process of inventory and weeding of the collection so that we really try to keep things focused on what is needed.

> More broadly, I am concerned about this in our culture. The broadest level is the degree to which we really care about and use information, use books, use libraries. I have a continuing concern that the television generation, the spontaneous generation, is not as careful about actually doing research as I would like to think they would be.

One dean gave an answer that reflected the view we found more typical among faculty members.

> There is some part of me that says, and this is going to sound awful, but I do not care how it is used. It should be there.

Another dean even thought use of the collection might be too high.

> If I am uncomfortable with it, it is because the level is way too high. From the level of use that is going on you think a large collection would be appropriate. That I cannot quantify, but that is my impression.

Seldom did any of the deans refer to quantitative data. When they did, none cited any specifics.

> I have seen the data that [the library director] has sent me but I do not recall.

Perhaps this reflects as much on the library directors and faculty members at these institutions as it does the deans. Quantitative data on library collection use may not be a high priority with any of these groups.

Computerization of the Library

In recent years, college libraries have made increasing use of the computer. We ask the deans, "What impact do you think computerization of certain library procedures and operations will have on the role of the library in undergraduate education?" Perhaps more on this question than any other, the deans' answers varied. About one-third of the deans viewed computerization quite favorably.

> If I were not confident that the money were going to be spent on that which was going to help our mission directly, as well as our faculty and students, I probably would not be pushing it as hard.

> I think automation for the humanities is revolutionizing how we are going to be learning and teaching. It has not occurred yet, but I cannot help think there will be a revolution going on.

Many of these deans already had expressed their confidence by supporting computerization of the library.

Perhaps about another one-third of the deans expressed caution about computerization of the library. Those deans with a science or mathematical background, a small minority among the deans, expressed the strongest reservations about the impact of the computer on the library.

> We do not know the educational impact. There have been some historical circumstances in which technology has been oversold. I think we need to be careful about being oversold again.

> I think that ultimately it will have a broad and profound effect, but that it will be slow in coming. We have got to wait for the faculty to become truly comfortable with working with computer searching itself.

> I do not see what a librarian might see as a major revolution. It seems to have evolved over the years. I think it is an important development, but I do not see it as a revolution.

> The technology will help people get to the information they need better, but it's hardly going to be a significant percentage in the overall educational impact.

> I am very old-fashioned in that I think the student needs to confront the collection directly. Real scholarship is messier and less systematic than the computerization of the library would suggest.

Some deans wondered about the computer's impact on interpersonal relations.

> Now what I would love to have a [terminal to the online catalog] within each department, but I am mixed minds of this because then faculty members would not go over to the library.

> The nightmare part of it is that we will have these individual scholars all in his or her own room, never getting out of this space for face-to-face communication with people.

Many of these deans expressed strong views related to the cost of computerization of the library.

> I think that, for example, those institutions that end up making major investments in computerization and, as a result, find themselves cutting back on people standing there helping, that is a bad trade off.

> I hope the net impact will be to make it easier and more exciting in someways to use the library. I think that we have to be very careful about the huge investments and what you do not do when you make those investments.

> I worry very much about the resource allocation in changing technology and how much it will balloon the library budget in relation to other things.

> I am not aware of any of these computers around here saving us a cent. I have the impression of endless amounts of money going towards computerization and we have the same number of secretaries and everything else. We are just drowning in paper.

In fact, none of the deans we interviewed believed the computer would save money.

Finally, perhaps another one-third of the deans accepted the computerization of the library reluctantly. They considered it inevitable. Some felt overwhelmed by the technology. Others believed they had to computerize the library to remain competitive with other institutions. It had become a symbol by which perspective students judged the institution.

> I think we will spend millions of dollars to get only marginally better. We have to be a participant in the technological revolution.

> I think that everybody will do it whether it will result in anything, won't they? Isn't there a technological imperative?

> If you don't go ahead and automate the library now when you have the money, then it is going to look like you are slipping into the nineteenth century and people may change their attitude towards it.

I do not know. What is driving us as an institution is our general competitive posture vis-à-vis other institutions and libraries and a clientele that is very sophisticated about consumer decisions. They look at the library as part of a check off as they look at athletic facilities, parking, dormitories, etc.

Whether or not it saved money or made library use more efficient and effective, many deans found themselves compelled to support the computer to compete for students.

Resource Sharing

Librarians often promote computers by pointing to the advantages of increased resource sharing through enhanced educational and financial benefits. Therefore, we asked the deans, "What impact do you think increased resource sharing through computer data bases will have on undergraduate libraries?" Again, most deans expressed cautious optimism. They usually viewed resource sharing as a "good thing." Nevertheless, many expressed reservations.

The more we can do to share resources to tie in with networks out there the better off we are going to be and in providing our students with an enormously broad data base.

It doesn't make any sense for libraries not to do these kinds of things in these expensive times, but there are some potential perils involved. You got to find some definition of how you are going to make decisions and to emphasize certain needs of the collection.

I think that futuristic people will be able to say yes to that question, and there are important sharing and exchanging that goes on within [local consortium] that are really marvelous. I do not believe that the electronic mail and the technological impulse sending it will be able to defeat distance.

Surprisingly, most of the deans expressed doubts about any momentary savings as a result of resource sharing made possible by the computer.

[It will] probably cost us more. Again, I do not think I know the answer to that question. Sharing resources sounds like such an obvious solution to the problem, but it is so hard to do.

I am very reluctant to think that it will save us money. Every thing that was ever proposed to me as money saving technology turned out not to be.

The tragedy of the commons takes over. It is not clear to me yet that institutions have worked out very well collaborative relations. I guess I am least optimistic about our saving money. I suspect that the expenses of all this will continue to rise.

The pervasiveness of this response makes us caution librarians about trying to promote the computer based on economic benefits.

The Dean's Responsibility

By this point in the interviews most deans had warmed to the topic. We next asked one of the more provocative questions of the interview, "What is your responsibility to be sure that the library plays the role you want it to have at this institution?" Most deans first responded by describing their role in the budgetary process.

> [My] most direct involvement is in the budget priority process which I allocate more resources to the library.

One dean explained this budgetary emphasis, 'Obviously the main one is to provide them with money. Almost everything else stems from that." Another dean confirmed some librarians' fears that deans sometimes view the library budget as an emergency fund.

> Make sure it gets its lion's share of resources in the good times because when you get to the bad times you can be sure that the library is going to be one of the things that is looked at as expendable.

Often we had to probe further to find other ways deans ensure that the library plays the role they want it to have.

Frequently deans referred to the informal and indirect ways they operated.

> My particular style is to try to be somewhat low key and try to work on an individual basis and not to use the pulpit that much and to work individually with department chairs and faculty as the occasion presents itself.

> My role is indirect rather than direct. Only a foolish dean would jam new ideas down the throats of unwilling departments, but you can certainly suggest.

> My less direct role is to be self-conscious as I interact with departments about their own curricular modeling with anticipating the library needs associated with changes.

> There are many things we can promote very subtly and I think most deans do that on a regular basis. It is an element that is always in the forefront and it interacts in the decisions that are made in many ways. The library is not something that I have on the back burner. It is a part of many things that enter into most decisions that I have to make. It has to be an organic whole. You cannot isolate any element. You certainly cannot isolate the library.

Perhaps deans must be careful to avoid any appearance of intruding in areas that faculty members believe protected by academic freedom (Dearing, 1968, pp. 120-132).

A few deans, in response to more specific questions, referred to other ways they involve themselves with the library.

> I can make sure that in the process of faculty governance and in tenure and evaluation the teaching aspects of the librarians' jobs are taken seriously.

> The academic dean can play an important role in facilitating this by recruiting, encouraging, and supporting the library staff in playing this kind of active role and in encouraging, educating, and leading the faculty in seeing the library in this kind of active role.

Few deans, however, provided examples of their leadership in this area.

Several deans believed they had a responsibility in working with the faculty to include the library in their teaching.

> I think I have a major role to play in moving faculty to integrate their work more with what is available in the library and involve their students in the library.

One dean even mentioned direct discussions with the faculty.

> If I wanted to draw the library more prominently into discussions ... it would have to be done on an ad hoc basis department-by-department rather than in the governance system.

This same dean, however, pointed out that he did not do this. In fact, we do not recall any dean describing conversations with faculty members on how to involve students in the library. While it may occur informally, none of the deans appeared to include it as part of evaluation discussions or any other formal meetings.

Several deans mentioned their role in recruiting a good library staff, particularly a good library director.

> I think first of all it is to make sure in our situation ... that we have someone in that position [library director] who has the energy and vision, and the managerial competence and all the other qualifications that we want in a librarian.

In planning this project, we discussed our questions with a well-respected library educator, who had been an academic library director. He predicted that deans essentially wanted library directors "who would take care of things in the library so the dean would not have to do so." We found considerable truth in this statement.

I do not take an active role. If I felt there were problems I guess the way staff functions in working with students and faculty I would talk with [the library director] about it, but I have not.

In fact, most deans believed that they had a library director who did "take care of things."

Most deans expressed strong confidence in their library director.

The librarian reports to me. I am very lucky. I can let him do pretty much what he wants to do and not worry about it. He and I think the same way on most things and he manages the library beautifully and deals with the personnel beautifully.

I regard [the library director] as a first rank professional who has thought of these things.

[The library director], in my judgment, is an excellent librarian, so he and I cover a lot of ground in our conversations. We meet often and he is a member of my immediate staff.

I think my first responsibility is to support [the library director]. If he is good, and he is in this case, then I delegate almost everything to him. I must back him both with respect to my commentary, my public pronouncements, and the kind of resources that I either allocate or seek.

A third role would be as mediator and an advocate for the faculty, but I do not feel in the current situation that is needed. [The library director] does good work with all the faculty and so backing him becomes my primary job.

With [the library director] I work much more with him as a peer. He answers to me, but... I trust him and rely on him for a whole range of issues that keeps me out of the nitty gritty of the library. I am very concerned about the overall direction, policy and that sort of thing. But I guess I am saying that I relate to it at a different level than I relate to academic departments.

In fact, most deans thought highly of the library.

It is not a library in need of rehabilitation. If there were anything I thought I could do, I would do it. But I think it is just a first-rate place.

As a result, most deans dealt little with the day-to-day operations of the library. They viewed their responsibilities toward the library in more general terms.

Several deans mentioned their role in speaking for the library to boards of trustees and to other college administrators.

A second specific responsibility I think is for advocacy with the board of trustees where I think a great deal of the future resources of the college will be coming.

I have to be the advocate for the library with the rest of the college administration and with the board of trustees.

As Munn noted, library directors often do not serve in the inner administrative circles. Therefore, they seldom see deans in their role as advocate for the library to administrators or trustees. This may be one reason why some library directors are unaware of just how much support deans give the library.

Computerization has drawn some deans into a more active role toward the library. The costs and complexities of this process have made many deans much more informed about the library.

I have been pretty much involved with the library because of automation in the last few years. If it had not been for automation I would probably know a lot less about libraries and what they are doing than I do now.

One dean even described the education he received when he attended the technical services presentation on the computer by mistake instead of the public services presentation.

To be sure, some deans felt strongly about the importance of the library and aggressively promoted it. Most gave strong verbal support for the library.

I think the library is so crucial that when I came for my interview I was supposed to be here for two-and-a-half days and I asked to stay for another day because I wanted time by myself in the library.

I put a lot of pressure on [the library director]. If he goes to sleep, then the faculty will forget about the obligation of teaching people about the library.

The quickest way not to support the library is to let it become noneffective and have it become an institution that everyone pays homage to, but no one goes to unless forced to.

The library and computer center report to this office. Both are important, but if I ever had to choose I certainly would choose the library over the computer sciences.

Others tried to fit the library within the larger institutional mission without particular emphasis on it.

I am provost of the college and I have no first priorities. I have no last priorities. My priorities are to make sure that the overall culture of the institution functions proportionally and comfortably.

Most librarians probably would welcome, as a minimum, the dean who stated, "My chief responsibility is to listen and to learn. To listen to the librarians and their perception of where the library is going and should go."

Determination of Library Needs

Because the deans' primary support for the library came through the budget, we asked them, "How do you determine how much the library needs?" One dean expounded on an elaborate planning process.

> We function in a macrobudgeting process with a faculty committee that works very well. It starts meeting very early in the fall to think of macrobudget allocations of the next fall. Often they look more than a year ahead.

Other deans referred to information provided them by library directors.

> We look at material [the library director] was able to get for us from several consortia interests. We made some calculations about collection size relative to size of student body, rate of acquisitions and so forth .... On the basis of those comparisons, the budget priority committee made some decisions last fall.

Elaborate planning processing involving careful weighing of information seemed the exception rather than the rule.

Most deans appeared to rely heavily on more subjective criteria.

> We know that the college budget is increasing across the board and we try to put more than that into the library. Is that rationale? No, it is simply an arbitrary decision, but we figure we can't go wrong if we do twice as much in the library as every place else.

Most deans relied heavily on informal information, particularly from faculty members.

> I get plenty of data. I still go by my instincts and emotions quite a bit. I get a sense from talking with people and from watching from what happens in the library and from eavesdropping on student comments and on faculty comments and just again from wandering around, and I factor that in a great deal. In the end I make judgments based on my instincts.

> The sign of our inadequacy, I think is if there are substantial student and faculty complaints that what they need to deliver the courses they are teaching is not present.

> The real test of the adequacy of the library is the faculty impression. If they do not have it they will complain about it.

> The reality check I mention is to watch when the rate of orders slow down in the library and to see how much screaming in the faculty to see how much is not getting ordered and what kind is.

Are the librarians complaining about the workload? That is always a good sign that things are hopping.

Perhaps there are at least two reasons why deans rely heavily on subjective information and their instincts in determining the library budget. One reason is that they believe they do not have objective data to help them.

I have said to the president that the requests made in a library budget are the most difficult for me to either defend or refute.

A second reason relates to simply the size of these institutions. These deans probably have considerable contact with faculty members. The deans may believe there is adequate flow of information to them through the faculty members, and, to a lesser degree, from librarians and students about the library.

In many ways, some of the criteria deans used in budget making are not readily subject to formal assessment. Particularly at the less endowed institutions, the deans referred to the library waiting until it had its "turn" at the budget. At these institutions, the deans could not well fund every program or department every year. Instead, a particular program or department might get an extra amount every four or five years or so.

Deans also often referred to the overall needs of the institution and to the need for balance among programs and departments.

Knowing there are specific needs is not all that important. That sort of nitty gritty has to be used in developing a request. But when you are sitting down arguing the library versus athletics or versus computers or versus faculty salaries for that matter, the big picture is much more important.

How the library fits into "the big picture" or the determination of when is the library's "turn" probably results more often from subjective value judgments than careful analysis of objective data.

Use of Comparative Data

Do deans make use of statistics, such as comparative data with other institutions? Their responses to this question varied considerably. Many paid considerable attention to such information.

I try to use comparable data effectively. [The library director] is very good in showing us the results of the Bowdoin surveys and comparing us.[3]

Two years ago we spent an entire year working on a long-range plan for the college. We selected some schools against which to compare [the institution].

I follow that Bowdoin list, and I look at it quite carefully every year. I do not see anybody cutting back. We think that we have put an extraordinary amount of resources in the library and then we look at our standing on the list and we do not even move because everyone else is doing the same thing.

I tend to lean very heavily on comparative statistics at virtually every area of the college. We have a set of sixteen colleges and sixteen universities with which we compete most directly for students.

I tend to look at Art Monk's data available through the Higher Education Data sharing group. I am on the national advisory panel of that so I encourage the librarians and the library staff to look at those numbers.

Enough of those figures look to me that they are relatively hard that I find them quite useful.

A large minority of deans expressed little confidence in comparative data.

What faculty and students are saying are more important than comparative numbers.

You can never tell whether the institutions are putting together the figures in the same way.

There is not a set of ratios that are compelling about how many catalog items an institution needs to attain a certain level of quality.

Sometimes the particular circumstances of an institution made comparative data less useful.

I must tell I really don't [use comparative data]. I used to do that a lot..., but I am finding those kinds of standards less and less useful. We after all have a huge special collection ... that so widely distorts comparative numbers.

We suspect, however, the dean's view of the usefulness of comparative data is highly dependent on his or her relationship with the library director. Several deans confirmed our hypothesis.

I think so much depends on the relationship between the dean and the director of the libraries that those things are not ... going to persuade somebody that does not trust the person who is using them.

The first thing I have to do before making those decisions is figuring out whether I am going to have confidence in the person I am talking to or not. And do I have confidence in that persons' values or my values. If I can't figure out whose values are right..., then I will assume mine are.

Perhaps library directors need to keep in mind the three most important things in the library budget-making process are: confidence, confidence, and confidence!

Outcome and Performance Measures

Because of the deans' mixed responses to comparative data, we wondered if they looked for specific outcome or performance measures in assessing the library. The response to this question, particularly as it relates to different regional accreditation agency requirements, also varied considerably. Many deans responded negatively to the question.

> I am bothered or irritated by this whole movement in the [name of regional accreditation agency]. Although I recognize those are the right questions to ask, I do not think we have the technology to answer them.

> I am very hostile to assessment. I do not like assessment. I think there is a way that we are an intellectually responsible community that assesses itself over and over. If you listen to our faculty, we drown them in a sea of paperwork to assure that they are doing excellent teaching and good scholarship.

> I am quite skeptical of those sorts of things [quantitative assessments], but we will do it. We doubtless will have to come to terms with that sort of issue. We have been avoiding it because most of the faculty and the administration are highly skeptical of those things versus the amount of time and resources it takes to do it.

In addition to opposition based on time and resources, some deans spoke of their philosophical opposition to quantitative evaluation of the library.

> No, I do not think we should ask that question. I think Jefferson was right when he said, "We hold certain truths to be self-evident." The intellectual and educational health of the institution depends on sharing certain convictions at a level of belief and at a level of consensus that do not have to be exact. At this institution, the centrality of the library is one such truth.

> I think when you start measuring use of the library and relative degree of its involvement you are in trouble because you have lost the faith. These institutions depend on a set of convictions which, for me, are almost religious like.

Again, we suspect that among small institutions, interpersonal relations and direct observations play a major role in any evaluation.

Other deans speculated on what "might" serve as performance measures of the library. However, few actually had used these measures to evaluate the library:

> My ultimate measure of the output is the productivity of the faculty in terms of the classroom performance in teaching, recognition of its excellence in teaching, and in its research productivity. So output for us consists of books and articles and lectures and so on.

I would be interested in some formal way of measuring the important variables on the library edge of the public service functions. I don't know what those would be at the moment. I is important because use of the library is one clear indicator of how well the academic enterprise is being carried out at large.

I think there are also ways, of course, to try to measure how effectively the faculty make use of the library in the curriculum and that would have to come through a study of syllabi to see whether or not library projects and research were actually included.

Many deans stated that they had little idea how to assess the library.

Frankly, that is the only variable we ought to use in judging the library. How effective is it for the users? How much do they use it? Do they get the kind of support they need when they go in there? Is it a place that invites people in and makes them want to stay around and explore? I don't know how you measure it.

In a way the library is like the academic disciplines. We all know that we have got to do a better job of measuring outcomes, but the big challenge before us is exactly what is the best way to do that. How do we measure the outcomes of a philosophy program or a theater program?

Not that we do not think outcomes are important, but we have never gathered information or asked questions or analyzed what we are doing with those outcomes.

Even those deans who accepted the inevitability of quantitative assessments did not know how to apply the techniques to the library.

I know that we are going to have to do whatever must be done to develop a sense of the quality of the use of the library. But in all candor I do not have a sense of it at the moment. I really don't.

In fact, some deans did not know how to apply outcome analysis to other sectors of their college.

I thank my lucky stars that I did not have to do quite so much outcome analysis for anything else either because I find that particularly difficult.

We did find a deans that supported careful analysis of library use.

The fact that we do pay attention to usage has allowed us to be wise in buying and in utilizing our space and things like that. I am convinced that it pays to have people who are serious about learning how it is used—not to satisfy external examiners but simply to allow us to work smart.

Nevertheless, even these deans referred to traditional measures of library use, such as circulation figures. We found little evidence of highly sophisticated analyses of the library's contribution to the educational program.

The "Bottomless Pit"

From these responses, we believed they had not completely answered the question, "How do deans decide the limits of support the library should have?" Munn claimed that academic administrators could not determine the limits of library needs:

> They [academic administrators] have observed that increased appropriations one year invariably result in still larger requests the next. More important, there do not appear to be even any theoretical limits to the library needs. Certainly the library profession has been unable to define them (1968, p. 52).

Did the deans interviewed consider the college library a "bottomless pit"? Some deans emphatically denied the validity of this view.

> I do not think so. I do not think it is a perception at all. I do not think anybody who perceives the library as that way. It is a vital resource that needs to be kept up to date.

One dean replied with particularly colorful language in describing the relationship between library needs and budgetary control.

> Bottomless pit is not a phrase I would use, but it is a kind of "river" of words and images, and of activities. You want to control the flow of that river and the depth of it at any given point, but it must keep moving.

Often deans from less endowed institutions would not accept the bottomless pit description because of the limited funds they had to support the library.

> I do not think it is a problem here because my perception here is that we are not purchasing enough.

> It is not a bottomless pit because there is only so much we can give to the library.

Most deans, however, accepted the bottomless pit analogy in describing the library.

Unlike Munn, however, the deans who agreed with the bottomless pit description viewed it as neither unique to the library nor necessarily pejorative.

All important academic enterprises are bottomless pits. Every department is a bottomless pit. Every department thinks it should have three times as many faculty as it does. If one was to respond [affirmatively] as a provost or dean to all the requests one would be impossibly over budget all the time.

I think at one level the library is and should be a bottomless pit. What you are talking about there are learning resources for both faculty and students.

The whole academic institution is a bottomless pit. I do not think [the library] is a bottomless pit, except to the extent that we all have needs that will never be complete. We are always in a position where we follow needs with too few resources. It is always going to be that way.

It may be a bottomless pit. So is computers. So is athletics. There are a number of areas in the college where you can always spend more.

Yes, the libraries are a bottomless pit. They share that with a great many parts of the college. Music is a bottomless pit.

Science is a bottomless pit. The way pits are constructed are a little different, but everything is a bottomless pit. So accept that now and you simply have to go through some sensible way of sorting out your resources so you optimize the system.

I would not use those sorts of pejorative terms, but your definition is accurate. I don't have any substitute language to use, but I never use bottomless pit. It is a constantly expanding need for funds, all of which is valid need, and it has to compete with other needs across the campus. Almost never do I think a dollar spent on books and journals as an unwise expenditure.

Perhaps librarians have been too sensitive or apologetic about the portrayal of the library as a bottomless pit.

In response to this question, a few deans singled out the faculty's demands for library materials.

In a sense, when you say libraries may be a bottomless pit, if faculty drive the accession process, it may be that the faculty are insatiable. If somebody else is paying for it, who does not want a book? I do not see it as bottomless because we have defined the bottom ourselves as an institution and try to maintain it.

Again, deans reflected their sensitivity to budgetary issues.

Frequently, deans referred to the computer center as the institution's bottomless pit.

Not any more than you could say the same about the computer center, which probably is a bottomless pit.

[The library] looks a lot less bottomless since the computer services have come along. I think if you want a bottomless pit, it is computing.

Despite increases in recent years in periodical prices, computer costs (not periodical prices) have captured more of the deans' attention. Perhaps as college libraries become increasingly computerized, the library again truly will compete with the computer center for the dubious distinction of the campus's bottomless pit.

The Dean and the Library Director

In responding to the bottomless pit question, deans often referred to the management skills of the library director.

> The library in that sense is very much like the natural sciences' appetite for equipment. The appetite is, in my experience, insatiable. There is always the need for more. And in a way, this is healthy and is not to be lamented, but I do not think that it greatly helps an academic administrator who is responsible for a budget [and] to have from the director of the library some clear sense of what the most important needs are.

Therefore, it followed naturally to ask them, "What do you look for in librarians, in particular, the library director?"

The deans also provided a wide range of answers in response to this question. Some deans listed numerous characteristics they looked for in library directors.

> The library director has to got provide a clear vision of the physical plant, relationship of the physical plant to the social purposes of the library, and the budget. The library director is responsible for managing the budget, for providing a budget projection that seems to be congruent with the goals that it is going for, needs to be a long-range planner, needs to be a compassionate manager of people, needs to be a public relations representative of the library to the administration, to the student body, and to the faculty. There are a lot of skills involved. It is a tough job.

> [I want] somebody that is systematic about what they want as the objectives of their particular area; pretty good at delegating and supervising, who has some experience in doing the things we want them to do; must be bright and able to work with faculty.

Most frequently, the deans mentioned the importance of the interpersonal skills of librarians.

> I think that in a small college that interpersonal skills are important.

> We are small enough that one of the things we will look for is literally personality.

> In my interviewing I look at personality types and how they relate to the faculty.

Being comfortable with students is pretty important.

I want [librarians] to be skilled in the art of librarianship or the various areas
of it in which you are going to spend your time. But we also want you to care
about this community and be an active participant in it and to be student oriented.

Some deans pointed out that good interpersonal skills alone are not enough
for a library director these days.

We had a Mr. Chips here for years and everybody loved him and he certainly
was a book person, but the library all but fell apart and we got terribly behind
in all methods of information retrieval. You just cannot afford that in a library.

On the other hand, some deans occasionally found librarians overemphasized
technology.

In this new world of librarianship, you get the impression from time to time that
you have people who never go near books.... You are hearing about online,
offline, and output and the camp of librarianship that is very discouraging.

Most frequently, deans wanted librarians and library directors who understood
the role of the library in the college community and actively promoted the
library.

I then look for, assuming that they have the educational background, the degrees,
the skills to do the job, I look for qualities that demonstrate that they too
understand what we mean by a liberal education.

I want a librarian who will be aggressive in a certain way. I want a librarian
who will not let me forget how important the library is.

In a larger sense, they have to understand the function of the library and how
it is vital to the support of the overall instructional program of the college. It
is hard to pin that down as exactly what that means, but it is best if librarians
and library staff talk to the faculty and get to know the faculty as well as the
students. They will come to appreciate just in conversation the kind of
requirements being placed on the faculty for research or requirements being
placed on students for assignments. The more interaction the better.

The only thing that will keep the expansion of the library staff a low priority
item is if the perception is that librarians are essentially people who sit around
without a great deal to do simply to respond to occasional and casual requests
that students and faculty bring to them.

If you got a librarian who has limited vision and limited energy and limited
integrity and the dean of the faculty who does not understand or appreciate the
library and who is handling his responsibilities poorly, both the college, at large,
and the library in [and] of itself can suffer.

Again, many deans referred to the importance of the relations between the dean and the library director.

> I have to view the librarian as on the same side of the desk or we are in trouble. He can't just be a money grubber who is trying to build a damn empire and drive the institution into the ground any more than the person who runs the E&G [educational and general budget] can have that attitude.

Most agreed that the library director had a difficult job.

> I think it is an extremely complex job with multiple responsibilities.

> [The library director] probably has to play the most difficult public political role of anybody outside of the president and the chief academic officer in the administration.

From these responses, we concluded that considerable potential exists for closer communications between deans and library directors.

Faculty Status

Although we did not ask about faculty status, many deans brought up the subject without our prompting. Because controversy often surrounds faculty status for librarians, we found surprising the support many deans gave to it.

> We have to bring them [librarians] back to more of a faculty role. That is going to be difficult because for some reason that has changed. They should have faculty status. We have a phrase: teacher-coach, student-athlete. We need to do it, teacher-librarian.

> I think this is important. Here at [name of institution] librarians are on a tenure-track or tenured. For tenured faculty, we expected them to be serious about their professional scholarship. We do not expect them to publish at the same rate as they would be expected to in a university setting, but we do want them to be active and productive professionally. I think it is important for library faculty that they identify some area in which they are going to be active in their profession.

> In the professional staff of librarians we expect librarians to be faculty members. We have the same expectations of professional library staff as we do of the faculty in the departments and that means to be and conceive of themselves as teacher/ scholars.

> The librarians become an integral part of the instructional staff. Any questions of whether they should have faculty rank and things like that virtually disappear because of the obvious instructional character of their roles.

Librarians, though they are not eligible for tenure, have full faculty status. They are among other things, eligible for election to the faculty affairs committee, which is the personnel committee of the faculty. In fact, [the library director] was on it when I was hired. You do not need to tell me that [the library director] was an important person here, and it was not just that he was appointed by somebody. He was elected by the faculty.

Four of the staff of the library have faculty status and although they do not teach in the classroom, there is a signal to be given by that.

I think faculty status for our librarians, plus also they go through the tenure and evaluation process, has contributed to that visibility.

First, our librarians are faculty and are respected and treated as such.

Faculty status is an enormous help. Librarians have to know what is going on in the curriculum. Curricular decisions are made at faculty meetings and committees and they should be very much involved in that.

We struggle with what it means to have librarians as members of the faculty, particularly at evaluation time.... We come down on the notion that we call them faculty and hold expectations that include professional activities and scholarship, and include collaboration with faculty where appropriate.

Not every dean strongly supported faculty status for librarians.

At that level that kind of faculty status is enormously important. On the other hand, it seems to me that it is a service organization and their job is to function as librarians as distinct from scholars.

Sometimes we received the impression deans considered the faculty members less supportive of faculty status for librarians than did the deans.

None of our librarians, including [the library director], has faculty rank, which is a constraint. The faculty does not think of them as peers; that has ... potential for undermining morale of librarians, which I am very self-conscious about, but again this is part of the culture.

A few deans believed librarians had not fulfilled their faculty responsibilities:

To some extent I am expressing exasperation with our librarians to some degree. Not individually, professionally they are quite competent. They have faculty status, evaluating them is very difficult because they don't do the kinds of things faculty do. Our faculty have said that we will not have two different criteria or two different levels of application of criteria for evaluating people. Yet, our librarians themselves have resisted getting academic credentials and doing the things which faculty recognize as being academic.

For us, one dean summarized the issue of faculty status quite well, "If an individual ... has the manner and education and interests of faculty members, then the faculty will treat them like a faculty member. If they don't, the faculty won't."

Library Personnel Problems

In our discussions, some deans seemed particularly sensitive to personnel problems of librarians.

> Librarians are easily isolated. They are in a building all by themselves nine to five. It is very easy for them to get demoralized and to feel that they are not part of the faculty or part of the institution—some conspiracy to get them somewhere or to deprive them of something. You really do have to watch out to keep up their morale and make sure they do not get isolated.

> I worry about librarians at times because I think as a group they have an inclination to feel under appreciated, overworked, not valued in the way academic faculty are valued, to feel somehow marginalized.

> I think that librarians have to have the desire to serve people even though it is going to be difficult because both faculty and students get frustrated because of the roles they have. I think it is hard for librarians sometimes.

> By-in-large librarians are bright, interesting people who are involved in the life of the mind and they can stagnate very easily if the library stagnates. So I think there is a responsibility not only to make sure that you have those qualities in people coming in, but that you sustain them over the years.

In general, we found most deans had considerable respect for the librarians, particularly the library director. Deans, of course, have more contact with the library director than any other of the librarians.

Nevertheless, we did find problems between library directors and deans. Early retirements, unexpected terminations, and other signs of difficulties have occurred among these 36 institutions in recent years. Occasionally the deans referred to the difficulties. One dean described the library director as "too political." Another dean characterized the library director as ahead of institutional priorities. Yet another reported that his library director "sometimes ... comes after you driving a bulldozer when he might just come in quietly on a bike." This dean added, "It is rather exciting." Nevertheless, these problems existed at only a handful of the institutions. Our interviews left us very encouraged about the relationships between deans and librarians.

The Ph.D. Degree

Part way through our interviews we begin asking deans (at the suggestion of Dr. David Kaser, Distinguished Professor of Library and Information

Science at Indiana University), "Do you look for someone with a Ph.D. degree?" We hypothesized that responses to this question would relate to faculty status issues. However, again the deans' responses surprised us. Very few deans believed the Ph.D. degree necessary or sometimes even desirable for the college library director.

> A Ph.D. is not a requirement for being a librarian at this college. I think that it probably or appropriately might be in a university setting, but here I think the masters is sufficient.

> We worked all that through. No, we wold not expect a doctorate. I would view that as something appropriate for someone who would want to teach in a library school.

> Ph.D.s in library science are relatively rare and tend to be perceived in my experience as wanting to teach in library schools.

> I assume people with Ph.D. in library science maybe go to teach in library science departments or at the research libraries, but we did not think it would be an appropriate credential in today's market.

> So a Ph.D. might also be a liability—not quite I am sure, but it does suggest a kind of focus that we thought was simply not necessary.

> I am not thinking of a Ph.D. in library science because I think those kinds of degrees would be irrelevant to our kind of institution.

> It seems to me that the Ph.D. might be more appropriate for the research library where they needed to have a better command of a particular subject matter or really going to teach library science than direct the library.

The answers to this question have important ramifications both to library educators and to librarians hoping to become college library directors. The paradox is that the Ph.D. degree may help librarians gain status in the eyes of faculty members but deans may be reluctant to hire librarians with Ph.D.s.

Some deans, of course, valued the Ph.D., such as the one who responded, "Absolute advantage, it lends distinction." Interestingly, the more prestigious the institution the less the deans valued librarians having the Ph.D. Perhaps at these institutions, the possible enhanced status offered by a library director with a Ph.D. mattered less.

Physical Characteristics of the Library

At this point in our interviews we switched to a different area. We asked, "How important are the physical characteristics of the library, particularly in relation to other aspects of the library, such as developing the collections and the staff?" We found this probably the most difficult question to get carefully thought-out answers. Typically, deans responded, "Of course they are important?" Frequently we had to rephrase the question to probe further.

Most deans held that a positive relationship existed between the physical characteristics of the library and its role in the educational process.

> I have argued that a handsome library is even more important than a handsome entrance to a campus because it in many ways is the gateway to the learning process.

> I think there is a direct relationship between esthetics and learning.

> It is very important that the library be a friendly and inviting place. It really is devastating to intellectual art not to have easy, friendly, comfortable access to new books and new titles.

> You only build a library once. I have seen libraries put up in sort of post-Soviet architecture period that we went through in the 60s and early 70s. The people saddled with those libraries know now that they are. The problem with a library to me and any big facility is that it's a morale loser unless it is done right.

> It is almost more important than those other things. If the students will not come to the library because the ambiance will not bring them in, they will not discover sufficiently all these other resources and the people who work there. So I think it is paramount.

Deans also pointed out the importance of the physical characteristics of the library in the admissions process.

> To be competitive in admissions, we must have a library that is open a lot of hours, has a warm feel to it, is attractive and the material is available. All those things shape the image and reputation of the college. The image aspect is very powerful.

Many deans could not separate the physical characteristics of the library from the other attributes of the library:

> In the first place, it is not disconnected from those other sorts of things. All these things are interconnected.

We probably received the least satisfying answers to this question out of all the questions.

Erosion of Support for the Library

Library literature is full of information about the erosion of support for libraries. We sought to confirm whether this was happening at these selective liberal arts colleges. We quickly discovered most libraries at these institutions well supported. Even when some of the colleges made cutbacks in the early 1980s, often the library suffered less than other parts of the institution. Consistently, deans responded about the strong support libraries received at these institutions.

> The library would be one of the last things to go in a financial pinch.

> No, the library during the twelve years I have been here has consistently got bigger increases than most of the general academic departments.

While computer, periodical, and other costs related to the library frequently have captured the attention of these deans, seldom have the libraries suffered.

Symbolic Role of the Library

In fact, we gained a sense that at these colleges, the library received considerable support because of its symbolic role. At the risk of asking a leading question, part way through our interviews, we begin asking some deans, "Does the library have a symbolic role at this institution?" The deans responded almost universally that it did.

> It is a major symbol and that is one reason why we are proud of building a new library. It is something [name of college] will use from now in its publicity about itself.

> I think it is. Certainly this institution could not parade its strength as an academic institution with a certain sense of intellectual values without having a library at least as strong as the one we have.

> Maybe that is unusually true of colleges of the kind you are talking to.

> I have implied it and I meant it. It is symbolic in a way that is particularly resonant and particularly important now.

> The president shares this attitude about the symbolic role of the library. We have put the library in a very central place in our planning for our next campaign.

Several deans also pointed out that support of the library for its symbolic role is not without problems. As one asked, "How does one measure symbols? You cannot really calibrate that."

Support for the symbolic role of the library can lead an institution to spend funds far beyond utilitarian need.

> In selective liberal arts colleges there is no question there is a psychological need to have resources in the library to keep you high on some symbolic list by which the prestige of the institution is measured—regardless of whether they have value.

We just don't have the resources to pay the outrageous prices in science and engineering periodicals—incredibly expensive stuff that is there for symbolic rather than utilitarian purposes. It is sort of driving us crazy.

Who says that [another institution] needs all those periodicals subscriptions. I will lay you odds that a lot of them are never used. They are there for the prestige of the institution and really nothing more than that.

Nevertheless, even those deans who complained about supporting the symbolic role of the library provided evidence of continued financial support for it. Perhaps this is because of the financial strength of most colleges we visited.

The Privileged Library Budget

Through our interviews we concluded that often the library's budget has almost a privileged status. We tested this conclusion by asking many deans directly the question, "Does the library have a privileged role in the budgetary process?" Typically, they responded:

Yes, I cannot remember a year since I have been dean that the library increase has not been above the average increase for departments.

Some deans reported on the strong support faculty members and other members of the academic community expected the deans to give the library.

The library is different only in [that] there is such a broad consensus that it is a central player that it would be very easy to give it an unfair share because nobody will ever criticize you for ever giving the library too much.

Yes, I think that is true here. Whenever we get a request from [the library director], our executive vice-president, who really handles the budget, and I try to work out a way to fund it. The faculty expects that.

Not every area of the library budget, however, is privileged. Most frequently, deans mentioned the materials budget.

Yes, it is privileged in that the books and periodical budgets are generally treated outside the established budget parameters. In our case in being outside means that the increases there are larger than are the increases allocated for most other areas of the budget.

Library directors, of course, would point out the need for larger than usual increases in these areas to sustain purchase power.

There, of course, are exceptions to support of the library. We found at one wealthy liberal arts college, with an exceptionally strong library, a rethinking of the library budget's "privileged status."

That has been the case and that issue is being confronted in the current budgetary planning process. The question is to what extent should that privileged position be maintained.

At the other end of the financial spectrum, we found a dean lamenting his inability to provide even more support for the library.

There is another way of answering the question, however, which is to say that the library here is not nearly as privileged as it needs to be.

At most of these selective liberal arts colleges the library does hold a strong position in the budgetary process.

Do Deans Talk to Each Other about the Library?

Robert Munn reported that academic administrators do not talk about libraries to each other. He wrote, "Libraries are almost never discussed at the national meetings of presidents, provosts, deans, and other academic luminaries" (1968, p. 52). We found many deans who agreed with Munn, particularly those deans from the more affluent colleges.

When we, deans from strong colleges, get together, we all tend to say we have good libraries. We have libraries that we do not have to worry about. It does not mean that we are not concerned. We have managed to hire good people and to have good people. It is a general consensus of the faculty and so forth that we need to support them.

Most of the deans at other schools, like [name of institution], that I know, are pretty happy with their librarians. They are pretty happy with their library services, and its role in the institution. So if it is not a problem, it does not get a lot of discussion. It is not because it is not important to each of us. It is just it is not giving us any trouble.

Some deans, however, reported discussion about the library problems. In general, libraries become topics only when they become problems.

It is probably true, in a general sense, the library is not a source of great anxiety among academic deans and provosts. So when we get together, our time is usually consumed by things which are more pressing.

Maybe the best answer is that libraries are so well run, so professional, there is never any problem. Most things come to the attention of deans when they become problems.

They do not. I think the reason why is because academic dean culture is always predisposed towards the discussion of personnel problems in faculty, the curriculum, relationships with your president, ... a whole series of things that are most difficult and intractable.

The library would not be in the top ten or twelve [topics]. The top things deal with the policies on learning disabilities, the difficulty of finding faculty in certain areas now as opposed to other areas, study abroad, legal questions dealing with confidentiality.

Several deans responded that discussion of the library "is more common than it used to be."

A few deans, especially in the midwest, reported talking with their peers about the difficulty of finding good library directors. They reported a "conservatism of head librarians" and expressed "the hope that a new generation will arrive that will at least convert people." These deans referred to the slowness of some library directors to adopt new technologies and formats and to assume new responsibilities.

[Deans talk about] the difficulty in having a reasonable pool of people in jobs like yours. There is a great shortage of people qualified to be head librarians. I am thinking of an aggressive and flexible spirit coupled with enough administrative experience so they are ready to move into head librarianship.

Occasionally there is a discussion of librarians and some of my colleagues have definite problems with their library personnel. I think simply because they do not pay them enough.

It is difficult, by the way, to find good people in library science at the present time. That is because this profession is not sufficiently valued in the salaries, the beginning salaries, for people in this area. [The salaries] simply do not attract the caliber of people who should be going into library science and so it gets very difficult to find the kind of people you want to find to staff a library.

Even discussions among deans of library personnel often focused on budgetary matters, as did most of the deans' library-related concerns.

Deans most frequently mentioned computer costs and periodical costs as the major budgetary items discussed.

One is how frightened they are of the level of investment in computerization over the past ten years.

The computerization of the library is one of those questions that deans talk about to each other.

In recent years there has been a rising level of concern among academic deans and provosts about the library. It has to do with two things. One is the enormous rise in the cost of periodicals.... The other has to do with ... the advance in technology and what should happen about the library there.

One dean lamented the emphasis on budgetary concerns:

> Unfortunately, deans tend to focus far too much attention on libraries as
> budgetary items. So the main thing one hears when talking with other deans about
> libraries is how much it costs to fund the development of the collection.

Finally, we found a few deans who talked with their colleagues a lot about
the library.

> I am in three relationships right now with deans who, as we confide in one
> another, find their libraries very exasperating. I would say, at the moment, when
> we get on the phone that is all these deans want to talk about.

Nevertheless, we agree with Munn in that most deans do not talk a lot about
the library with the fellow deans. Deans do not perceive the library as a major
source of problems.

> To put it bluntly, ... our jobs are not on the line because of the library. Things
> like tenure, affirmative action, fiscal survival, and integrity ... tend to get our
> major attention.

Because they consider it well-managed and reasonably stable, most deans
viewed the library as one element of the college about which they did not have
to worry.

CONCLUSIONS AND RECOMMENDATIONS

Perhaps because of this satisfaction, Munn found a strong element of "benign
neglect" in most deans' relationships with the library. Throughout our
interviews we also found evidence of this same "benign neglect." Only
infrequently did library directors meet regularly with deans. Any meetings
occurred typically only "when the need arises"—that is, when the dean and
the library director need to discuss problems.

Even the strongest relationships can deteriorate when individuals meet only
infrequently and then only to discuss problems. Most deans expressed strong
confidence in and respect for the library director and the library staff.
Nevertheless, we found they also seldom communicated these thoughts to the
director and the rest of the library staff. We found this benign neglect troubled
even the most competent library director. As one library director wrote us,
"Communicating only budgetary concerns is bound to make a library director
feel paranoid and isolated from the institution's missions and goals."

Despite the problems we found and contrary to many of Munn's and
Moffett's earlier observations, the 39 interviews left us very encouraged about
the relationships between deans and librarians. We found most deans at these

selective liberal arts colleges considered themselves part of the faculty. Many planned to return to the classroom after a temporary stint in administration. In fact, many continued to teach part-time. Most expressed genuine interest in undergraduate education.

The deans, themselves, expressed an awareness of the problems of benign neglect.

> The critical step is to make sure that the actors go on the stage and play the roles. And I think a lot of institutions don't do that. They set the stage and walk away from it and assume that people are going to use the library spontaneously. I know for a fact that they are not. They are going to come and badly use the library or use 1/100 of the material in there and be intimidated of it and be intimidated of the librarians.

In general, the deans recognized the important role the library plays in undergraduate education. The deans also provide support for both the library's utilitarian and symbolic roles in liberal arts education.

Perhaps part of some library directors skeptical view toward deans may be because they fail to understand deans. Library directors seldom serve in the inner administrative circles or work with boards of trustees. They seldom directly see the support deans claim to give the library in working with fellow administrators or trustees.

In addition, library directors operate in a more formal bureaucratic organization. They may not fully appreciate the limits of the dean's formal authority in the incomplete bureaucracy of academia. Most frequently deans must seek compliance from faculty members through persuasion and consensus-building. Seldom can they intercede directly with faculty members successfully to promote a particular teaching methodology, such as use of the library.

Despite some differences in our findings, we agree with Moffett and Munn in at least two areas. Munn found that the library director "does not often carry great weight in the academic power structure" (1968, p. 53). We found this situation continues at most colleges we visited. Moffett (1982a, 1982b) found that problems often occur when library directors do not educate their colleagues about the library. We also agree.

Deans and library directors miss an excellent opportunity to educate each other when they do not have frequent, regularly scheduled meetings and when library directors do not serve in the upper levels of the academic power structure. A dean at a prestigious eastern college aptly described the importance of regular and frequent meetings with the library director.

> If you don't meet with the librarian weekly you forget that you have a library. [If] you wait [to meet] until you have a humongous crisis come up, ... as soon as it goes away you go back to sleep and forget that you have a library.

Face-to-face discussions are particularly invaluable to the regular flow of information to and from the library.

Library directors and deans should more assertively cultivate the natural affinities they have with each other. Both have campus-wide responsibilities and share many of the same constituencies. They struggle with the same problems, such as the need to establish priorities in the face of increasing costs and finite budgets, to placate sometimes intractable faculty members, and to motivate often indifferent students. Informed library directors and administrators can make better decisions affecting each other.

How far can we generalize from the experiences at these 36 selective liberal arts colleges? Since the Council on Library Resources announced the availability of the report of this study, we have responded to almost 150 requests from librarians, administrators, and faculty members. Replies by library directors from liberal arts and community colleges tend to support our conclusions. Typically, library directors from these institutions responded, "The conclusions conform well with my observations over the years"; "Your findings seem to reflect my personal experience"; and "I found myself nodding in agreement and repeatedly thinking, 'Yes, this is true.'"

The responses of library directors from research and comprehensive universities varied. Some agreed with the library director who wrote, "It [the report]... was much more in keeping with what I had personally discovered in my own career than Munn's or Moffett's writing would verify." Others shared the thoughts of the library director who wrote, "My own sense is that college administrators may be more knowledgeable and sympathetic to the library than is the case in research universities." A library director from a comprehensive university recommended replication of my study at comprehensive and research institutions. He wrote:

> I suspect that such studies would show that differences among types of school do affect how library directors work in with administrators. I'd also guess that chief academic officers in all kinds of schools are very much alike in their understanding of and commitment to libraries.

Partially explaining this situation, another well-respected academic librarian wrote:

> My suspicion is that provosts in larger institutions start out thinking that they are only moments away from the classroom, but before they know it, demands of the job turn them into professional administrators. Serving as provost at a large institution is no piece of cake.

Without direct evidence from this study, we suspect that size and type of institution does make a difference about the relationships between library directors and administrators. At the smaller institutions, for example, administrators can rely more on informal information gathering and interpersonal relationships in decision making. This may be why many college deans resisted quantitative measures of the library and other elements of the academic enterprise.

We, of course, recommend further studies in this area. "At most institutions," commented one dean, "the library is not the center of the institution. It only gets in the center of the institution if somebody is trying aggressively to put it there." While many individuals share this responsibility, including the dean, library directors have most of the responsibility. Library directors must not only understand the library but also how to work aggressively to promote the library within the framework of academia and their particular institution. If academic administrators do not think very much about the library, the library director must rise to the challenge and educate them.

ACKNOWLEDGMENTS

The author gratefully acknowledges the support of the Council on Library Resources through Cooperative Research Grant 8018-A. He expresses his appreciation to Evan Farber, David Henderson, Dr. David Kaser, John Sheridan, and Dr. John Mark for editorial and other assistance. The assistance provided by numerous other librarians and chief academic officers in the completion of this research is very much appreciated. A copy of the full report is available from the author.

NOTES

1. Institutions included: Albright, Augustana (IL), Beloit, Capital, Colgate, Coe, Cornell (IA), Davidson, Denison, Earlham, Eckerd, Franklin and Marshall, Furman, Grinnell, Gustavus Adolphus, Kenyon, Lafayette, Lake Forest, Lawrence, Macalester, Mills, Mount Holyoke, Oberlin, Occidental, Presbyterian, Ripon, Rollins, St. Johns (MN), St. Olaf, Skidmore, Swarthmore, Union, Whittier, Wittenberg, Wofford, and Wooster.

2. Fall 1987 enrollments ranged from 872 to 3,696 students—with an average of 1,891 (*Voluntary Support of Education, 1987-1988,* 1989); library book volumes ranged from 100,141 to 961,194—with an average of 298,219; current periodical subscriptions ranged from 646 to 2,656—with an average of 1,375 (*American Library Directory, 1988-89,* 1990); endowments ranged from $7.4 million to $273.5 million—with an average of $71.3 million (*Voluntary Support of Education, 1987-1988,* 1989). The National Center for Education Statistics classified all except two of the institutions as general baccalaureate institutions (IIB). The center classified two institutions as comprehensive institutions ("Mastering the Academic Marketplace," 1988).

3. Arthur Monk, library director at Bowdoin College, for many years has compiled comparative library information among a select group of liberal arts colleges.

186   LARRY HARDESTY

REFERENCES

American Library Directory, 1988-89. 41st edition. New York: Bowker, 1990.
Dearing, G. Bruce. "The Relation of the Dean to the Faculty." In *The Academic Deanship in American Colleges and Universities,* ed. Arthur J. Dibden. Carbondale, IL: Southern Illinois University Press, 1968.
Hardesty, Larry. "Book Selection of Undergraduate Libraries: A Study of Faculty Attitudes." *The Journal of Academic Librarianship* 21 (March 1986): 19-25.
Katz, Daniel and Robert Kahn. *Social Psychology of Organizations.* New York: John Wiley, 1966.
"Mastering the Academic Marketplace: The Annual Report on the Economic Status of the Profession, 1987-88." *Academe* 74 (March-April 1988): 74.
Moffett, William A. "Don't Shelve Your College Librarian." *Educational Record* 62 (Summer 1982a): 46-50.
————. "What the Academic Librarian Wants from Administrators and Faculty." *New Directions for Higher Education: Priorities for Academic Libraries,* eds. Thomas Galvin and Beverly Lynch, San Francisco, CA: Jossey-Bass, 1982b.
Munn, Robert F. "The Bottomless Pit, or the Academic Library from the Administration Building." *College & Research Libraries* 29 (January 1968): 51-54.
————. "The Bottomless Pit, or the Academic Library from the Administration Building." *College & Research Libraries* 50 (November 1989): 635-637.
Stewart, Charles J. and William B. Cash. *Interviewing Principles and Practices.* Dubuque, IA: Wm. C. Brown, 1974.
Voluntary Support of Education, 1987-1988. 29th edition. New York: Council for Aid to Education, 1989.

GENERAL EDUCATION IN COLLEGES AND UNIVERSITIES:
AN ANNOTATED BIBLIOGRAPHY OF JOURNAL ARTICLES, 1985-MARCH 1990

Sandra Yaegle, Faith Jack, Polly Mumma, and Rashelle Karp

This bibliography was commissioned by William N. Ross, faculty member in the College of Business and Chair of the General Education Subcommittee of Clarion University of Pennsylvania. In preparation for the University's deliberations and revision of its general education curriculum, Ross, with funds from a grant through the university, hired Polly Mumma (a graduate student in the Department of Libriary Science) to develop a bibliography of journal articles which would serve as source readings for the university faculty. After the bibliography was compiled, Rashelle Karp (a faculty member in the library science department) took on the responsibility for abstracting each of the listed articles. With the help of two graduate assistants in the department of library science (Sandra Yaegle and Faith Jack), the abstracting project was completed.

Advances in Library Administration and Organization,
Volume 10, pages 187-249.
Copyright © 1992 by JAI Press Inc.
All rights of reproduction in any form reserved.
ISBN: 1-55938-460-3

Adams, K.H. & Cotton, W.T. (1989, March). Cultural literacy (symposium). *Clearing House,* 62, 285-287+.
   Disagreements with the views presented by E.D. Hirsch concerning the teaching of cultural literacy are voiced. It is felt that factual content material should be included in the teaching of cultural awareness skills.

Adeniyi, E.O. (1987, July). Curriculum development and the concept of "integration" in science—some implications for general education. *Science Education,* 71, 523-533.
   The integrated science curriculum in Nigerian secondary schools promotes the general education of individuals.

Akpe, C.S. (1989, No. 2). Using respondents' free comments to improve college curricula: A case study of Rivers State College of Education NCE Primary Programme. *Studies in Educational Evaluation,* 15, 183-191.
   Goal-free evaluation of curricula allows respondents to freely comment about a program rather than restricting responses to official questions. This type of questioning takes into account the actual effects as well as intended effects of curricula. A case study of a Nigerian college of education reinforces this concept.

Alexander, Francie & Crabtree, Charlotte. (1988, September). California's new history-social science curriculum promises richness and depth. *Educational Leadership,* 46, 10-13.
   California hopes to enrich students' understanding of the entire world by emphasizing history and geography in its school curricula.

Alexander, H.A. (1989, Spring). Criticism and curriculum: Between Phillips and Eisner. *Curriculum Inquiry,* 19, 67-70.
   The theory of relativism in education is explored. The author compares his viewpoints to those of Phillips and Eisner.

Alexander, H.A. (1989, Spring). Liberal education and open society: Absolutism and relativism in curriculum theory (with discussion). *Curriculum Inquiry,* 19, 1-9; 11-32; 51-70.
   Two traditional philosophical theories in education, relativism, and absolutism are described. A balanced view that incorporates both viewpoints is recommended.

Anrig, Gregory R. & Lapointe, A. (1989, November). What we know about what students don't know. *Educational Leadership,* 47, 4-9.
   The results of the NAEP (National Assessment of the Educational Progress) report are analyzed within subject areas. The article concludes by suggesting ways by which instructional practices can improve student performance.

Appleton, J.R. & Wong, F.T. (1989, Spring). Freshman ethics course influences students' basic beliefs. *Educational Record,* 70, 29-31.
   A mini ethics course taught by the University of Redland uses the themes of identity, good and evil, the search for success, and cultural diversity to encourage students to apply their academic education as they arrive at personal convictions.

Archer, J. & Freedman, S. (1989, November). Gender-stereotypic perceptions of academic disciplines. *British Journal of Educational Psychology,* 59, 306-313.

A study conducted to investigate gender stereotyping among academic disciplines concluded that engineering, the physical sciences, and mathematics were perceived as masculine, whereas English, biology, psychology, French, and sociology were perceived as feminine.

Arden, E. (1988, July 13). There's no reason why our core curriculum should make freshman year a purgatory. *Chronicle of Higher Education,* 34, B2.

The distribution of required courses over a four-year college career, rather than in the first year, is advocated.

Arens, K. (1985, No. 4). Between disciplines and methods: A proposal for the curriculum. *Journal of General Education,* 36, 280-292.

Advocated is an approach to interdisciplinary education which focuses on examples of research model in disciplines (rather than traditional coverage of a discipline); active student participation and monitoring (as opposed to an authority role for the instructor); the validity (rather than the result) of research; the significance of a research model (rather than its master); and the use of competency criteria rather than "background required" criteria in the selection of faculty. A course which embodies this philosophy (at the University of Texas/ Austin) is described.

Ariss, Sonny S. & Timmins, Sherman A. (1989, Spring). Employee education and job performance: Does education matter? *Public Personnel Management,* 18, 1-9.

A study of 66 city government managers in positions that did not exclusively require a business degree indicates that the level of a college degree has no impact on a person's managerial performance at work. It is suggested that the values and attitudes of an individual toward life have more to do with job performance.

Armistead, L. Pendleton & others. (1989, No. 2). The amount and importance of general education in the two-year occupational curriculum according to corporate employers. *Community/Junior College Quarterly of Research and Practice,* 13, 91-99.

A survey of corporate employers indicates that they value communication competency, critical thinking skills, and vocational adjustment capability most highly in new employees. Five general education courses were also ranked as important: English, mathematics, computer literacy, career management, and economics.

Armour, R.A. & Fuhrmann, B.S. (1984, Winter). Integrating liberal learning and professional education (symposium). *New Directions in Teaching and Learning,* 40, 1-99.

The question of whether liberal arts and professional faculty can work together to devise coherent curricula is dealt with. Various educators write about aspects of the issue. Their articles are annotated under the appropriate authors' names.

190   SANDRA YAEGLE, FAITH JACK, POLLY MUMMA, and RASHELLE KARP

Arons, A.B. (1985, Summer). "Critical thinking" and the baccalaureate curriculum. *Liberal Education,* 71, 141-157.

"Critical thought" is operationalized as the process of (1) asking what, how, and why; (2) becoming aware of information gaps; (3) discriminating between observation and inference; (4) recognizing the difference between words and the ideas they express; (5) probing for the assumptions behind a line of reasoning; (6) drawing firm inferences; (7) applying relevant knowledge to abstractions; (8) discriminating between inductive and deductive reasoning; (9) developing intellectual self-reliance; and (10) developing an awareness of one's own thinking and reasoning processes.

Astin, Alexander W. (1987, September/October). Competition or cooperation? Teaching teamwork as a basic skill. *Change,* 19, 12-19.

Institutions of higher education should emphasize a cooperative world view which stresses the importance of working together in society, as opposed to promoting a competitive world view which fosters passivity.

Astin, Alexander W. (1988, January/February). The implicit curriculum: What are we really teaching our undergraduates? *Liberal Education,* 74, 6-10. [Also printed in (1989, July/August). *AGP Reports,* 34, 6-10.]

Undergraduate values are shaped by implicit curricula of colleges and universities which foster competition (i.e., through testing and grading) over cooperation. It is stressed that the formal liberal arts curriculum should be overhauled to encourage trust, empathy, cooperation, and teamwork.

Ayers, W. & Schubert, W.H. (1989, Summer). The normative and the possible: Values in the curriculum. *Educational Forum,* 53, 355-364.

The values promoted in curriculum innovations can be interpreted in the light of three theories: intellectual traditionalism, social behaviorism, and experimentalism.

Bailey, A.L. (1988, September 21). More scholars, colleges taking an interest in the study of philanthropy and non-profit organizations. *Chronicle of Higher Education,* 35, A34+.

Various centers, projects, and grants focusing on "the study of philanthropy and non-profit organizations" are discussed as is opposition to the study of philanthropy.

Balch, P.M. (1989, Spring). Matching school curricula to future employment trends: Just whose responsibility is it? *Education,* 109, 340-342.

Thirteen suggestions are given to adjust the school curriculum to better prepare students for the future job market.

Baldwin, Roger C. (1987). Professors and professional programs: Fostering mutually beneficial development. *New Directions for Higher Education,* 57, 83-90.

The implications for faculty members as they add career programs should be evaluated before committing to the new programs. Suggestions are made which may assist the institutions in answering questions regarding professional development and staffing needs.

Balentine, M.B. & Henson, K.T. (1985, Summer). Back to basics: Skills needed for the information age. *Contemporary Education,* 56, 213-216.
> The return to the teaching of basic skills should also include teaching students to be computer and technology literate, to think critically, to generalize information, and to properly express emotions.

Banner, J.M. Jr., Ed. (1985/1986, Winter). Is a liberal arts education passe? *College Board Review,* 138, 2-3.
> A European observer of American education indicates that American educators focus too much on whether liberal arts education is passe, and not enough on how the liberal arts, humanities, mathematics, and sciences help students understand and prepare for life. Instead of pandering to a market-driven society by promoting the liberal arts as a possible means to a practical end, educators should emphasize the innate value of such an education and promote it accordingly.

Banner, J.M. Jr., Ed. (1988, January/February). Mutual responsibilities: Society and the arts and sciences. *Liberal Education,* 74, 1-5.
> Banner states that rather than liberal education bearing a responsibility to society, society bears a responsibility to liberal education. Both educational institutions and society must commit to liberal education.

Barham, I. (1985, June). Review and redesign: Beyond course evaluation. *Higher Education,* 14, 297-306.
> In this teaching model, small-scale course evaluation is carried out by a team that analyzes the aim of the evaluation process, the characteristics of the review process, the methodology, and the process of reflection.

Bauman, M. Barrett. (1989, Spring). Interdisciplinary studies for the twenty-first century. *National Forum: Phi Kappa Phi Journal,* 69, 38-41.
> Bauman discusses some shortcomings of liberal arts education and suggests curricular changes designed to meet social needs.

Beauchamp, B. & Wheeler, B. (1988, Fall/Winter). From Achilles to the heel: Teaching masculinity. *Women's Studies Quarterly,* 16, 100-111.
> The goal of a course taught by a male/female team at Southern Methodist University was to inquire into male gender roles in Western culture by examining their representations in literary "masterpieces." The course content, as well as the issues surrounding its unique nature are detailed.

Beck, P. (1987, June 5). Signals failure on jobs. *Times Higher Education,* 761, 17.
> Despite the British government's emphasis on science and engineering degrees over humanities and social science degrees because such degrees are more

employable, the author claims that personal qualities are more important in a job search than expertise.

Bedient, D. & others. (1987, No. 2). An evaluation of student attitudes toward self-instruction materials presented in two different formats. *International Journal of Instructional Media,* 14, 117-124.

A study comparing computer-assisted instruction to a format using slides and audio tapes concludes there was positive student acceptance of self-instruction materials, but there was not a strong preference for the computerized format.

Belford, F.M. (1987, March/April). Liberal arts and leadership. *Liberal Education,* 73, 16-19.

Liberal arts education must be based on values including respect for diversity, conviction and commitment, and character.

Benjamin, Ernst. (1985, September/October). Expanding the content of curriculum reform. *Academe,* 71, 28-31.

Recent reports have laid the blame for the inadequacies in American undergraduate education on undergraduate curricula and instruction. The author contends that the real issues arse funding, teaching conditions, and bureaucracy. Reform should evolve from the ranks of the faculty and faculty should protect their instructional and curricular authority.

Bennet, William J. (1989, Summer). Why western civilization? *National Forum: Phi Kappa Phi Journal,* 69, 3-6.

Bennet expounds on his belief that colleges and universities must educate today's youth in the background of our culture.

Benoist, H. (1985/1986, No. 2). Planning and academic program review. *Planning for Higher Education,* 14, 22-25.

The academic program review, a process used to evaluate programs completed in the past, can be linked with formal planning processes to produce more effective future academic programs.

Bergenhenegouwen, G. (1987, No. 5). Hidden curriculum in the university. *Higher Education,* 16, 535-543.

A University of Amsterdam study explores the effects of the "hidden curriculum" phenomenon which comprises underlying attitudes and expectations of the students.

Berlin, Barney M. & Jensen, Kathleen. (1989, November). Changing teachers. *Education and Urban Society,* 22, 115-120.

The Concerns-Based Adoption Model (CBAM) and Michael Fullan's Model of the School Improvement Process state that teachers need support as they experience the changes that occur during the implementation of a new program or curriculum.

Besvinick, Sidney L. (1988, September). Twenty years later: Reviving the form of the '60s. *Educational Leadership*, 46, 52.
  Current methods of teaching science have not retained the emphasis on problem solving that was developed in the 1960s.

Beyers, C. (1988, April 15). Stanford eurocentrists focus on third world. *Times Higher Education Supplement*, 806, 10.
  Stanford University's decision to alter its Western Civilization class to include more women's and minority issues, as well as works from non-European cultures is reviewed.

Bigelow, B. (1989, November/December). A geographical perspective of world history: Contribution to an interdisciplinary course. *Journal of Geography*, 88, 221-224.
  "Change and Tradition: Historical and cultural Perspectives," a course developed at Butler University (Indiana) to cultivate understanding of the tradition of Western civilization and how it has changed, integrates non-Western cultures into its overall perspective by stressing geographical themes.

Blanchard, R.O. & Christ, W.G. (1985, Autumn). In search of the unit core: Commonalities in curricula. *Journalism Education*, 40, 28-33.
  The fields of journalism and mass communication are affected by changing technology and by reforms calling for higher education to focus on the "basics." In response to this, a core curriculum should be offered that emphasizes similarities within communication fields. A core model is presented.

Blatz, Charles V. (1989, Spring). Contextualization and critical thinking: Programmatic investigations. *Educational Theory*, 39, 107-119.
  Debate about the benefits of teaching critical thinking in the curriculum may be resolved through a more complete understanding of the elements involved in critical thinking.

Blood, D. & Zalewski, L.J. (1989, November). Developing science curricula. *School Science & Mathematics*, 89, 590-597.
  Broad goals of science curricula (meeting personal and social needs, providing career education and awareness, and facilitating academic preparation) are operationalized in the Illinois State Board of Education "Sample Learning Objectives."

Boehnert, J.B. & Moore, G.A. (1985). From research to practice: Tying it all together. *New Directions in Teaching and Learning*, 23, 85-93.
  The experiences of the University of Guelph with the initiation of formal procedures for improving teaching and learning are described.

Boles, M. & others. (1984, Winter). Lessons learned the hard way: The making of a new general education program at Bradford College. *Liberal Education*, 70, 375-381.
  Bradford College's general education curriculum, which is based on a core curriculum rather than a distribution requirement, is described.

194   SANDRA YAEGLE, FAITH JACK, POLLY MUMMA, and RASHELLE KARP

Boli, J. & others. (1988, January/February). Analyzing academic research records for informed administration: The Stanford curriculum study. *Journal of Higher Education,* 59, 54-68.

Analysis of the academic records of graduating seniors at Stanford University has yielded a great deal of useful information, including information about (1) trends in student choices of majors set in the context of national trends regarding major choices, (2) relationships between major choices and trends in course choices, (3) sex differences in classroom performance, and (4) differences in grading standards and the effect of class sizes on grading standards. It is recommended that more colleges engage in such institutional self-study.

Bonnstetter, Ronald J. (1989, November). Teacher behaviors that facilitate new goals. *Education and Urban Society,* 22, 30-39.

Teaching traits that maximize the learning process are based on (1) understanding the students; (2) knowing the subject; and (3) appreciating which teaching behaviors best tie together the curriculum and the students.

Botstein, Leon. (1989, March/April). Learning and doing: The arts in liberal learning. *Liberal Education,* 75, 29-34.

It is not enough to cultivate future consumers of art through passive instruction; the real value of the arts can only be learned if the teaching of the arts is integrated into the active "making of art and music." Aesthetic literacy must be a goal of general education.

Bowen, Howard K. & Schuster, Jack H. (1985, September/October). Outlook for the academic profession. *Academe,* 71, 9-17.

Colleges and universities will lose the brightest and best faculty members and students if the present deterioration in working conditions for faculty continues.

Bowker, L.H. & others. (1987, No. 4). Support for teaching the liberal arts: An institutional dilemma. *Higher Education,* 16, 379-392.

A survey of support for liberal arts teaching in American colleges and universities indicates categories of support having good or excellent funding include library books, graduate courses, library journals, computer purchases, and sabbaticals for the purpose of knowledge acquisition or research. Categories least likely to receive good or excellent funding include research graduate assistants, travel to develop grants, full professors' salaries, grant development personnel, research by senior professors, research by untenured professors, and the purchase of research equipment. The size, location, sponsorship and degree level of the institution are associated with pronounced variations in funding support in the areas of research and grants. Concentration of discretionary support researches in a few large institutions, and the use of part-time faculty to teach one-quarter of liberal arts courses were noted as symptomatic of inadequate support for liberal arts teaching.

Boyer, C.M. & Ahlgren, A. (1987, July/August). Assessing undergraduates' patterns of credit distribution: Amount and specialization. *Journal of Higher Education,* 58, 430-442.

A study of the patterns of undergraduates' general education credit-distribution behavior in mathematics, political science, and English indicates that math students show very low credit distribution outside of the science and mathematics category; English majors show greater credit distribution outside of literary and artistic expression. It is felt that universities should carefully examine the ways in which undergraduates respond to general education distribution requirements.

Boyer, Ernest L. (1989, March/April). Connectedness through liberal education. *Journal of Professional Nursing,* 5, 102-107.

Five essentials of equality undergraduate education that relate to the profession of nursing are highlighted. The emphasis is on the importance of connectedness so that students can see the relationship between theory and its application.

Brady, Laurie. (1986, No. 1 & 2). Models for curriculum development: The theory and practice. *Curriculum & Teaching,* 1, 25-32.

The author created the Curriculum Model Questionnaire (CMQ), the first known tool to measure the process of curriculum development. She concludes that tools can be designed to study the curriculum development process and more should be developed in the future. Samples from the CMQ, a table of factor loadings, and twenty-five references complete the paper.

Brandt, Ron. (1988, April). New possibilities. *Educational Leadership,* 45, 3.

To teach critical thinking, instructors must teach *for* thinking, *about* thinking, and *of* thinking.

Brandt, Ron. (1989, November). On curriculum in California: A conversation with Bill Honig. *Educational Leadership,* 47, 10-13.

Bill Honig discusses changes in California curricula which have centered around preparing students for work, citizenship, and individual attainment.

Brandt, Ron. (1989, September). On liberal education for tomorrow's world: A conversation with Douglas Heath. *Educational Leadership,* 46, 37-40.

Douglas Heath discusses how schools can prepare students to be effective, adaptable adults by teaching character building as well as content, and by developing in their students self-awareness, self-confidence, other centeredness, interpersonal skills, and the ability to continue educating themselves.

Brandt, Ron. (1988, September). On philosophy in the curriculum: A conversation with Matthew Lipman. *Educational Leadership,* 46, 34-37.

Elementary and secondary school students should learn philosophy to increase their abilities to think critically.

Brandt, Ron. (1988, September). On the high school curriculum: A conversation with Ernest Boyer. *Educational Leadership, 46*, 4-9.
Ernest Boyer calls for curriculum reform that includes requiring students to perform community service activities in an effort to encourage students to become culturally literate.

Brandwein, Paul. (1989, November). Toward a permanent agenda for schooling. *Education and Urban Society, 22*, 83-94.
Crises in education have alternated back and forth between pushing basic skills for everyone and emphasizing academics. To minimize these crises in the future, the author proposes that schools develop a supportive network of relationships called SCHOOL (School, Community, Home, Organizations, Opportunities, Life and Living), in which the developmental tasks of youth, the implemental tasks of the society that supports youth, and the implemental tasks of a culture which fosters appreciation of other cultures are emphasized.

Breyer, R. & Moller, P. (1989, February 1). The liberal-arts curriculum should include a requirement to study television and its special language. *Chronicle of Higher Education, 35*, B2-3.
A "television-literate" society is discussed and the impact of television is compared to the impact of various literary genres.

Brint, Steven & Karable, Jerome. (1989, Fall). The community college and democratic ideals. *Community College Review, 17*, 9-19.
Two-year community colleges are facing a crucial question. Should the focus of their programs be to prepare students to transfer into four-year programs, or should the emphasis be on vocational-oriented programs?

Brubacher, J.S. (1986, Spring). Secular humanism and higher education. *Educational Forum, 50*, 291-293.
A democratic, pluralistic society such as ours calls for an educational system that is secular in philosophy.

Brubaker, D. (1989, September). A curriculum leader's search for meaning. *Journal of Instructional Psychology, 16*, 107-111.
The definition of curriculum as a planned course of study is expanded to also incorporate what each person experiences as a learning setting. Educators are urged to recognize the culture of curricula.

Bruder, Isabelle & Goodspeed, Jonathon. (1989, March). Personal computers for K-12: A guide to help you make the right choice. *Electronic Learning, 8*, 34-39.
This buyer's guide for computer hardware includes a list of 55 computers targeted to be sold to schools.

Burhans, C.S., Jr. (1984, No. 3). The demise of the cultural core: Whatever happened to general education. *Journal of General Education,* 36, 154-166.

Undergraduates' ignorance of their own culture and civilization (revealed in a survey by the author) reinforces the need for general education which combines traditional disciplines in a series of one-year courses, constituting a core program which all students must take each year throughout their undergraduate careers.

Burke, Paul E. (1989, November). A different interpretation of the data: Most students know a lot. *Educational Leadership,* 47, 6.

Analyzing how many students answer each question correctly (rather than grouping all questions into one scale), and excluding the questions at the end of the test not reached by 7-8 percent of the students shows that various analysis results of the Nation's Report Card are consistent whether success or failure is stressed. Eighth and ninth grade is a time for a numeracy course that includes using sample surveys, logic, basic computer commands, and percents.

Burke, T. (1986, Fall). Changing the curriculum: A contemporary approach. *College Student Journal,* 20, 312-314.

In an attempt to encourage new nontenured faculty, concrete strategies for implementing curricular change are provided.

Burns, D.E. & Olenchak, F.R. (1989, Summer). A buyer's guide to thinking skills programs. *Education,* 109, 445-454.

A study of 10,000 students who took the New Jersey Test of Critical Thinking showed only a 1 point difference between mean scores of 6th grade students and college freshmen. Students performed well on tasks that required paraphrasing and literal comprehension, but stumbled over test items that required inference, analysis, or evaluation. A buyer's checklist is presented to evaluate the purchases of first rate curricular materials which teach thinking skills.

Caissy, Gail A. (1989, Fall). Curriculum for the information age. *Educational Horizons,* 68, 42-45.

Microcomputer skills, including computer ethics and information processing skills must be integrated and learned at all levels of the curriculum in order for students to live, work, and adapt successfully in the information age. Teachers must give students opportunities to practice classifying, identifying alternatives, or collecting data dealing with a problem.

Campbell, D.F. & Wood, M.T. (1987). General education in the occupational curriculum: Why? To what extent? With what results? *New Directions for Community College,* 58, 65-75.

Community colleges are making progress in strengthening their general education programs and in integrating these programs with occupational education curriculum. More stringent national standards are needed.

Canon busting: The basic issues: An interview with Stanley Fish. (1989, Summer). *National Forum: Phi Kappa Phi Journal,* 69, 13-15.
The underlying question in the canon debate is the residence of values.

Canon busting and cultural literacy (symposium). (1989, Summer). *National Forum: Phi Kappa Phi Journal,* 69.
Various authors in this issue speak to the canon and cultural literacy debates. Their articles are annotated individually under the appropriate author's name.

Canon, cultural literacy, and the core curriculum: An interview with Lynne V. Cheney, Chairman. (1989, Summer). *National Forum: Phi Kappa Phi Journal,* 69, 10-12.
Cheney opines on the canon, cultural literacy, and core curriculum debates.

Carlock, Laneta L. (1989). Developing and coordinating the business education curriculum. *National Business Education Yearbook,* 50-56.
Business education needs a common curriculum that is coordinated to meet articulation needs at every educational level. The article suggests resources to help business educators implement effective programs.

Carroll, J.A. (1987, November/December). Censorship: Toward a rhinestone curriculum. *Curriculum Review,* 27, 28-30.
The analogy is made that the practice of censoring curriculum is like taking a diamond and replacing it with a rhinestone. A call is made for strong action to protect the curriculum from censorship.

Carson, Emmett. (1988, September/October). Black philanthropy. *Liberal Education,* 74, 8-10.
The study of philanthropy must include the study of other than monetary donations, especially the benefits derived from the nonmonetary philanthropy of black Americans.

Carter, Carol J. (1987). Strategies for recruiting and retaining minorities and women in nontraditional programs. *New Directions for Higher Education,* 57, 75-82.
Strategies are provided to assist planners in developing programs that will attract and retain minority women students in higher education. The roles of the administration, faculty, and student support services are outlined.

Carter, Jack. (1985, Summer). Internationalizing curriculum in the natural sciences. *Liberal Education,* 71, 121-126.
The teaching of science must include consideration of more than structure and function. It must also consider the human perspective and the global implications of science and technology. The author, a scientist, teaches (jointly with a philosophy professor) a course titled "Conflicts in the Modernization of India" which embodies this approach.

Carter, Lindy Keane. (1989, June). Charting a new course of study. *Currents,* 15, 26-47.

   Hamline University has implemented a curriculum revision plan that will broaden the liberal arts program to include work related experiences without resorting to vocationalism.

Cashion, S.V. (1989, March/April). Continuity and change: Dance in higher education. *Liberal Education,* 75, 18-22.

   Among other benefits, dance "reaches out to college students who are socialized to be competitive and fiercely independent and provides them with a structured context of interdependence and cooperative effort." This experience is essential for good general education.

Cere, R.C. (1988, January). A new dimension for international and professional studies: Foreign language intercultural courses (FLICS). *Canadian Modern Language Review,* 44, 316-333.

   For United States businesses to successfully compete in a foreign market, it is important that employees have a working knowledge of the language and culture surrounding different foreign markets. A model is provided for establishing foreign language intercultural courses.

Chambers, John H. (1988, April), Teaching thinking throughout the curriculum—where else? *Educational Leadership,* 45, 4-6.

   Thinking skills must be taught within the content of knowledge forms. Students must learn how to think within each discipline because the appropriate skills cannot always be transferred to other subject areas. Teachers must make students aware of the distinctions and similarities of the disciplines and how to think within them.

Christensen, Bryce J. (1987, No. 3). Oedipus and the sophomore. *Journal of General Education,* 39, 164-172.

   Undergraduates' disenchantment with tragic literature is linked with their inexperience and illusions of immortality, which are also reasons that they should study it.

Cianni, M. & Keiser, P. (1987, Spring). Career planning: A required course at Susquehanna. *Journal of Career Planning and Employment,* 47, 19-21.

   Susquehanna University has established a career planning course to assist freshmen and sophomores in reaching career goals and increasing career awareness.

Clabaugh, G.K. (1989, Fall). The pitfalls of sloganeering. *Educational Horizons,* 68, 5.

   The system of using slogans or statements with undefined key terms in educational mandates creates ambiguity and serves as a cover up for existing problems.

Clark, Mary E. (1988, May). What is science for? Re-introducing philosophy into the undergraduate classroom. *Journal of College Science Teaching,* 17, 452-457.
   A holistic interpretation of science is advocated as a way of combatting the view of science as value-free.

Coburn, T.B. (1985, Spring). Nattering nabobs, habits of mind, persons in relation: The future of liberal arts education in a specialized society. *Liberal Education,* 71, 1-11.
   The practicality of the American character tends to downplay the role of ideas and liberal education. However, liberal education may provide an antidote to much of what is wrong with contemporary life.

Coghlin, Ellen K. (1989, September 13). Scholars in the humanities are disheartened by the course of debate over their disciplines. *Chronicle of Higher Education,* 36, A1, 14-15.
   Scholars speak out on the debate, introduced by William J. Bennett (then chairman of the National Endowment for the Humanities) "that too much of their research and teaching is politicized, trivialized by a fascination with popular culture, and preoccupied with questions of race, gender, and class."

Coleman, Robert J. & Toenjes, Richard H. (1989, Fall). Integrating liberal learning into technical education. *Thought & Action,* 5, 49-54.
   Students enrolled in professional courses in technical fields (e.g., engineering) often negate the value of studying the humanities and the social sciences. A successful pilot program used documentation from real life situations to demonstrate to students that a liberal arts education is important.

Coles, Robert. (1988, September/October). Community service at work. *Liberal Education,* 74, 11-13.
   Study of philanthropy in the undergraduate curriculum should include field experiences as community volunteers.

Conrad, C.F. & Pratt, A.M. (1985, November/December). Designing for quality. *Journal of Higher Education,* 601-622.
   A five-part approach to improving the quality of American higher education is presented. Basic to the approach is the need to bring medium and message together. Equally important is the need to move away from reputational studies and toward direct self-evaluation which includes both quantitative and qualitative assessment.

Coon, A.C. & Birken, M. (1988, Spring/Summer). The common denominators: A collaborative approach to teaching reasoning skills through literature and mathematics. *Innovative Higher Education,* 16, 91-100.
   A creative problem-solving course is described in which academically at risk students studied the uses of analogy in education, politics, religion and advertising. The emphasis on cross-discipline collaboration helped students develop stronger reasoning skills.

Cooper, W.E. & Fobian, C.S. (1987, No. 1). Long-range course planning by college students. *Higher Education,* 16, 95-102.
    A study of 633 college students in a large midwestern university revealed that student planned courses of study are influenced by factors such as commitment to career choices and motivation.

"Core" in Texas. (1989, September). *Humanities,* 10, 12.
    In 1987, the state of Texas mandated the implementation (in 1989) of an undergraduate level core curriculum. Each college and university had the flexibility to develop a curriculum that best suited their needs and each had to evaluate its curriculum every five years.

Craige, Betty Jean. (1989, Summer). Curriculum battles and global politics: Conflict of paradigms. *National Forum: Phi Kappa Phi Journal,* 69, 30-31.
    The debate over curricular reform is "a predictable effect of the change in paradigm from dualism to holism."

Crabtree, Charlotte. (1989, November). Improving history in the schools. *Educational Leadership,* 47, 25-28.
    The effectiveness of the teaching of history will be enhanced with better textbooks, improved teacher training, and increased instructional time.

Cranton, P.A. & Smith, R.A. (1986, Spring). A new look at the effect of course characteristics on student ratings of instruction. *American Educational Research Journal,* 23, 117-128.
    A study of 55,000 student ratings over three years indicates that student ratings are influenced by class size and levels of instruction. The results imply that student ratings should not be used for faculty promotion or tenure.

Creamer, E.G. & Creamer, D.G. (1989, January). Testing a model of planned change across student-affairs and curriculum-reform projects. *Journal of College Student Development,* 30, 27-34.
    This preliminary study supported earlier studies that have concluded that the Probability of the Adoption of Change (PAC) model is an effective measure for predicting the likelihood of change occurring in student affairs. The study also found the PAC model to be weaker in predicting the likelihood of change occurring in the curriculum.

Cummings, Richard J. (1989, Spring). The interdisciplinary challenge: Connections and balance. *National Forum: Phi Kappa Phi Journal,* 69, 2-3.
    Cummings advocates interdisciplinary education, citing the Honors Program at the University of Utah.

Curriculum in the year 2000. (1989, January/February). *Liberal Education,* 75, 26-35.
    Various leaders in higher education look forward to the year 2000 with suggestions for curriculum including renewed emphasis on values, mastery of the

basics, respect for human diversity, continued liberal education, recruitment of a diverse student body, and in interdisciplinary approach.

Curry, W. & Hager, E. (1987). Assessing general education: Trenton State College. *New Directions in Higher Education,* 59, 56-65.
A survey of faculty at Trenton State College (NJ) concluded that the college's general education program emphasizes communication, research, and problem solving, but deemphasizes the arts and nonwestern civilization. The survey methodology is described.

Davis, Blaine E. (1989, May/June). International awareness in American management education. *Liberal Education,* 75, 28-31.
Higher education must overcome ethnocentricity by teaching all courses in a global context. Strategies for accomplishing this in a business school are outlined.

Deboer, George E. (1986, No. 4). Perceived science ability as a factor in the course selections of men and women in college. *Journal of Research in Science Teaching,* 23, 343-352.
Three hundred and two upper level undergraduates were surveyed regarding science and math courses that they took during their high school years. It was found that although women performed better than the men in biology and chemistry, women curtailed their study of science after completing these courses. It is suggested that women be encouraged to take more science courses in high school, as this type of participation results in more female science majors at the college level.

Deboer, G.E. (1987, September). Predicting continued participation in college chemistry for men and women. *Journal of Research in Science Teaching,* 24, 527-538.
A survey of 214 freshmen and sophomores indicates that participation in science by men and women is not just a function of their success in previous science courses, but is also dependent on their belief in their ability, belief in the effect of effort on performance, and expectations concerning future performance.

Dede, C. (1987, September). The evolution of information technology: Implications for curriculum. *Educational Leadership,* 47, 23-26.
Schools must shift their curriculum to meet the evolving transformation of work due to changing information technology. Two categories of cognition enhancers—empowering environment and hypermedia—will impact on the workplace.

DeLoughry, T.J. (1988, November 9). Professors try to assess the impact of computers on liberal education. *Chronicle of Higher Education,* 35, A15+.
The debates over computers' benefits and detriments to education are outlined.

DeLoughry, T.J. (1989, January 18). Study of transcripts finds little structure in the liberal arts. *Chronicle of Higher Education,* 35, A1+.
　　Robert M. Zemsky, professor at the University of Pennsylvania, in reviewing student transcripts from 28 higher education institutions, found that liberal arts curricula are weak in the areas of science and math.

DeNitto, J.F. & Strickland, J. (1987, Summer). Critical thinking: A skill for all seasons. *College of Student Journal,* 21, 201-204.
　　Critical thinking skills must be integrated into subject matter, not taught in special courses that may be artificial and inert. Using the Givens-Operations-Goals paradigm and the Scientific Method, students can be taught to apply the attitudes of critical thinking throughout their lives.

Desruisseaux, P. (1990, January 24). Undergraduate curriculum out of touch with academic knowledge, colleges told. *Chronicle of Higher Education,* 36, A13+.
　　Leon Botstein, president of Bard College, opines that colleges need to develop a curricular "balance between general education and the academic major." He calls for reforms in graduate programs and faculty hiring. William M. Chace, president of Wesleyan University, opposes Botstein's views.

Dick, B. Gale. (1989, Spring). Marrying science and the humanities: A new approach to teaching western civilization. *National Forum: Phi Kappa Phi Journal,* 69, 26-27.
　　Dick reports on interdisciplinary education in the Honors Program at the University of Utah.

Dickey, J.S., Jr. (1988/1989, Winter). A question of degrees: New possibilities for higher education. *College Board Review,* 150, 28-29+.
　　Enhancement of the liberal studies degree will better accommodate the diverse student body at colleges and universities.

Doeringer, Franklin M. (1985, Summer). International perspectives on campus. *Liberal Education,* 71, 127-134.
　　Adding an international perspective to liberal education should be accomplished through integration rather than through the addition of discreet courses.

Dohn, H. & Wagner, K.D. (1987, No. 2). Learning problems—when arts students encounter computer science. *Higher Education,* 16, 231-235.
　　A computer science and information technology course was introduced to arts students at the University of Copenhagen to increase their employability. Students in their final term were surveyed three times and interviewed once. The response to one question (Have you experienced special acquisition problems of computer science deviating substantially from those that you have met in your main study?) was analyzed; 80 percent of the students reported having special problems. The study indicates that different thinking skills are needed for learning arts and science information.

Donald, J.G. (1987, No. 2). Learning schemata: Methods of representing cognitive, content and curriculum structures in higher education. *Instructional Science,* 16, 187-211.
> Assessing the cognitive, content, and curriculum structures of a field of knowledge leads to a clarification of the learning tasks involved.

Dossey, John A. (1989, November). Transforming mathematics education. *Educational Leadership,* 47, 22-24.
> Changes recommended by the National Council of Teachers of Mathematics should be initiated by school personnel who must analyze the content of the curriculum, allow the use of calculators and computers, make curricular material relevant, participate in professional development programs, and include teachers, administrators, and parents in curriculum revision.

Douglas, Ronald G. (1986, February). The importance of calculus in core mathematics. *Journal of College Science Teaching,* 15, 250-251.
> Calculus should continue to be taught in the undergraduate mathematics program because it is a key to understanding many issues in science and technology.

Drabek, T.E. (1988, January). Teaching the sociology of complex organizations: Issues and strategies. *Teaching Sociology,* 16, 1-7.
> Critical issues of course design include student characteristics, the curricular environment, and methodological training. Strategies for dealing with these issues are presented, along with some questions that should be asked before curriculum design occurs.

Durham, Taylor R. (1984, Winter). Business and the liberal arts: Managing the constructive tensions. *New Directions in Teaching and Learning,* 40, 31-38.
> The study of management in historical and comparative perspective can help resolve tensions between business and the liberal arts in undergraduate education.

Edgeman, R.L. (1988, Fall/Winter). Quality, reliability, and productivity education: America's hope for enhanced competitive position. *Innovative Higher Education,* 13, 21-26.
> Academic programs stressing quality, reliability, and productivity are profiled. Similar programs have succeeded in Japan and could improve America's impact in foreign markets as well.

Edmisten, P.T. (1985/1986, Winter). Bringing global education to the university and community. *Journal of Environmental Education,* 17, 11-13.
> The existence of critical issues such as overpopulation, food shortages, and environmental concerns dictate the need for global awareness and understanding. The University of West Florida at Pensacola initiated a model program titled "Humanity and Global Resources: Education for Tomorrow," to increase international awareness among its students.

Eisner, E.W., ed. (1989, March/April). The arts in the context of the liberal arts curriculum (symposium). *Liberal Education, 75,* 2-34.
    Various educators discuss the issue of the arts in liberal education. Their articles are annotated separately under the appropriate authors' names.

Eisner, E.W. (1989, March/April). The polite place of the arts in American higher education. *Liberal Education, 75,* 2-7.
    Because many faculty consider the arts to be an arena for the "development or display of refined sensibility," the arts are not considered to be at the intellectual heart of universities, and so are not often included in the core of general education. The author contends that this does a great disservice to the world.

Eisner, Eilliot. (1989, Spring). Slippery moves and blind alleys: My travels with absolutism and relativism in curriculum theory. *Curriculum Inquiry, 19,* 59-65.
    The curricular theories of relativism and absolutism are compared and contrasted. A curriculum theory that is based on relativism is preferred.

Ellsworth, E. (1989, August). Why doesn't this feel empowering? Working through the repressive myths of critical pedagogy. *Harvard Educational Review, 59,* 297-324.
    The experiences of a class of students attempting to develop an antiracist course point to the need for social change and action in education as opposed to critical pedagogy that is based on assumptions that are biased.

Entrekin, D.N. & others. (1987, Spring). A model for evaluating a competency based curriculum of a professional school. *College Student Journal, 21,* 69-77.
    A survey instrument designed to assess graduating pharmacy students' perceptions of their own professional competency is reproduced, as are the results of its distribution to 96 students. Overall, it was found that the students perceived themselves as competent.

Estes, Thomas H., Gutman, Carol J., & Harrison, Elise K. (1988, September). Cultural literacy: What every educator needs to know. *Educational Leadership, 46,* 14-17.
    An analysis of Hirsch's *Cultural Literacy: What Every American Needs to Know* shows that Hirsch recognizes the problem that many of today's graduates are not literate; however, his solution of list learning aggravates the problem. Learners must participate actively in education by reading, listening, writing, and speaking in order to learn and contribute to culture.

Ettinger, B. (1989). Basic skills and core competencies. *National Business Education Yearbook,* 107-118.
    The current and future employment patterns in the workplace indicate that employers exhibit deficiencies in reading, writing, speaking, listening, computing, and personal development skills. Instructional strategies are suggested which would incorporate these basic skills into business education programs.

Evangelauf, J. (1986, March 12). Many colleges found heeding calls to reform undergraduate studies. *Chronicle of Higher Education, 32,* 1+.

   Survey results show that colleges and universities are adapting their curricula to meet the charge of the "national education-reform reports." This includes a back to basics approach as well as a concentration on the institutions' personal missions.

Feather, N.T. (1988, September). Values, valences, and course enrollment: Testing the role of personal values within an expectancy—valence framework. *Journal of Educational Psychology, 80,* 381-391.

   A survey of 444 Australian university students enrolled in humanities, social science, or science courses indicates that higher expectations of success in a course of study positively relate to students' enrollment in that course of study. Interventions that are directed toward increasing perceived ability, especially in mathematics, are recommended.

Felder, R.M. & Soloman, B.A. (1988, Spring/Summer). Systems thinking: An experimental course for college freshmen. *Innovative Higher Education, 12,* 57-68.

   An interdisciplinary experimental enrichment course called "The Systems Approach to the Universe" (taught at North Carolina State University), is described, as are its effects.

Feldman, Edmund B. (1989, March/April). Idealogical aesthetics. *Liberal Education, 75,* 8-14.

   Students must be exposed not only to "classic" art, but also to many forms of ideologically motivated art.

Feldman, Reynold. (1988, November/December). Reforming general education: Lessons from practice. *Liberal Education, 74,* 24-37.

   Educators discuss various issues of general education curricula including open curriculum, core curriculum, integrated core curriculum, interdisciplinary "cluster schools," and the motivation of faculty who teach general education courses.

Fichter, Lynn S. (1987, September/October). Teaching the deep structures of the natural sciences. *Journal of College Science Teaching, 17,* 11, 87-88.

   In liberal arts science courses, the deep structure of the various science disciplines should be taught through activities and questions that encourage critical thinking.

Figuli, David J. and others. (1987). Legal issues: Identification and management. *New Directions for Higher Education, 57,* 39-47.

   The increasing demand for accountability calls for institutions of higher education to be aware of the legal issues that may develop as faculty restructure or add career programs. Suggested policy guidelines are offered.

Fincher, C. (1988, No. 3). Provisional variation and selective retention in curricular change. *Research in Higher Education,* 28, 281-285.
    College curricula are typically reformed through the processes of provisional variation and selective retention. For curriculum reform to be effective it must be directed and supported from within.

Finn, Chester E., Jr. (1989, Summer). A truce in the curricular wars? *National Forum: Phi Kappa Phi Journal,* 69, 16-18.
    Finn lists "eight tenets" in a compromise between cultural literacy and canonist approaches.

Fleming, John P. & Hollman, Carolyn S. (1989, September). The self-study as catalyst: Evaluating a college business communication program. *Bulletin of the Association for Business Communication,* 52, 10-15.
    A business communication curriculum that emphasizes the development of oral and written communication skills is outlined.

Fong, Ho-Kheong. (1989, No. 2). Models for the integration of computing into mathematics curricula. *Computers and Education,* 13, 157-166.
    A teaching model for incorporating the use of computers into the mathematics program is presented.

Fortune, J.C. & McKeen, R.L. (1987, Fall). Curriculum building: Start to finish evaluation instrumentation and the management information system. *Education,* 108, 81-86.
    To successfully implement a Management Information System (MIS), educators should consider the community's values, the desirability of the curriculum's objectives, the teachers' attitudes and expectations, the materials necessary, and the teaching skills needed to present the material.

Fox-Genovese, Elizabeth. (1989, Summer). The feminist challenge to the canon. *National Forum: Phi Kappa Phi Journal,* 69, 32-34.
    The author discusses the feminist view of the literacy canon stating that "a collective culture" and "common ideals" are needed "to defend the claims of the individual against oppression."

Franklin, P. (1988, 87th part 2). The prospects for general education in American higher education. *Yearbook (National Society for the Study of Education),* 198-210.
    Methods that teach cultural literacy through facts, people, movements, and ideas ignore that cultural awareness develops gradually by assimilation.

Gabelnick, F. (1989). Curriculum design: The medium is the message (honors curriculum). *New Directions in Teaching and Learning,* 25, 75-86.
    The University of California/Los Angeles uses team teaching, interdisciplinary seminars, core courses organized around categories of knowledge, upper-level honors seminars, and honors versions of disciplinary courses to foster undergraduate intellectual development in its honors educational program.

Gaff, Jerry G. (1989, July/August). General education at decade's end: The need for a second wave of reform. *Change,* 21, 10-19.

A second wave of educational reform (which focuses on the entire college culture) is needed to broaden existing reforms, encourage more colleges to reform, raise new perspectives and strategies for improvement, and break down the barriers to implementation. Strategies for reform include determining what undergrads should know about the college culture, working to assure that all aspects of college life will further the values of the college, and staffing and funding the core curriculum so that it becomes the core of the institution. The result should be a blend where college catalogs, freshmen orientation, college life, and the core curriculum all lead to a well-rounded, generally-educated student who will be able to put her/his major in perspective.

Gaff, Jerry G. (1988, September/October). The Hamline plan (at Hamline, University in St. Paul, MN). *Change,* 20, 18.

The Hamline Plan is based on the premise that students need to receive practical experience in the workplace as part of an effective liberal arts education.

Gaff, Jerry G. (1989, October). Interdisciplinary studies in higher education. *Education Digest,* 55, 57-60.

There is renewed interest in designing college level curricula that are interdisciplinary in scope. This process may correct the problems that accompany programs that are organized around specific subject disciplines.

Gaff, Jerry. (1988, November/December). Reforming undergraduate general education. *Liberal Education,* 74, 4-10.

The primary emphasis of general education reform on content, coherence, and comprehensiveness has led to reforms in many areas, including (1) higher standards and requirements, (2) a move away from distribution requirements, (3) a move toward fundamental skills, (4) more integration of knowledge through interdisciplinary courses, (5) the fusion of values into curricula, (6) an extension of general education through all four years, and (7) the establishment of new administrative positions to coordinate general education.

Gaff, Jerry G. (1989, Spring). The resurgence of interdisciplinary studies. *National Forum: Phi Kappa Phi Journal,* 69, 4-5.

Gaff advocates curricular reforms that promote interdisciplinary education.

Garafalo, A.R. & others. (1988, October). Student evaluation of an integrated natural science curriculum. *Journal of Chemical Education,* 65, 890-891.

Student evaluations of a college freshman integrated natural science curriculum indicate that a cross-disciplinary presentation of various subjects increases their ability to make cross-disciplinary connections, decreases their fears of college level science courses, and results in more interest in the sciences.

Gardner, H. (1989, November 8). The academic community must not shun the debate over how to set national educational goals. *Chronicle of Higher Education,* 36, A52.
  Gardner encourages scholars to become active in solving the "nation's educational crisis" rather than leaving it to the politicians. He calls for an "intermediate path between 'uniformity' and 'pluralism,'" citing the Chinese educational system as a model. He states that teaching thinking skills is more important than teaching "national facts."

General education in postsecondary institutions (symposium). (1987, Spring). *North Central Association Quarterly,* 61, 454-480.
  Is liberal education essential, or is it a nuisance and a waste? In order for general education to be essential and valuable it must be coherent for each student, have commonality for a large number of students, represent a pervasive commitment from the institution, allow for choice on the part of students, constitute a major portion of the total undergraduate experience, and be politically responsive.

General education: New support growing on campuses. (1985, November/December). *Change,* 17, 27-30.
  A survey by the Carnegie Foundation of four-year colleges' and universities' academic officers reveals that 60 percent of institutions surveyed are reviewing their basic education requirements. Tables highlight requirements by institution; changes in requirements from 1970-1985; institutions' goals and students' achievement of those goals; and effectiveness of, obstacles to, and influential factors involved in general education programs. Although schools and their faculties are demonstrating a greater commitment to general education, students' own commitment has not increased proportionately.

Gigliotti, R.J. (1987, November 4). Expectations, observations, and violations: Comparing their effects on course ratings. *Research in Higher Education,* 26, 401-415.
  This study compares the effects of fulfilled expectations and violated expectations on the final evaluations given by students upon completing a course. It is concluded that student ratings are not affected by student expectations, nor are they affected by violations of student expectations. Classroom activity and the quality of the instruction account for variations in student ratings.

Girioux, H.A. & Kaye, H.J. (1989, March 2). The liberal arts must be reformed to serve democratic ends. *Chronicle of Higher Education,* 35, A44.
  The authors encourage a broader look at "the debate about the humanities curricula." The main question is, "What [does] it mean to educate students to be critical citizens[?]?"

Glatthorn, A.A. (1988, September). A curriculum for the twenty-first century. *Clearing House,* 62, 7-10.
  Plans for a two-year incremental educational reform of English, social studies, mathematics, and science curricula include achieving a balance between content and process. This is to be achieved in part through the use of the computer

instructional programs that emphasize critical-thinking skills, in part by demanding that students make choices involving ethics, and in part by stressing global education.

Glatthorn, Alan A. (1988, September). What schools should teach in the English language arts. *Educational Leadership, 46,* 44-50.
Grades 5-12 should employ a whole language approach to English. This will empower teachers to take small steps to make improvements as opposed to completing major overhauls. The English curriculum is divided into six strands that include literature, language, composition, speaking and listening, critical thinking, and vocabulary development. Basic concepts to be covered, recommended readings, and special units are indicated for each strand.

Goldberg, T. & Lamont, A.E. (1989, Spring/Summer). Curriculum change as viewed by students: A three year study. *Journal of Social Work Education, 25,* 150-159.
A three-year study of curriculum change contrasted Master of Social Work students enrolled in a new, integrated curriculum with students who had taken an earlier method sequence program. The authors found no major differences in the students' interest, knowledge, or their perceptions of faculty instructional competencies.

Goldenstein, Erwin, Ronning, Royce R., & Walter, L. James. (1988, September). Course selection across three decades as a measure of curriculum change. *Educational Leadership, 46,* 56-59.
School districts desiring to obtain more information for use in curricular decision making are provided with a readily adaptable model that was developed through a study that compared Nebraska high school curricula between 1953 and 1983.

Goodlad, J.I. (1987, May). A new look at core curriculum. *Education Digest, 52,* 6-9.
It is difficult to define and teach a core curriculum that is equitable in terms of content, time frame, presentation, and accessibility.

Goodlad, J.I. & Oakes, Jeannie. (1988, February). We must offer equal access to knowledge. *Educational Leadership, 45,* 16-22.
The educational needs of minorities and financially disadvantaged individuals must be met through curricula focus on centralized concepts grounded to reality. An experiment conducted by Deer Valley Unified School District in Phoenix indicates that a school district can rid itself of tracking and, with the assistance of a team learning process, discover that all students in mixed-ability classes are able to grow academically.

Gow, Haven Bradford. (1989, March). The true purpose of education. *Phi Delta Kappan, 70,* 545-546.
The qualities of virtue and wisdom should be cultivated by institutions of learning through the study of classical literature.

Graff, Gerald & Cain, William E. (1989, Summer). Peace plan for the canon wars. *National Forum: Phi Kappa Phi Journal,* 69, 7-9.
The authors discuss myths regarding curricular reform which must be dispelled before progress can be made.

Green, C.S., 3rd. & Salem, R.G. (1988). Assessing the prospects for liberal learning and careers. *New Directions in Teaching and Learning,* 35, 5-19.
Purely vocational training overlooks many intangible outcomes of liberal education in lieu of monetary, tangible outcomes. The two philosophies of education must be synthesized.

Green, K.C. (1989, Summer/Fall). Children of the upheaval. *Educational Research,* 70, 30-31.
College faculty must help students deal with today's economic upheaval by providing information, building their self-confidence, and encouraging flexibility.

Greenberg, N. (1986, Spring). Science and technology as human endeavors. *Liberal Education,* 72, 35-41.
Liberal education must include the study of science and technology.

Greene, E. (1987, November 11). Business is most popular major, but many recruiters stress liberal arts. *Chronicle of Higher Education,* 34, A38.
The popularity of business courses has caused colleges and universities to offer "business-related degree programs." Qualifications demanded by prospective employees in business often include a liberal arts background.

Greene, E. (1986, November 5). Shifts in students' attitudes seen as threat to liberal arts. *Chronicle of Higher Education,* 33, 32-35.
Findings of *The American Freshman: Twenty Year Trends, 1966-1985* include changes in focus among freshmen from service professions to those of corporate money makers. Statistics suggest a crisis for liberal arts.

Greene, E. (1988, September 28). Under siege, advocates of a more diverse curriculum prepare for continued struggle in the coming year. *Chronicle of Higher Education,* 35, A13+.
Conference attendees debate the call for curricular changes in liberal arts education. The majority favor a fusion of many schools of thought.

Gronbeck, Bruce E. (1989, July). Rhetorical criticism in the liberal arts curriculum. *Communication Education,* 38, 184-190.
Effective training in rhetorical criticism necessitates a two-tiered approach in which rhetorical criticism is taught both in foundational curricula as well as in upper division curricula. Such training should focus on the ability of students to critically describe, contextualize, and judge rhetoric.

Grosvenor, Gilbert M. (1989, November). The case for geography education. *Educational Leadership,* 47, 29-32.

The National Geographic Society's plan to increase geographical literacy involves teachers by providing them with funding, advocates, inservice training, lesson plans, and state-of-the-art educational technologies. The U.S. Department of Education's National Diffusion Network and the Society are joining forces to integrate geography education in all curriculum areas.

Gudgin, A.N. (1987, May). Computer-assisted learning of introductory economics. *British Journal of Educational Technology,* 18, 84-93.

Research indicates that students find computer-assisted learning activities helpful in the study of economics.

Haemmerlie, Frances M. & Matthews, Janet R. (1988, December). Preparing undergraduates for paraprofessional positions: What, where & how are ethical issues taught? *Teaching of Psychology,* 15, 192-194.

Ethics should be taught to undergraduate psychology students. A practicum format is one possible method of presentation.

Harris, John. (1987). Assessment: Providing quality assurance for students, programs, and career guidance. *New Directions for Higher Education,* 57, 65-73.

To assure the quality of graduates, colleges and universities must test students separately from the award of credit. Guidelines for this type of testing are presented.

Harrison, J.D. (1987, No. 4). Changing tides and liberal studies. *Journal of General Education,* 38, 262-271.

Courses in human ecology and energy conservation are being included in college curricula to revitalize the liberal arts program.

Hart, E.P. (1989, September). Toward renewal of science education: A case study of curriculum policy development. *Science Education,* 73, 607-634.

Science curriculum reform in Saskatchewan, Canada, is described in this essay which includes a great number of historical and state-of-the-art citations.

Harter, Paula & Gehrke, Nathalie J. (1989, Fall). Integrative curriculum: A kaleidoscope of alternatives. *Educational Horizons,* 68, 12-17.

Relying on the research of Paul Dressel and other proponents of integrated curriculum, the kaleidoscope is symbolically used to illustrate how alternative integrative curriculum structures can make sense of lessons that were previously taught as an unrelated jumble of facts. As the learner looks through the opening of the kaleidoscope, he can perceive knowledge as organized by topics, concepts, great ideas (generalizations of powerful concepts), life problems, mind constructs, and the disciplines.

Hay, Leroy E. & Roberts, Arthur. (1989, September). Curriculum for the new millenium. *Educational Leadership,* 7, 12.

>   The Connecticut Association for Supervision and Curriculum Development (ASCD) report, which identified ten trends that will affect the nation's schools in the next decade, is summarized.

Hayes, Floyd W., III. (1989, Summer). Politics and education in America's multicultural society: An African-American studies; Response to Allan Bloom. *Journal of Ethical Studies,* 17, 71-88.

>   Criticizing Alan Bloom's ideas because they place the blame for racial impasse on African-American students, Hayes examines and responds to these ideas from a historical perspective.

Hayford, Elizabeth R. (1985, Summer). Liberal arts in new international perspective (symposium). *Liberal Education,* 71, 93-140.

>   Various articles discuss this issue. They are annotated separately under the appropriate authors' names.

Healy, L.M. (1988, Fall). Curriculum building in international social work: Toward preparing professionals for the global age. *Journal of Social Work Education,* 24, 221-228.

>   Social work education in the United States needs to achieve an international perspective. The results of an expert study have produced suggestions for strengthening the content areas and learning objectives of graduate social work curriculum.

Hearn, J.C. (1985, No. 4). Determinants of college students' overall evaluations of their academic programs. *Research in Higher Education,* 23, 413-437.

>   A study of 775 university students indicates that the major determinants of college students' overall evaluations of their academic programs are stimulating coursework and good teaching. Significant gender and field differences were also found. These differences are identified as especially important avenues for further investigation.

Hearne, J. Dixon & Cowles, R. Vern. (1987, Fall). Curriculum development: A critique of philosophical differences. *Education,* 108, 53-56.

>   Changes within schools often result from outside political and social forces rather than from curriculum planning. These forces are reflected in three schools of thought regarding education: transmission, transformation, and individual development.

Heath, Phillip A. (1989, November). Societal issues as the missing link. *Education and Urban Society,* 22, 22-29.

>   The rationale for incorporating the study of social issues, referred to as S.T.S. (science/technology/society), throughout the entire school curriculum is presented.

Heller, Scott. (1989, October 4). Colleges told to stress tradition and shared views even as they bring more diversity into curricula. *Chronicle of Higher Education, 36,* 13.
> Leon Botstein (president of Bard College) urges conference participants to "stress what is common." Botstein believes students will be confused by the curricular reform which emphasizes diversity.

Heller, Scott. (1988, January 13). General-education reform should stress how students learn, report says. *Chronicle of Higher Education, 34,* A11+.
> An Association of American Colleges report, *A New Vitality in General Education,* urges educators to consider students' thought processes and to employ "active learning."

Heller, Scott. (1989, October 11). Model curriculum for colleges proposed by humanities chief. *Chronicle of Higher Education, 36,* A1+.
> Lynne V. Cheney (National Endowment for the Humanities) presents a "structured core" for undergraduate education in her report "50 Hours: A Core Curriculum for College Students."

Heller, Scott. (1987, September 2). A new wave of curricular reform: Connections between disciplines. *Chronicle of Higher Education, 34,* A28-30+
> Colleges are answering the call for curricular reform by placing emphasis across the curriculum on the basics.

Heller, Scott. (1988, June 8). Reform of undergraduate education requires integration of professional and liberal arts studies, report says. *Chronicle of Higher Education, 34,* A11+.
> The Professional Preparation Network's *Strengthening the Ties that Bind: Integrating Undergraduate Liberal and Professional Study* calls for a fusion of the two educational branches through a change of mindset from administrators to accrediting agencies.

Heller, Scott. (1988, September 7). Universities grapple with academic politics as they strive to change their curricula. *Chronicle of Higher Education, 35,* A12-13+.
> Problems of curricular reform in general education are discussed with the University of Washington serving as a model.

Henson, L. (1987, Winter). Preparing students to write in major-field courses: A faculty questionnaire for data-based instructional design. *Technical Writing Teacher, 14,* 108-110.
> A faculty survey designed to determine the writing skills which students need in science, engineering, and technology curricula is presented, along with suggestions for its effective use.

Herrold, William G. Jr. (1989, Fall). Brain research: Brain-compatible learning. *Educational Horizons, 68,* 37-41.
> Recent studies indicate that the brain functions holistically rather than through one hemisphere, therefore teachers must understand students' individual differences in cognitive learning.

Hertzberg, Lanny. (1989, March). Software to make life a little easier. *Electronic Learning,* 8, 47-49.

The software programs *Thoughtline* from Xpercom, *Grammatik II* from Reference Software, *Emul 3* by MAP Systems, and *Twist and Shout* by Software Toolworks are reviewed.

Hetherington, N. & others. (1989, November). Liberal education and the sciences. *Journal of College Science Teaching,* 19, 91-93, 124-127.

Curriculum reform is needed in the teaching of science and technology in the college liberal arts program to increase student aptitude and literacy in the sciences. One innovative program reform involves the integration of clumping (the process of incorporating clumps of information as a nonscientist solves problems) with climbing (the vertical integration of knowledge used by scientists) as a teaching technique for nonscientists.

Hill, A.D., ed. (1989, December). Rediscovering geography (symposium). *NASSP Bulletin,* 73, 1-7+.

Considerable progress is being made in the development and reform of educational programs in the field of geography. A major focus of these programs is to teach the five "fundamental themes" of location, place, relationships within places, movement, and regions.

Hill, John C. (1989, April). A matrix for curriculum evaluation: The author's approach. *NASSP Bulletin,* 73, 84.

Hill presents a matrix which can be used to redesign curricula.

Hilton, T.L. & Lee, V.E. (1988, September/October). Student interest and persistence in science: Changes in the educational pipeline in the last decade. *Journal of Higher Education,* 59, 510-526.

Based on census data and various studies over the past 10 years, the authors conclude that the numbers of graduates in the fields of math, science, and engineering will increase with a substantially higher representation of women and minorities.

Hirschorn, M.W. (1987, June 24). Working science into a liberal arts education: "Why, when we teach, do we make it so dull." *Chronicle of Higher Education,* 33, 29-30.

Conference participants debate "whether liberal-arts science education should teach students to 'do' science or teach them 'about' science."

Hlebowitsh, P.S. (1989, No. 4). The rise of the conservative agenda and the fall of the curriculum. *American Secondary Education,* 17, 21-25.

The reduction of high school curricula into a main or one track system is detrimental because the resulting curriculum is not broad enough or integrated enough to meet students' needs.

Holmes, M. (1988, 87th, part 2). The fortress monastery: The future of the common core. *Yearbook (National Society for the Study of Education)*, 231-258.

The common core of schooling comprises allocation (to jobs), basic skills (reading, writing, and the manipulation of numbers), and custody (the length of time required for mandatory school). Today's crisis in education is caused by the clash between the common core and the move toward differentiated schooling.

Holton, G. (1988, September/October). Raising awareness. *Liberal Education*, 74, 14-16.

The role of philanthropy must be made clear to college and university students while they are in school, not just after they graduate.

The hope of radical education: A conversation with Henry Giroux. (1988, No. 2). *Journal of Education*, 170, 91-101.

Radical education is interdisciplinary in nature, aims to make society more democratic, and questions the fundamentals of all disciplines.

Hope, Samuel & others. (1989, Summer). Civilization and arts education (symposium). *Journal of Aesthetic Education*, 23, 83-102.

The contents of the report titled *Toward civilization: A report on arts education* from the National Endowment for the Arts are discussed.

Hruby, Norbert J. (1985, September/October). MIA: The nontraditional student. *Academe*, 71, 26-27.

An attack on the Bennett, NIE, and ACC reports indicates that they are missing the mark by ignoring the older, nontraditional student, who is usually over 22 and often female.

Huber, Bettina J. & Laurence, David. (1989, Fall). Report on the 1984-1985 survey of the English sample: General education requirements in English and the English major. *ADE Bulletin*, 93, 30-43.

The statistical data are presented from a 1984-1985 survey conducted by the Modern Language Association which studied faculty salaries, institutional general education requirements in English, and the English major.

Hunkins, Francis P. & Ornstein, Allan C. (1989, November). Curriculum innovation and implementation. *Education and Urban Society*, 22, 105-114.

Curriculum implementation is a change process that depends on communication, incrementalism, cooperation and support.

Hutchings, P. & Wutzdorff, A., ed. (1988). Knowing and doing: Learning through experience (symposium). *New Directions for Teaching and Learning*, 35, 1-77.

This symposium has articles focusing on the task of involving students in their own learning, overcoming passivity in the classroom, making knowledge personal and important for students, and helping students to apply the knowledge gained in the classroom. Articles are written from the perspectives of a school of engineering, an urban university, a nontraditional university, and a liberal arts college for women.

Isakson, R.L. & others. (1987, Summer). Student development and the college curriculum: What is the connection? *NASPA Journal,* 25, 70-78.
Students can be promoted through skill development courses, career development courses, courses which apply human developmental theory within their content, and broad-based developmental programs which take into account the social environment of students.

Jacobson, R.L. (1986, January 22). Academic leaders showing new optimism about reform of undergraduate education. *Chronicle of Higher Education,* 31, 1+.
Scholars at a meeting of the Association of American Colleges believe that integrating general and professional education is a viable solution to the call for curricular reform.

Jacobson, R.L. (1986, September 10). Group of executives wants to make liberal arts part of the preparation for business careers. *Chronicle of Higher Education,* 33, 42.
Business leaders urge colleges and universities to integrate liberal arts education and career training. Communication and critical thinking skills are qualities sought in prospective employees.

Jacobson, R.L. (1985, October 9). Leading advocates of reform in undergraduate education find that it's not so easy to move from rhetoric to action. *Chronicle of Higher Education,* 31, 24.
Impediments to curricular reform include government mandates, financial concerns, and relegation of responsibility.

Janosik, S.M. & Sina, J.A. (1988, Winter). A comprehensive planning model and delivery system for leadership training programs. *NASPA Journal,* 25, 180-184.
The author's eight-step model for developing a campus-wide leadership training program includes assessing the environmental climate, identifying methods of training, targeting the population, developing leadership teams, developing the programs, implementing the programs, and evaluating the programs.

Jewett, Ann E. (1989, No. 1). Curriculum theory in physical education. *International Review of Education,* 35, 35-49.
To analyze the theory of physical education curricula, one must analyze the values which underlie curricular decision making; curriculum goals; program content; and the process of curricular change. Lifetime sports participation and lifetime wellness are two key goals.

Johnstone, Alex H. & Leton, Kirsty M. (1988/1989, December/January). Teaching the large course: Is practical work practiceable? *Journal of College Science Teaching,* 18, 190-192.
> Effective programs in laboratory chemistry should allow for the psychological capacities of students' short-term memories. Techniques such as organizing laboratory exercises according to skill levels can help reduce the psychological load on students.

Jurasek, R. (1988, Spring). Integrating foreign languages into the college curriculum. *Modern Language Journal,* 72, 52-58.
> Earlham College has developed a program in which foreign language studies are integrated into regular classes in the existing curriculum as well as being taught in separate classes. The program has demonstrated to students and faculty the meaningfulness of language study.

Kallendorf, Craig. (1987, No. 3). Ancient, renaissance, and modern: The human in the humanities. *Journal of General Education,* 39, 133-151.
> A comparison of ancient, renaissance, and modern thought in regard to the humanities is presented as the author addresses whether the humanities are linked to values, and if so, to which values are they linked.

Keohane, Nannerl O. (1988, January/February). Creativity, the classics, and the corporation. *Liberal Education,* 74, 31-35.
> Good liberal education is not a dress rehearsal for anything. It is an education that gives students the critical capacity for distancing, assessing, making judgments, and developing perspective. People who lack such liberal education will become obsolete "overnight."

Keohane, N.O. (1986, April 2). Our mission should not be merely to "reclaim" a legacy of scholarship—We must expand on it. *Chronicle of Higher Education,* 32, 88.
> Women's studies can add insight to the classics and stimulate student thinking.

Kemp, J.E. (1987, Fall). Providing for quality in teaching. *College Teaching,* 35, 152-155.
> Case studies illustrate that although an instructor has undoubted subject competence he/she may need some guidance to teach that subject. Instructors, working with experts in the areas of faculty development and instructional development, must learn how to motivate and encourage student participation and how to design and develop curriculum.

Kessler, G. (1988, February 18). Where is the liberation in liberal arts physics? *Journal of College Science Teaching,* 17, 271-273.
> This approach to liberal arts physics emphasizes balanced study which includes scientific premises as well as study of historical and philosophical issues to facilitate a global focus.

Kiely, Robert. (1988, No. 4). Should it be kept a secret that everyone (even in universities) isn't sure God is dead? *Journal of General Education,* 39, 222-226.
   Throughout history, religion has been both the victim and the cause of oppression. The study of religion is controversial and uncertain. However, important cultural phenomenon as well as scholarly need necessitate study of religion in an open, tolerant format.

Kimball, B.A. (1988, January/February). The ambiguity of logos and the history of liberal arts. *Liberal Education,* 74, 11-15.
   The debate over the importance of grammar and rhetoric versus the importance of mathematics and logic stems from the ambiguity of the Greek term, *logos.*

Kimball, B.A. (1986, No. 3). Legal education, liberal education, and the trivial *artes. Journal of General Education,* 38, 182-210.
   The author argues that the nature of liberal education influences the character of legal education, especially in terms of whether rhetoric or dialectic dominates.

Kindleberger, Charles P. (1989, May/June). Historical economics: Testing models for generality. *Liberal Education,* 75, 7-9.
   Historical economics (the process of using historical episodes to test economic models for their generality) can serve as a bridge between liberal arts studies (which may have too much ambiguity) and business studies (which may have too little ambiguity).

King, Maxwell C. & Fersh, Seymour H. (1988/1989, December/January). International education: Its future is now. *Community, Technical, & Junior College Journal,* 59, 28-29.
   The scope of the curriculum for community colleges should be expanded to incorporate issues that are international in dimension.

Klein, T. (1985, Winter). What one academic department in a university learned from general education. *Liberal Education,* 71, 327-334.
   The lessons learned from the experiences encountered in recent years by departments of English, as they have dealt with declining student enrollments, are applicable to reforms in general education.

Kliebard, H.M. (1988, 87th, part 2). The liberal arts curriculum and its enemies: The effort to redefine general education. *Yearbook (National Society for the Study of Education),* 29-51.
   The philosophy of liberal arts education has been impacted by the inclusion of science and has been influenced by reformers such as Herbert Spencer, Thomas Huxley, Matthew Arnold, and Charles Eliott.

Kliebard, H.M. (1989, Fall). Problems of definition in curriculum. *Journal of Curriculum and Supervision,* 5, 1-5.
   The definition of curriculum development centers around the main question of what should be taught. Curriculum development comprises four main

dimensions: the justification of what is studies; the consideration of who is taught; the methods used to transfer knowledge; and the interrelationships between the components of the curriculum.

Klinkenborg, Kay F. (1989, Spring). A selected bibliography for integrating women's studies into the college curriculum. *Feminist Teacher,* 4, 26-31.
This bibliography (1975-1988) on women's studies was produced by the Sangamon State University Women's Studies Sequence Incorporation Project for the university's liberal arts curriculum.

Knox, A.B. (1989, Winter). Designing comprehensive programs in adult and continuing education. *New Directions in Continuing Education,* 44, 47-54.
Compared are two approaches to adult education: the comprehensive approach (where emphasis is placed on activities at a community or organizational level) and the individual approach (where the learner is the main planner of the activities). The advantages of the comprehensive approach are described, as are some strategies for its implementation.

Komoski, P.K. (1989, No. 7/8). Curriculum alignment: The systematic solution? (Excerpts from educational technology: The closing-in of the opening-out of curriculum and instruction). EPIEgram, 16, 1-7.
Imbalances in curriculum are caused by the lack of a well developed curriculum statement, computer-based integrated systems that are compatible with other systems, and the lack of adequate information about teaching strategies.

Kridel, C. (1986, No. 2). General education as a component of teacher education. *Journal of General Education,* 38, 134-143.
Students enrolled in teacher education programs need general education as much as they need professional education.

Kuh, G.D. & others. (1987, May). Student affairs and liberal education: Unrecognized (and unappreciated) common law partners. *Journal of College Student Personnel,* 28, 252-260.
Student affairs work is not perceived to be central to the mission of higher education, even though student affairs workers and proponents of liberal education share similar goals in the development of the student's personal identity, esthetic sensibility, moral reasoning, social perspective, and intellectual and academic skills. This results from the widely shared view of faculty that the intellectual and affective are mutually exclusive domains, and the consequent development of a system of dualistic education which separates intellectual functioning and personal development. Student affairs workers are advised to evaluate the current strength of the dualistic structure, promote contributions made by student affairs to the quality of campus life, collaborate with faculty to develop creative learning environments inside and outside the classroom, and participate in review efforts to articulate curriculum revisions with student service efforts.

Labianca, D.A. & Reeves, W.J. (1985, May). Writing across the curriculum: The science segment: A heretical perspective. *Journal of Chemical Education, 62,* 400-402.
It is advised that writing across the curriculum, especially in the sciences, be resisted. Recommended is a series of required writing courses that culminate in an advanced, discipline-oriented course.

LaFeber, W. (1989, May 24). We need fresh scholarship to understand changed world realities. *Chronicle of Higher Education, 35,* A40.
Curricular reforms must consider the shift in political power of Russia, the United States, Japan, and the European nations. Background in Western civilization is required along with studies of other cultures.

Lambert, D.A. (1988, Winter). Students still fail important tests of general facts. *Journalism Educator, 42,* 21-23.
The question is asked, are teachers of journalism doing enough to impress upon their students the importance of a wide, general fund of knowledge? Journalism students in general appear to be the weakest in the area of knowledge that pertains to the arts.

Lasch, C. (1986, March). Education as a public ritual. *Education Digest, 51,* 2-5.
Reforms in general education are futile until the larger social questions of the depoliticalization of society and the deskilling of the workplace are addressed.

Lawson, H.A. (1988, April). Physical education and the reform of undergraduate education. *Quest, 40,* 12-32.
Reformers are calling for more precision in the study of the learning process. The discipline of physical education reflects the reforms that are occurring in the spheres of general, liberal, and professional education.

Lee, Barbara A. (1985, September/October). Faculty involvement in enhancing student learning. *Academe, 71,* 22-25.
This study prepared by the National Institute of Education study group points out that college faculty are primarily responsible for maintaining performance standards and implementing reforms in curriculum.

Leming, James S. (1989, October). The two cultures of social studies education. *Social Education, 53,* 404-408.
The social studies professor is endangered by the division that exists between the theorists and those who teach. Issues that need to be resolved concern perspectives on politics and economics, conceptions about citizenship, and the balance between commitment and critical thought.

Lenn, Marjorie Peace. (1987). Accreditation, certification, and licensure. *New Directions for Higher Education, 57,* 49-63.
The procedures for accreditation and the costs involved are outlined. A list of career programs and the corresponding recognized accrediting bodies is provided.

Levine, Arthur. (1985, November 6). Undergraduate reform: A time for readjustment. *Chronicle of Higher Education,* 31, 44.
    Comparison is made between educational reforms of 1827 and the present.

Levine, Arthur E. (1987). Career education: A prospective, a retrospective, and a few guesses. *New Directions for Higher Education,* 57, 13-20.
    Undergraduate education in America has historically had the goals of intellectual advancement and utility. Career education must be continually updated to meet the needs of society.

Liberman, M. (1985, November 13). Yes, Secretary Bennett, college professors feel the pull of academic tradition too. *Chronicle of Higher Education,* 31, 96.
    Liberman disagrees with William Bennett's assessment of higher education and his call to return to a quality traditional curriculum which demands conformity.

Lin, Eugene. (1989, Summer). Something deep . *National Forum: Phi Kappa Phi Journal,* 69, 42-43.
    The author believes that philosophy should be part of the core curricula.

Lincoln, James R. (1989, May/June). Stimulating cooperation between sociology and business. *Liberal Education,* 75, 13-17.
    The author urges sociology and business faculty to add international perspectives to their research and instruction as a way to foster interdivisional cooperation among the disciplines.

Lipman, Matthew. (1988, September). Critical thinking—What can it be? *Educational Leadership,* 46, 38-43.
    The integration of critical thinking into curricula involves an understanding of (1) the outcomes of critical thinking, or judgments, (2) the criteria used to form judgments, (3) the self-correcting nature of critical thinking, and (4) the context specific, or holistic nature of critical thinking.

Lochhead, Jack. (1988). From words to algebra: Mending misconceptions. *Yearbook (National Council of Teachers of Mathematics),* 127-135.
    The translation process in algebra word problems can be taught to students by the three-step method of qualitative understanding, quantitative understanding, and conceptual understanding.

Lochhead, Jack. (1981, October). Research synthesis on problem solving. *Educational Leadership,* 39, 68-70.
    Two steps in the process of teaching problem solving include actively involving students and teaching specific strategies.

Locke, Lawrence. (1989, July/August). General education: In search of facts. *Change,* 21, 20-23.

Data from six studies on the status of general education indicates that lost ground has been regained, and more fundamental skills are being required. Programs vary from school to school and are affected by environmental factors.

Logan, R.D. & Mannino, J.A. (1988, January/February). The two pillars of wisdom and the dummying-down of higher education. *Liberal Education,* 74, 36-40.

The trend toward a "social sciences" liberal education as a middle ground between the humanities and the sciences represents anti-intellectualism because it has a leveling effect on how we view knowledge and makes all domains of knowledge more similar than they are different.

Lohrmann, D.K. & DeJoy, D.M. (1987/1988, December/January). Utilizing the competency-based curriculum framework for curriculum revision: A case study. *Health Education,* 58-77.

A study of the graduate and undergraduate levels of the health and safety education program at the University of Georgia was conducted using a competency-based curriculum framework. The information gained was especially beneficial in restructuring the graduate program. Progress was attributed to strong faculty cooperation.

Loo, C.M. & Rolison, G. (1986, January/February). Alienation of ethnic minority students at a predominantly white university. *Journal of Higher Education,* 58-77.

A research study at a small university in California demonstrates that the sociocultural alienation of minority students in a predominantly white university is greater than that of white students. Reasons include the cultural dominance of white, middle-class values on campus and the ethnic isolation of minorities. Research also suggests that positive student-faculty relationships and quality of education might counterbalance alienation.

Lopez, A.M., Jr. (1988, July). Developing a low-cost expert system in a liberal arts environment. *Educational Technology,* 18, 33-36.

The use of computer-oriented expert systems in the liberal arts setting is best achieved by attempting to keep the system as simple as possible.

LoPresti, V.C. & Garafalo, A.R. (1987, September/October). A new interdisciplinary course in the natural sciences. *Journal of College Science Teaching,* 17, 36-39.

The Massachusetts College of Pharmacy and Allied Health Sciences offers a course called Perspectives in Natural Science. The course is an integrated study of natural science that incorporates physics, chemistry, and biology.

Lopushinsky, T., ed. (1988, May). General education science (symposium). *Journal of College Science Teaching,* 17, 429-457.

Various educators explore the issue of general education in science. Their articles are annotated under the appropriate authors' names.

Lopushinsky, Theodore. (1988, May). General education: An introduction. *Journal of College Science Teaching,* 17, 429-431.
    The author outlines the recommendations he received from experts on the subject of teaching general education science throughout the K-12 education system.

Louis, Karen Seashore. (1989, Summer). Surviving institutional change: Reflections on curricular reform in universities. *New Directions for Higher Education,* 17, 9-25.
    To survive undergraduate curriculum reform, colleges and universities must look beyond the technical aspects of organization. Political and cultural problems and solutions must also be examined, including our market-driven higher education system, its need to be consumer-flexible, the relative weakness of faculty bodies, the isolation of faculty, and the power of external funding agencies over curriculum. Focused models for change are outlined.

Lunneborg, P.W. (1986, Winter). A solution to the liberal arts employment dilemma. *Journal of Career Planning and Employment,* 46, 24-26.
    A booklet developed by the placement center of the University of Washington provides advice for liberal arts graduates on securing employment.

MacIsaac, Teresa. (1986, Nos. 1 & 2). The impact of politics on curriculum decision-making. *Curriculum Teaching,* 1, 43-54.
    The integrity of both the school system and the political system will remain intact if school authorities recognize the right of political authorities to make demands on school programs, and conversely, if political authorities respect the decision-making realm of the school system and the political system will remain intact if school authorities recognize the right of political authorities to make demands on school programs, and conversely, if political authorities respect the decision-making realm of the school authorities.

Magner, D.K. (1989, July 5). Specific disciplines are the new focus of movement to assess colleges' effectiveness. *Chronicle of Higher Education,* 35, A25-26.
    Curricular reform in general education has inspired colleges and universities to evaluate the quality of education in field majors.

Malaty, G. (1988, January/February). What is wrong with the "back-to-basics" movement, and what was wrong with the "new-math" movement. *International Journal of Mathematical Education in Science and Technology,* 19, 57-65.
    Lessons learned from the "back to basics" movement and the "new math" movement are used to formulate the direction that should be taken in mathematics education.

Malone, M.E. (1986, Summer). What could a philosopher teach? *Liberal Education,* 72, 125-1237.
    Education in philosophy should teach students to have respect for reason, respect for the classics, and respect for radical criticisms and perspectives. It should also enable students to gain a critical perspective on the subject matter presented to them in other courses.

Mangan, Katherine S. (1987, May 24). Colleges introduce undergraduates to research with eye to building future pool of professors. *Chronicle of Higher Education, 35,* A29-30.
> Undergraduate research is used as stimulus for enticing students on to graduate schools. College and university officials see this as a way to stop the steady decline of faculty members.

Manson, N. (1989, September/October). Philanthropy studies. *Liberal Education,* 32-39.
> The courses in philanthropy of six different schools are outlined. A common feature of these courses is that the students are required to become active volunteers in local nonprofit public service organizations.

Martin, E.S. (1989, January). The relationship among college student characteristics and their assigned importance to dimensions of course choice information. *Journal of College Student Development, 30,* 69-76.
> The relationship between psychological type, ego development, and educational aspiration for college freshmen and their preference for different kinds, sources, and delivery services of pre-registration course choice information was examined. Two trends revealed were that (1) students with no aspiration for advanced degrees but with Intuitive/Feeling preference combinations considered information about the professor important, while advanced-degree aspirants with Sensing/Thinking and Sensing/Feeling preference combinations valued information about career relatedness of courses; and (2) nongraduate degree aspirants with lower ego development and Intuitive/Feeling personality types placed greatest importance on information about course requirements and practical aspects delivered in a group format, and conversely, graduate school aspirants with higher ego development and Intuitive/Thinking personalities placed importance on administrative and printed sources delivered individually.

Marx, Leo. (1989, Spring). A case for interdisciplinary thinking. *National Forum: Phi Kappa Phi Journal, 69,* 8-11.
> Generalist and specialist education are contrasted. Marx compares specialist education to the development of artificial intelligence and calls for a fusion of "the two forms of knowledge throughout professional education, the liberal form serving as the framework within which expert knowledge is acquired."

Mathison, C.I. (1989, January). Checklist for content of introductory geology courses. *Journal of Geological Education, 37,* 18-19.
> This checklist, which incorporates the major themes of geology, has been developed to assist teachers, planners and students in planning the content of geography courses.

Mayhew, L. & others. (1984, Winter). Beyond breadth: General education in the research university. *Liberal Education, 70,* 383-400.
> The curriculum at the University of California (Davis) has been reformed to incorporate a campus-wide general education curriculum. The new model is presented.

Mazurek, Kas & Dawson, Don. (1989, No. 2). Leisure as a field of study in higher education. *Canadian Journal of Higher Education,* 19, 59-71.
> The emerging field of leisure studies is struggling to achieve credibility in the academic community. Further development of the basic principles and theories of the field is needed to establish a well-defined paradigm.

McCall, J.M. (1987, Summer). Liberal arts focus provides training for media careers. *Journalism Educator,* 42, 17-21.
> The focus of programs in journalism and mass communications is switching to an approach based on liberal arts philosophy. The DePauw plan is an example of such a change in focus.

McCarthy, Robert. (1989, March). A heated race that shows no sign of letting up. *Electronic Learning,* 8, 26-30.
> While computer manufacturers are fighting for control of the hardware and software markets, schools are searching for applications to integrate the numerous systems these companies have created.

McComas, William F. (1989, November). The issue of effective and valid student evaluation. *Education and Urban Society,* 22, 72-82.
> The most effective student assessment schemes assess cognitive knowledge (the cognitive domain), student attitudes (the affective domain), and manipulative or fine motor skill development (the psychomotor domain).

McDavid, Alex. (1988, Fall/Winter). Feminism for men: 101. Educating men in "women's studies." *Feminist Teacher,* 3, 25-33.
> A case is made for encouraging men to take courses in women's studies, and a sample course outline is presented.

McDonough, P. & McDonough, B. (1987, No. 4). A survey of American colleges and universities on the conducting of formal courses in creativity. *Journal of Creative Behavior,* 21, 271-282.
> A survey of four-year accredited colleges and universities indicates that only a small number of colleges and universities conduct formal courses in creativity. Reasons cited for not offering such a course focus on its nontraditional aspects.

McKeen, Ronald L. & Fortune, Jim L. (1987, Winter). Curriculum building: Start to finish knowledge, learning and the design of curriculum. *Education,* 108, 220-227.
> Designing a coherent rather than eclectic curriculum requires knowledge of student, teacher, and societal characteristics. A flowchart describing the steps involved in building a curriculum is presented.

McKernan, Jim. (1987, Winter). Action research and curriculum development. *Peabody Journal of Education,* 64, 6-19.
> The historical and philosophical development of critical action research as a problem-solving method is presented, as is its impact on curriculum development.

McLeod, S.H., ed. (1988, Winter). Strengthening programs for writing across the curriculum (symposium). *New Directions for Teaching and Learning,* 36, 5-130.

This symposium on the issues and problems of writing across the curriculum programs has articles on how to translate the enthusiasm generated by faculty development workshops on WAC into curricular change, WAC programs in community colleges and research universities, cooperation between academic institutions and public schools, funding for WAC programs, evaluation, collaborative research regarding WAC programs, and the future of WAC.

McLeod, Susan H. (1989, October). Writing across the curriculum: Second stage and beyond. *College Composition and Communication,* 40, 337-343.

As the "writing across the curriculum movement" enters the second phase, programs that have successfully survived and adapted are outlined. The third phase will see the movement being permanently established in higher education.

McMillen, L. (1989, April 26). Foundations are being drawn into colleges' debate over cultural diversity in the curriculum. *Chronicle of Higher Education,* 35, A25-26.

Foundations are asked to evaluate endowments on the basis of "conflicting perspectives on the movement for cultural diversity."

McMillen, L. (1987, September 9). More colleges and more disciplines incorporating scholarship on women into the classroom. *Chronicle of Higher Education,* 34, A15-17.

Colleges and universities integrate women's studies across the curricu'um.

McPherson, M.S. (1986, Winter). Who needs liberal education? *Liberal Education,* 72, 331-333.

Liberal education should be widely available at the college level, but it should not necessarily be required, nor does it have to be made available to everyone.

McRae, L.S. & Young, J.D. (1988, March). Student satisfaction in introductory business courses taught by lecture and discussion methods. *Journal of Education for Business,* 64, 252-255.

Research was conducted to determine the effectiveness of discussion and the lecture methods of teaching introductory business courses. The results indicate no difference between the two methods when measuring student performance on tests.

Mears, J.A. (1986, No. 4). Evolutionary process: An organizing principle for general education. *Journal of General Education,* 37, 313-325.

The importance of a core curriculum is discussed, and a twelve-credit curriculum model is presented to show how a core curriculum might be developed.

Medve, R.J. & Pugliese, F.A. (1987, May). Science as a process. *American Biology Teacher,* 49, 277-281.

The process oriented biology course developed at Slippery Rock University is designed to help nonscience majors develop problem-solving skills.

Meller, M.L. (1988, November). Incorporate values education across the curriculum. *NASSP Bulletin*, 72, 110-11.
Values education contributes to the general good and the furtherance of democracy. Practical teaching ideas are listed to show how values can be taught through example.

Merriam, R.W. (1986, November). Academic research vs. the liberal arts. *Journal of College Science Teaching*, 16, 105-109.
The author questions whether research functions, especially in the scientific and technical disciplines, can be balanced with a liberal arts education. It is proposed that university faculty be divided into research and teaching faculty to allow for both the specialization necessary for effective research as well as for the interaction between teachers and students necessary for effective learning.

Met, M. (1987, September). Which foreign languages should students learn? *Educational Leadership*, 47, 54-58.
Valid reasons for language study include developing a better ability to communicate in the global marketplace, better cultural understanding and communication with international neighbors, an improved capacity to function in a multiethnic/multilingual society, or simply to achieve personal and intellectual benefits. Since one to two years of study do not lead to fluency in a language, careful level-to-level coordination from elementary school through college is necessary. While students should think carefully about which language to study, any language study is beneficial and crucial because through it students learn the fundamental process of all language study.

Meyer, Marshall. (1989, May/June). Finding the impetus. *Liberal Education*, 75, 18-20.
The author indicates that business schools should not have all the responsibility for internationalizing curricula. Other disciplines should also take initiative, especially sociology.

Miller, L.F. (1986, No. 4). Creativity's contribution to a liberal education. *Journal of Creative Behavior*, 20, 248-257.
Classes designed to teach the creative process, as demonstrated in models by Wallace and Motamedi, provide a foundation that allows students to develop into creative thinkings.

Miller, Robert J. (1989, No. 2). A systems model for curriculum decision-making. *Community/Junior College Quarterly of Research and Practice*, 13, 109-117.
A systems model is presented that incorporates environmental factors into the development of college level curricula.

Milner, J.O. (1987, September). The peripheral curriculum. *Clearing House*, 61, 4.
The wisdom of adding peripheral studies such as value clarification, thinking skills, visual literacy, and computer literacy to the English curriculum is question.

Minor, Robert O. (1989, December). Computer technology can manage curriculum, link learning to instruction. *NASSP Bulletin,* 73, 75-80.
> A computer program that facilitates faculty access to curricula, management of curricula, and linkage of curricula to instruction is described.

Mociun, Tony. (1989, November). Geography by cargo ship. *Educational Leadership,* 47, 33-34.
> A 4th-8th grade class visited, followed the course of, and communicated with the *President Kennedy,* a cargo ship with the American President Lines. The students were better able to envision and understand the larger world around them as well as to comprehend their own place in it.

Moheno, Phillip B.B. (1989, March). Classroom and curriculum management issues for humanities and confluent teachers. *Journal of Humanistic Education and Development,* 27, 98-104.
> Several approaches to classroom management and curriculum management are presented for humanistically oriented educators.

Monaghan, Floyd V. (1988, May). General education science. *Journal of College Science Teaching,* 17, 436-443.
> Survey courses and a distribution requirement approach to general science education do not work because these approaches emphasize vertical connections to advanced courses rather than lateral connections to other science courses. For nonmajors, this approach suffers from disconnectedness that "kills the vitality" of curriculum. An alternative which involves courses in science and courses about science is proposed.

Mooney, Carolyn J. (1989, July 5). Long-ignored interdisciplinary teachers seek support for changes in curriculum. *Chronicle of Higher Education,* 35, A11-12.
> Conference attendees discuss the pros and cons of interdisciplinary education.

Mooney, Carolyn J. (1988, December 14). *Chronicle of Higher Education,* A35, A1+.
> Sweeping curricular change is underway at Stanford as the university phases out its "western culture" program. Stanford is working to change its ethnocentric curriculum to meet student's calls for multicultural education.

Moore, John A. (1988, May). Teaching the sciences as liberal arts—which, of course, they are. *Journal of College Science Teaching,* 17, 444-451.
> To ensure that as many students as possible understand the sciences to a degree that will make them feel comfortable in the modern world and enable them to make informed decisions: (1) the sciences must have a greater emphasis in general education curricula; (2) courses should move away from facts and toward providing conceptual frameworks; and (3) subject matter should be integrated around themes.

Moore, Kenneth D. (1988, Winter). A model for teacher preparation. *Contemporary Education,* 59, 104-109.
    The issue of weak teacher training programs is discussed and a model program of study that stresses more field experience and liberal arts courses is presented.

Moore, Roy L. (1984, Winter). Journalism: Acquiring something to write about. *New Directions for Teaching and Learning,* 40, 59-66.
    A four-step plan is proposed for strengthening the ties that bind journalism education and the liberal arts: (1) establish an exchange program where faculty from other disciplines rotate teaching responsibilities with journalism professors; (2) require journalism students to take paired, cross-disciplinary courses; (3) incorporate liberal arts content into journalism courses; and (4) create a nonprofessional major in media studies.

Mullaney, N.M. (1986, No. 1). "From Plato to Pareto" the western civilization course reconsidered. *Journal of General Education,* 38, 28-40.
    Western Civilization, the standard history survey course, has been changed or discontinued on most campuses due to criticisms of ethnocentricity, an overemphasis on wars and the "do your own thing" philosophy of the 1960s. The challenge is to redesign and restructure the survey course.

Muller, R. (1989, September). A world core curriculum. *Social Education,* 53, 284-286.
    In 1982, recognition of the need for global education prompted the development of the World Core Curriculum. The framework and objectives on which this curriculum was designed are listed.

Muscatine, Charles. (1985, September/October). Faculty responsibility for the curriculum. *Academe,* 71, 18-21.
    The American college curriculum is in poor shape and the lion's share of the blame lies with American faculty, which has shunned its obligation to educate the whole student by offering a sound curriculum. Curricula that revolve around academic majors produce specialists instead of well-educated citizens, and educators who focus inward toward their field instead of outward toward the world. A balance between teaching and research can be reached and maintained if the educational community becomes committed to developing capable, responsible citizens.

Muther, C. (1987, September). What do we teach, and when do we teach it? *Educational Leadership,* 45, 77-80.
    Attacking textbook publishers for the spiraling of skills and sequencing in secondary texts, the author claims that using these textbooks throughout grades 7-12 leads to subject repetition and minimal progression of skills. She fears that series that follow this trend produce only student boredom—not a better understanding of the material.

Natriello, G. & others. (1982, April). On the right track? Curriculum and academic achievement. *Sociology of Education,* 62, 109-118.
   Research data is presented from a study on tracking systems in which the impacts of graduating from academic, general, or vocational tracks or dropping out of school were compared. Generally, students in the academic track showed the greatest academic achievement, and students who graduated showed an achievement advantage over those who dropped out.

Neusner, J. (1988, September/October). Righteousness, not charity. *Liberal Education,* 74, 16-18.
   The Judaic view of philanthropy is that it is not charity, but rather righteousness, a responsibility of very person.

Newell, L. Jackson. (1984, Winter). The healing arts and the liberal arts in concert. *New Directions for Teaching and Learning,* 40, 67-76.
   Humanities and nursing faculty must cooperate with each other to create imaginative integration of liberal education content and values in baccalaureate nursing programs.

Newell, W.H. & Davis, A.J. (1988, Fall/Winter). Education for citizenship: The role of progressive education and interdisciplinary studies. *Innovative Higher Education,* 13, 27-37.
   The combination of interdisciplinary and progressive education represents the best way to prepare future citizens to meet the six requirements for citizenship in the twenty-first century (civic literacy, critical thinking, social conscience, toleration and respect for diversity, global citizenship, and political action).

Newmann, F.M. (1988, October). Another view of cultural literacy: Go for depth (with discussion). *Social Education,* 52, 432, 434-436.
   Hirsch's proposal to use a core list as a basis for curriculum designed to teach cultural literature will not result in a curriculum which meets the standards of clarity, rationale, feasibility, and opportunity cost.

Newmann, F.M. (1988, May). Depth or coverage in the school curriculum. *Education Digest,* 53, 8-11.
   Emphasis on more thorough analysis of more limited subject matter will allow all students to master more important information, learn to ask the questions necessary for better understanding, and encourage a hunger for knowledge. To implement such an approach, schools must explain the benefits of in-depth study to the public, explore fewer issues in more depth in existing courses rather than eliminating them, and offer resources to help teachers as they restructure the content of these courses. Legislators should also affect curriculum content in a minimum of five areas: assessment, state curriculum requirements, textbook selection, school improvement programs, and teacher education.

Nichols, Robert L. (1985, Summer). How can one know America, who only America knows? *Liberal Education, 71,* 109-120.
Examination of the two societies can provide a base for clearer understanding of each. The author illustrates this with examples from a course on Russia, in which the American character was illuminated.

Niece, R. (1988, May). Facility planning and curriculum design—The impact of environment on teaching and learning. *NASSP Bulletin, 72,* 79-81.
School structures and designs should exist in harmony with instructional ideals. The environment they create should be pleasing, inviting, and exciting.

Nielsen, M. Elizabeth. (1988, Fall). Integrative learning for young children: A thematic approach. *Educational Horizons, 68,* 18-24.
Building on the theory that ever-increasing amounts of information necessitate systematic, integrated approaches to learning, the Thematic Webbing Model is stressed as a way to base a curriculum on broad concepts or themes. First explained is the hierarchical concept continuum (that concepts range from concrete to highly abstract) on which the selection of the themes for webbing is based. Succeeding steps in the webbing process include selection of a global (generalizable, abstract, and complex) theme, development of a thematic main idea, selection of subunit topics, development of main ideas for subunits (themes in the middle of the hierarchy), development of linking propositions between web areas, expansion of subunit topics into discipline areas, and outlining of activities or lessons within subunits.

Nohe, L.M. (1988, November/December). Grinnell College freedom of choice encourages active learning. *Liberal Education, 74,* 27-28.
A tutorial system utilized by Grinnell College allows students to select their courses, but it also potentially allows students to by-pass important coursework, and places a heavy advising load on faculty.

Ognibene, E.R. (1989, Summer). Integrating the curriculum: From impossible to possible. *College Training, 37,* 105-110.
Simply adding materials from female or minority perspectives to a curriculum is not integration. Instead, the underlying mindsets and assumptions of professors and courses must be changed so that alternative viewpoints are considered normative. Effecting such a change requires developing political commitment, a critique of traditional assumptions, and an interdisciplinary approach to courses. Case studies from political science, religion, and English support this argument.

O'Neill, M. (1988, Spring). Curricular reconstruction: Visions of the social frontier. *Educational Forum, 52,* 223-234.
The educational journal, *The Social Frontier* (published from 1934 to 1943), is lauded for its progressive philosophy and support of social activism.

Ornstein, A.C. (1989, September). Academic time considerations for curriculum leaders. *NASSP Bulletin,* 73, 103-110.
> To improve the outcome of student learning it is important to consider both the quality and the quantity of the allotted instructional time.

Ornstein, A.C. (1989, February). Emerging curriculum trends: An agenda for the future. *NASSP Bulletin,* 73, 37-48.
> The contents of the curriculum of the future will be multidimensional and multidisciplinary. Organizing the curriculum will require careful balance between selecting and integrating new knowledge and carefully removing old knowledge.

Ornstein, A.C. (1989, January). The irrelevant curriculum. *Education Digest,* 54, 21-23.
> Irrelevant curriculum is fixed or not relevant to society, is antiseptic, is trivial, or is right-answer oriented. Curricular emphasis should be on process rather than on products.

Ornstein, Allan C. (1989, November). Theoretical issues related to teaching. *Education and Urban Society,* 22, 95-104.
> Research on teacher effectiveness must allow for a variety of teaching styles; it should not be exclusively product oriented.

Osguthorpe, R.T. & Zhou, L. (1989, June). Instructional science: What is it and where did it come from? *Educational Technologies,* 29, 7-17.
> The field of instructional science is defined and the relationship of programmed instruction to instructional science is discussed.

Packard, Sandra P. (1989, March/April). Four questions. *Liberal Education,* 75, 14-17.
> Art contributes to general education because it is a uniquely powerful visual language that communicates perceptions, experience, facts, feelings, and ideas. Art has the capacity to transmit the whole of a culture.

Pajares, Frank. (1989, November). Geography in a fortnight. *Educational Leadership,* 47, 35-37.
> By devoting two weeks to a school wide effort to teach geography, an American school in Spain was able to bring its students up to a minimal level of competency without overhauling the existing curriculum.

Pankin, Jeff, and Newmark, Ami. (1989, March). Three top software programs you don't want to miss. *Electronic Learning,* 8, 46-47.
> *First Winter,* by Houghton Mifflin, *Taking Responsibility,* by Tom Snyder Productions, and *Tutor-Tech,* by Techware are described.

234   SANDRA YAEGLE, FAITH JACK, POLLY MUMMA, and RASHELLE KARP

Payne, H.C. (1986, Fall). Tradition, individual talent and the modern college. *Liberal Education*, 72, 205-211.
> Modern liberal arts institutions should commit themselves to the traditional notions of education for citizenship in part through the study of personal traditional (religious, ethnic, regional, and family) which allow people to be individuals.

Payton, R.L. (1988, September/October). Claiming a place: Philanthropy in the undergraduate curriculum. *Liberal Education*, 74, 1-7.
> The role of and most appropriate place for study of philanthropy in the undergraduate curriculum is discussed.

Payton, R.L. (1988, September/October). The role and place of philanthropy in the undergraduate curriculum (symposium). *Liberal Education*, 74.
> Various authors discuss the importance of philanthropy in undergraduate curricula. The articles are annotated under the appropriate authors' names.

Pazandak, C.H. (1989). Improving undergraduate education in large universities (symposium). *New Directions for Higher Education*, 66, 1-84.
> Various educators discuss how to improve undergraduate education. Their articles are annotated under the appropriate authors' names.

Peat, D. & others. (1989, No. 2). SPELT (Strategies program for effective learning/thinking): A description and analysis of instructional procedures. *Instructional Science*, 18, 95-118.
> The SPELT (Strategies Program for Effective Learning/Thinking) instructional model uses effective and efficient instructional procedures consistent with theories espoused by Bruner, Ausubel, and Gagne. The model is described in great detail.

Pederson, Tom. (1989, Summer). Liberal education: A literary black hole? *Review of Higher Education*, 12, 411-421.
> In this response to Kimball's article on the roots of liberal education, and the trivial *artes* (see first entry under Kimball), Pederson agrees that no curriculum change will emerge from higher education.

Pendergast, Richard J. (1988, No. 2). Reflections on the myth of the machine. *Bulletin of Science, Technology and Society*, 8, 163-166.
> The need for a return to liberal and moral education is propounded, and the writings of Cantore, Dawkins, Mumford, Ouchi, and Polanyi are cited as evidence.

Perkins, D.N. & Salomon, Gavriel. (1988, September). Teaching for transfer. *Educational Leadership*, 46, 22-32.
> Concepts of transfer, including transfer of skill, transfer of knowledge, low road transfer (reflexive), and high road transfer (reflective) are discussed. Teaching strategies which can stimulate transfer are suggested.

Perrin, Robert. (1989, March). Can cultural literacy be taught or tested? *The Clearing House,* 62, 284.

    Methods that teach cultural literacy through facts, people, movements, and ideas ignore that cultural awareness develops gradually by assimilation.

Perspectives on teaching from "integrity in the college classroom: A report to the academic community" (with discussion). (1985, Summer). *College Teaching,* 33, 117-128.

    College and university professors are central to the solutions and the problems existing in higher education. The profession of college teaching needs to develop more fully in terms of professional awareness, accountability, and responsibility.

Petroski, Henry. (1989, Spring). Teaching technology to nontechnologists. *National Forum: Phi Kappa Phi Journal,* 69, 29-30.

    Petroski discusses impediments to combining technology and liberal arts education and examines ways of overcoming such obstacles.

Phillipo, John. (1989, March). Videodisc technology and HyperCard: A combination that can't be beat. *Electronic Learning,* 8, 40-41.

    The recent advent of videodiscs such as *HyperCard* allows the computer to create multimedia-based lessons.

Phillips, D.C. (1989, Spring). Dialogue—Absolutism, relativism, and the curriculum—A response to Alexander. *Curriculum Inquiry,* 19, 51-57.

    In terms of curricular philosophy, criticism is leveled at both the "forms of knowledge" theorists and the Great Books theorists.

Phipps, R.A. & Romesburg, K.D. (1988, Spring). An assessment by alumni of college and university experience. *College and University,* 63, 284-295.

    In a study done by the Education Commission of the States, alumni were surveyed to assess the overall effectiveness of undergraduate education. The majority of graduates felt they benefitted from their undergraduate experience.

Pickering, J.W. (1986, December). A comparison of three methods of career planning for liberal arts majors. *Career Development Quarterly,* 35, 102-112.

    Effective career planning programs are comprehensive in scope and include directed self-study, peer tutoring, and courses on careers.

Pike, G.R. & Phillipi, R.H. (1989, No. 3). Generalizability of the differential coursework methodology: Relationships between self-reported coursework and performance on the ACT-COMP exam. *Research in Higher Education,* 30, 245-260.

    The Differential Coursework Patterns Project at Iowa State University attempted to explain how different patterns, or clusters, of collect coursework relate to student achievement. The procedures appear to have enormous potential but questions remain about their generalizability.

Pintrich, P.R. & others. (1987, April). Teaching a course in learning to learn. *Teaching of Psychology*, 14, 81-86.
   Course materials and laboratory sessions are outlined as part of the instructional techniques necessary to help college students who are at risk academically to develop more effective learning strategies.

Popkewitz, T.S. (1988, 87th, part 2). Knowledge, power, and a general curriculum. *Yearbook (National Society for the Study of Education)*, 69-93.
   The question of establishing a general curriculum is complicated by the relationship of knowledge to power, historical conditions that have developed, and inequalities found in the classroom setting.

Presseisen, Barbara Z. (1988, April). Avoiding battle at curriculum gulch: Teaching thinking and content. *Educational Leadership*, 45, 7-8.
   A call is made for the advocates of the teaching of thinking and the advocates of content to begin a discussion about combining process and content in the curriculum.

Pruitt, Randall P. (1989, Fall). Fostering creativity: The innovative classroom environment. *Educational Horizons*, 68, 51-54.
   The four main factors which either encourage or impede the creative process in learning are classroom control, habitual behavior, time, and student assessment.

Quattrone, David F. (1989, Fall). A case study in curriculum innovation: Developing an interdisciplinary curriculum. *Educational Horizons*, 68, 28-35.
   The Greenwich Public School System addressed curricular needs by developing an interdisciplinary approach.

Ramsey, John M. (1989, November). A curricular framework for community-based STS issue instruction. *Education and Urban Society*, 22, 40-53.
   The four goals of the STS (Science Technology Society) are to provide issue-oriented science instruction that comprises (1) foundations knowledge needed to understand and investigate issues; (2) conceptual knowledge needed to understand the "anatomy" of issues; (3) knowledge necessary to evaluate alternative solutions to issues; and (4) skills necessary to make responsible decisions.

Ravitch, Diane. (1989, Summer). Education and the public good. *National Forum: Phi Kappa Phi Journal*, 69, 35-38.
   Ravitch examines attitudes toward education in America from 1787 to the present.

Rehnke, Mary Ann F. (1987). Concluding notes and further readings. *New Directions for Higher Education*, 103-106.
   A bibliography of resources to aid in the college program planning process is provided.

Revans, Rej. (1989, Spring). Integrity in the college curriculum. *Higher Education Review,* 21, 26-62.

    The way to enforce the qualities of the new era of education, identified by the Association of American Colleges as integrity, intellectual rigor, and religion, is to achieve a balance between the learning factors of programmed instruction and questioning insight.

Rhodes, F.H.T. (1986, February). Fostering liberal learning in higher education. *Education Digest,* 51, 30-32.

    Rhodes cites hiring "faculty members who regard teaching as a moral activity and who embody and exemplify the liberal spirit" as the solution to the crisis in liberal education.

Rickard, C.E. & Waters, G.E. (1984, Fall). Academic programming: The key to enrollment growth. *College Board Review,* 133, 26-28.

    Planning processes that are well coordinated and involve both the campus and community will result in stronger academic programs.

Root-Bernstein, R.S. (1987, September). Tools of thought: Designing an integrated curriculum for lifelong learners. *Roeper Review,* 10, 17-213.

    The humanities, arts, and sciences should be taught in an integrated format that will allow students to become skilled polymaths who are able to utilize whole schools of thought as they become creative individuals.

Rothblatt, Sheldon. (1989, January/February). Merits & defects: The American educational system. *Liberal Education,* 75, 25.

    The American liberal arts educational system has many distinguishing features including a unique institutional structure and an emphasis on breadth of study over subject specialization.

Rudd, William J. (1984, Winter). Architecture education: The profundity of edifice. *New Directions in Teaching and Learning,* 40, 21-38.

    Both skills and liberal knowledge are necessary to an architect's professional preparation. Consequently, professional education must encompass both.

Russell, James D. & Blake, Bonnie L. (1988, September). Formative and summative evaluation of instructional products and learners. *Educational Technology,* 28, 22-28.

    A distinction is made between the formative and summative methods of evaluating the people and products involved in education. Both methods should be used in the evaluation process.

Russo, M.A. (1989, September/October). Communications: An undergraduate major for the liberal arts. *Liberal Education,* 75, 40-43.

    Effective programs in communications studies include the study of language or text analysis, the social sciences, and the humanities.

Ryckman, D.B. & Peckham, P. (1987, November/December). Gender differences in attributions for success and failure situations across subject areas. *Journal of Educational Research,* 81, 120-125.

Results of the Administration of the Survey of Achievement Responsibility scale in a large urban school district indicate that students appear to feel more in control in the area of language arts than they do in the areas of match and science. Females demonstrated more learned-helpless orientation in mathematics and science than did males.

Sachse, Thomas P. (1989, November). Making science happen. *Educational Leadership,* 47, 18-21.

California's experiment with a new science curriculum emphasizes thematic understanding by means of constructivist teaching (building on students' prior knowledge) rather than the teaching of factoids. State and national efforts are aligning texts, tests, and training so that these reforms are supported.

Salisbury, D.F. (1989, August). What should instructional designers know about general systems theory? *Educational Technology,* 29, 42-45.

The General Systems Theory (GST) is based on the belief that instruction is enhanced when knowledge from many different subject disciplines is combined in the instructional format.

Salisbury, R.H. (1988, September/October). Is active citizenship still possible? *Liberal Education,* 74, 19-21.

Effectively organized citizenship, responsible for American government as we know it, must be taught.

Sample, John. (1989, June). Civil liability for failure to train to standard. *Educational Technology,* 29, 23-26.

Law-enforcement agencies and other at risk organizations should use well-designed, job-related training programs to reduce the probability that they will face law suits based on the "failure to train to standard" statute.

Sangrey, Dwight A. & Phelan, Thomas. (1984, Winter). Liberal learning and engineering education. *New Directions in Teaching and Learning,* 40, 49-59.

The authors present strategies for capturing engineering students' interest in the humanities and social sciences component of their education as well as strategies for motivating engineering students to take general education as seriously as they take their professional education.

Schmidt, Charles P. (1989, Winter). An investigation of undergraduate music education curriculum content. *Bulletin for the Council for Research in Music Education,* 99, 42-56.

A survey of 180 music teacher training institutes was conducted to evaluate the contents of music education curricula. A degree of variability in some aspects of curricula was reported, and further study was encouraged.

Schwab, Joseph J. (1983, Fall). The practical 4: Something for curriculum professors to do. *Curriculum Inquiry,* 13, 239-265.
Four practical considerations are recommended when developing curricula: the overall objectives of the curriculum, the socio-ethnic background of the community, how to best constitute the membership of the curriculum planning committee, and the function of the committee chair.

Schwartz, Ruth. (1986, Winter). Computers and the arts. *College Teaching,* 34, 11-16.
The Art Department at the University of Southern California has integrated the use of computers into its art curriculum.

Seymour, Daniel. (1988-1989, No. 4). HODGE-PODGE: Or the unintended results from straying too far afield. *Planning for Higher Education,* 17, 3-11.
The recent proliferation of college programs has been spurred by the perceived needs of the faculty, the perceived market, competition among institutions, and competition within institutions. Program proliferation can create overspecialization, declines in educational quality, and limits to the allocation of resources.

Shane, H.G. (1990, January). Educated foresight to the 1990's. *Educational Leadership,* 55, 3-5.
The next decade will present numerous social and technological changes that will necessitate existing foresight in curriculum planning and policy development.

Shea, William M. (1988, Winter). John Dewey and the crisis of the canon. *American Journal of Education,* 25, 593-614.
The author feels that in the current educational "crisis of the canon," William Bennett and Allan Bloom's emphasis on the classics should be balanced with John Dewey's emphasis on the human experience.

Sherry, J.F., Jr. (1988, December). Teaching and international business: A view from anthropology. *Anthropology and Education Quarterly,* 19, 396-415.
A study of anthropologists who are also involved with business anthropology explored common characteristics of course design and implementation, content areas, course adjustments, and instructional materials. Directions for future research are suggested.

Shipps, J. (1988, September/October). Philanthropy, religion, and American Culture. *Liberal Education,* 74, 24-25.
The study of philanthropy is critical to an understanding of American culture.

Shoenberg, R.E. (1986, Fall). On intellectual adulthood. *Liberal Education,* 72, 189-197.
Required upper-level general education courses at the University of Maryland fall into two categories: the development of knowledge (courses here introduce students to epistemological questions), and analysis of human problems. The criteria which courses must meet to qualify as meeting the requirements for these categories are outlined.

Simpson, W.A. (1987, May/June). Tracking students through majors: Methodology and applications. *Journal of Higher Education,* 58, 323-343.
A new computer model that assesses the impact of the change that results when students decide to change majors is presented.

Sipple, Jo-Ann M. (1989, July/August). A planning process for building writing-across-the-curriculum programs to last. *Journal of Higher Education,* 60, 444-457.
A planning process that uses a heuristic, problem-solving approach provides the strategies needed to develop "writing-across-the-curriculum" programs.

Sjoberg, L. & Dahlstrand, U. (1987, No. 3). Subject matter attributes study interests in post-secondary education. *Higher Education,* 16, 357-372.
This study of M.B.A. students concluded that subject disciplines which have a logical appeal tend to elicit more student interest than those with practical value.

Slaght, R.L. (1987, February 18). We can no longer separate the thinkers from the doers in liberal arts. *Chronicle of Higher Education,* 33, 38-39.
To meet today's societal needs, colleges and universities are integrating liberal arts and technology.

Smith, Barbara Herrnstein. (1989, Summer). Contingencies of value. *National Forum,* 69, 22-24.
Smith gives a historical view of "literary education."

Smith, C. LeMoyne. (1988, September). Business education will prepare today's students for tomorrow's economy. *Educational Leadership,* 46, 55.
Business education should be included in the core curriculum for all secondary school students because the economy is shifting to service related employment.

Smith, Jeff. (1989, Summer). Cultural literacy and the academic "left." *National Forum: Phi Kappa Phi Journal,* 69, 19-21.
The author examines E.D. Hirsch's call for "cultural literacy."

Smith, Peter A. (1989, November). A modest proposal, or using ingredients at hand to make an art curriculum. *Art Education,* 42, 9-15.
A proposed art curriculum model contains an organizational framework that is based on selections from the disciplines of art history, technique, and criticism.

Smith, R.T. (1989, Summer). Canon fodder, the cultural hustle, and the Minotaur. *National Forum: Phi Kappa Phi Journal,* 69, 25-29.
Smith explores both sides of the cultural literacy debate.

Smith, Sally K. Sommers & Morrison, Dane A. (1989, March/April). The Boston scholars: An introduction to college science with an interdisciplinary focus. *Journal of College Science Teaching,* 18, 301-311.
The success of the Boston Scholars Orientation program is attributed to an interdisciplinary approach to the teaching of science at the introductory college level.

Smuckler, Ralph & Sommers, Lawrence. (1989, March). Internationalizing college curriculum. *Education Digest,* 54, 43-47.
 College curricula should be global in their focus. Practical methods are presented which involve students, faculty, and administrators in an effort to internationalize the curriculum.

Solomon, Gwen. (1989, March). A powerful, inexpensive Apple II compatible. *Electronic Learning,* 8, 44.
 The Laser 128EX/2, by Laser Computer, is compared with an Apple II computer.

Solomon, Gwen. (1989, March). Shift your Apple II into overdrive with the superfast Zip Chip. *Electronic Learning,* 8, 42.
 An analysis of the Zip Chip by Zip Technology, when installed in an Apple II computer, revealed little effect on software operation, but showed great value when working with large file listings and data bases.

Spalding, Jane R. (1989, May/June). Internationalizing higher education through business school liberal arts cooperation (symposium). *Liberal Education,* 75, 1-41.
 Interdisciplinary cooperation is the key vehicle for internationalizing higher education. Various educators (articles annotated separately under their names) expand this concept.

Spear, K. (1984, No. 2). The Paideia Proposal: The problem of means and ends in general education. *Journal of General Education,* 36, 79-86.
 Although the Paideia Proposal is fundamentally correct in its rationale for broad liberal arts education, its proposal of a uniform curriculum for everyone could result in a dangerous drift toward mediocrity.

Spear, Karen. (1989, Summer). Sources of train in liberal education. *Review of Higher Education,* 12, 389-401.
 The author opines that the back to basics movement, spurred on by structural, epistemological, and political pressures, is flawed because it does not consider the pluralistic, cultural context in which college students operate. Changes in general education must be made in terms of academic policy, a focus on values, curricular reform, and pedagogical reform.

Spete, Allen P. (1987). The presidential perspective on mission review for new career programs. *New Directions for Higher Education,* 57, 21-28.
 The mission review procedure to establish new career programs should aim to balance the needs of the institution with economic reality. Practical and philosophical considerations are discussed.

Stark, Joan S. & Lowther, Malcolm A. (1984, Winter). Exploring common ground in liberal and professional education. *New Directions in Teaching and Learning,* 40, 7-20.
 Professional and liberal education share common competency and attitude goals including communication competency, critical thinking, contextual competence,

aesthetic sensibility, professional identity, professional ethics, adaptive competence, leadership capacity, scholarly concern for improvement, and motivation for continued learning. Faculty must collaborate to fully achieve these goals.

Stark, J.S. & others. (1988, No. 3). Faculty reflect on course planning. *Research in Higher Education,* 29, 219-240.

Based on their survey of 89 faculty members, in which the authors studied how faculty planned introductory courses, an outline of a tentative course model and suggestions for further course planning strategies are presented.

Stark, J.S. & Lowther, M.A. (1988). Perspectives on course and program planning. *New Directions for Institutional Research,* 57, 39-52.

Viewing curriculum as an academic plan permits development of parallel course and program planning models that are dynamic, conceptually related to student learning, and familiar to institutional planners.

Stark, J.S. (1989). Seeking coherence in the curriculum. New Directions for Higher Education, 66, 65-76.

If colleges and universities begin the process of changing curricula by establishing clearly defined guiding models, the result will be a coherent curriculum. Examples of mock curriculum committee meetings are presented.

Stark, Joan S. (1987). Liberal education and professional programs: Conflict, coexistence, or compatibility? *New Directions for Higher Education,* 57, 91-102.

Professional education and professional education programs share mutual goals and objectives which can be blended together in ways that will benefit the students and the institution.

Stevens R. (1985, Summer). Restructuring the liberal arts: Synthesis rather than fragmentation. *Liberal Education,* 71, 163-165.

Strong high school education programs will allow college programs to be more tailored to individual students' particular fields of academic interest.

Stewig, John Warren. (1988, December). Oral language: A place in the curriculum? *The Clearing House,* 52, 171-174.

The major challenge in language arts and curricula is to include expressive oral language activities amid requirements for more written language activities. Teachers must develop rationales, plan curriculum sequences, and implement evaluation of programs to justify a secure place for oral language in the curriculum.

Stimpson, C.R. (1988, March/April). Is there a core in this curriculum? *Change,* 20, 26-31.

The use of core curricula is discouraged because they are rigid and exclusionary in their content. A broader, more coherent curriculum that is based on relativism is recommended.

Strand, Linda M. & Winston, Mark. (1984, Winter). Liberal arts in pharmacy education. *New Directions for Teaching and Learning,* 40, 77-86.
  It is suggested, among other things, that pharmacy programs admit freshmen so that better integration of professional and liberal studies throughout the curriculum can be achieved.

Strange, Susan. (1989, May/June). International political economy: Recruiting three fields of intellectual endeavor. *Liberal Education,* 75, 20-24.
  To combat curricular fragmentation among the disciplines of international relations, international economics, and international business, an approach to "international political economy," which involves the study of business history, general political and world history, and comparative demographics, is advocated. Ways in which this approach can be implemented are outlined.

Strassburger, J. (1988, January/February). Corporate thinking and the liberal arts. *Liberal Education,* 74, 22-26.
  The current favorable climate among corporate employers toward liberal arts education can be turned to the advantage of students if they are taught to demonstrate mastery of a certain field, to reflect on what they have accomplished, and to talk about their accomplishments with pride.

Sutton, Francis X. (1985, Summer). The liberal arts in new international perspective: Summary remarks. *Liberal Education,* 71, 135-140.
  The loss of Americans' confidence in their ability to mold the world in their image has led to a more realistic acceptance and understanding of cultural diversity.

Taking stock: A roundtable discussion on general education. (1988, November/December). *Liberal Education,* 74, 11-23.
  A roundtable discussion between members of the Association of American Colleges focuses on how institutions of higher education respond to changes in society through curricular reform.

Taylor, A.A. Basic skills and core competencies. *National Business Education Yearbook 1989,* 138-148.
  Business courses teach personal and professional skills that are vital to business and nonbusiness majors. Many strategies are suggested that can be used to promote business courses.

Tanner, Daniel. (1989, Fall). A brief historical perspective of the struggle for an integrative curriculum. *Educational Horizons,* 68, 7-11.
  The author reviews the history of curriculum development in the United States and proposes that the measure of any area of study in a curriculum should be through its relationship to neighboring fields.

Terry, Roger L. & McIntosh, David E. (1988, Fall). Do students' expectancies affect their course selection? *Educational and Psychological Measurement,* 48, 787-798.
  Students' written evaluations at the conclusion of a course do not appear to be significantly affected by their prior expectations of the course.

Thieblot, Bernice Ashby. (1989, September). A campus of many colors. *Currents*, 15, 12-16.
  A checklist to promote pluralism on campuses includes the areas of missions and goals, institutional history, admissions and financial aid policies, administration, student support systems, curriculum, campus community, campus activities, community environment, and educational benefits.

This we believe about the role of business education as a component of general education. (1989, October). *Business Educational Forum*, 44, 7.
  A statement issued by the Policies Commission for Business and Education calls for a balanced business curriculum that includes academic and employability competencies to assure credibility and to obtain full academic acceptance.

Thomas, Gail E. & Larke, Patricia J. (1989, May). Gender differences among blacks in education and career orientation. *Education and Urban Society*, 21, 283-298.
  Black students need systematic intervention that is sponsored by families and schools if they are to succeed in higher education and in the labor market.

Thornborrow, Nancy M. & Nathan, Laura E. (1986, Spring). An interdisciplinary approach to inequality. *College Student Journal*, 20, 60-65.
  An interdisciplinary approach to core curricula can strengthen quality liberal education while also addressing social issues. Described is a course on inequality taught at Mills College (CA) which used integrative team teaching to produce a beneficial interdisciplinary curriculum.

Tirozzi, Gerald N. & Sergi, Theodore S. (1989, April). Connecticut's common core of learning. *The Clearing House*, 62, 347-350.
  The Common Core of Learning (C.C.L.), developed by the Connecticut State Board of Education in 1987, is proving to be a successful standard for their educational programs.

Toole, W.B. (1987, Winter). The usefulness of useless knowledge: A perspective for the 1980's. *Educational Record*, 68, 26-31.
  The popularity of career-oriented education coupled with social change has influenced students to devalue a liberal arts education. Necessary are continuing communication and effective collaboration between schools, corporate entities, and the private sector to promote both liberal and professional learning.

Tucker, Marc S. (1987). The college market. *New Directions for Higher Education*, 57, 5-12.
  The increasing costs of education and changing economic structures will increase the demand on colleges and universities for liberal arts curricula and will produce changes in the market for higher education.

Turner, J.A. (1986, September 10). Professors find many obstacles to combining technology and liberal arts in single course. *Chronicle of Higher Education*, 33, 14-15.
  Impediments to integrating liberal arts and technology include logistical and traditional problems associated with interdisciplinary teaching.

Tyson, Harriet & Woodward, Arthur. (1989, November). Why students aren't learning very much from textbooks. *Educational Leadership, 47,* 14-17.

Textbooks are identified as the major contributor to American students' ignorance of important concepts and knowledge in economics, history, geography, and science. Better textbooks are possible, but only if those who select them start rejecting those textbooks with gross errors or serious omissions and demand that publishers produce better quality material.

Unks, Gerald. (1989, November). Educating consumers, not just practitioners: An education course for non-majors. *Education and Urban Society, 22,* 54-63.

Schools of education should offer specifically designed courses to noneducation majors to prepare them to become wise consumers of educational services.

Useem, M. (1988, January/February). Liberal education and corporate management. *Liberal Education, 74,* 16-21.

A study of corporations in America indicates that while liberal arts education is generally held to be valuable for people wishing to enter higher levels of management, training in practical skills, or technical arts, is also regarded as beneficial for preparing students for careers in corporate management.

Utterback, Phyllis H. & Kalin, Maurice. (1989, October). A community-based model for curriculum evaluation. *Educational Leadership, 47,* 49-50.

The school system of Howard County, Maryland successfully used volunteers from the community to assess the strength of its science, mathematics education, and guidance programs.

Vaala, Leslie. (1989, Spring). Preference of transfer students for a transfer program. *Community College Review, 16,* 28-37.

A study of 400 college transfer students attending a large university in western Canada indicates that students transferring from a nondegree college program to a degree granting university generally need special assistance from the faculty to be successful.

Vann, Allan S. (1988, September). The curriculum cup runneth over. *Educational Leadership, 46,* 60.

Curriculum overcrowding is occurring because state departments of education are calling for the implementation of new curriculum without providing effective time guidelines.

Vulgamore, M.L. (1985, Summer). The rhetoric of being and becoming. *Liberal Education, 71,* 167-172.

There is a need to return to the classical roots of the liberal arts: logic (the signifying of some particular things through other particular things in discourse); grammar (the operation of particular things in discourse); and rhetoric (the relation of all things to universals).

Waetjen, W.B. (1989, November). Harmony and discord: Technology and liberal arts. *Technology Transfer,* 49, 3-5.
The liberal arts curriculum should include the study of technological reasoning and decision making, because practice results in long-term learning.

Walters, K.S. (1986, Fall). Critical thinking in liberal education: A case of overkill? *Liberal Education,* 72, 233-244.
After defining critical thinking, the author propounds that our current focus on critical thinking needs to be balanced by training in alternative methodologies such as synthetic, dialectical, and creative modes of awareness and expression.

Ward, F. Champion. (1969, July/August). Requiem for the Hutchins College: Recalling a great experiment in general education. *Change,* 21, 22-33.
The experiment to promote general liberal arts education that was attempted by the University of Chicago by Chancellor Robert Maynard Hutchins in the 1940s and 1950s is analyzed.

Ware, Norma C. & Lee, Valerie E. (1988, Winter). Sex differences in choice of college science majors. *American Educational Research Journal,* 25, 593-614.
Data drawn from a nationally representative sample of high-achieving college students reveals that for men, predictors of a science major choice included positive assessments of the high schools, attending a four-year college, and relatively high socioeconomic status. Women who were influenced by high school teachers and counselors in making college plans, who attended a four-year college, and who placed a high priority on future family and personal life were less likely to major in science than other women.

Waters, G.L. (1985, Winter). Implementing general education. *Liberal Education,* 71, 335-339.
In 1981-1982, the University of Michigan at Flint conducted a curriculum revision process that applied the arts and science program to the needs of the career and professional education programs. A unique feature was the joining together for the first time of the faculty and staff.

Watson, Fletcher G. (1988, May). General education in the sciences in transition. *Journal of College Science Technology,* 17, 432-435, 483.
Faculty have a central role in the implementation of a successful general education science program, as does a university polity willing to consider curricular and academic structural change. The main question over history has been "what should the educated layperson know of the sciences."

Wells, Louis T. (1989, May/June). Supping with the devil: Another interpretation. *Liberal Education,* 75, 25-27.
Strategies for ways in which collaboration among disciplines may be achieved are presented. The author especially focuses on the role of business school faculty as identifiers of research areas for other faculty.

White, Edward M., et al. (1989, September/October). European vs. American higher education: Two issues and a clear winner. *Change*, 21, 52-55.

American universities offer a general curriculum, geared toward mass education, while European universities are more specialized and more selective in admissions. The American perspective is lauded.

Wiggins, Thomas, and Seaberg, John. (1988, Summer). Initiating curriculum change through multiple method inquiry. *Education*, 108, 522-527.

Multiple Method Inquiry is a method of curriculum evaluation that is used to assess needs, to plan programs, and to determine if programs are being implemented effectively. The model utilizes five processes: needs assessment, program planning, implementation evaluation, progress evaluation, and outcome evaluation.

Wilkins, Mira. (1989, May/June). Economic historians: Their interdisciplinary nature and dilemmas. *Liberal Education*, 75, 10-12.

Economists push historians to seek models, while historians lead economists to respect diversity and tolerate ambiguity. The two must work together.

Willinsky, John M. (1987, Fall). The seldom-spoken roots of the curriculum. *Curriculum Inquiry*, 17, 26-291.

The philosophies underlying the Romantic movement in British literature are compared to the philosophies of the new movement in language education called the New Literacy.

Wilson, Glenn T. (1987, Spring). Coping with changing student demands. *College Board Review*, 143, 24-27, 39-40.

College administrators must evaluate changing student demands for courses in terms of whether surges in demand are fads or long term. To cope with the problems, the administration can elect to either restrict enrollment, allow large classes, add faculty to high demand areas, or retain/relocate faculty. The choice depends on whether the changes are expected to be long or short run.

Winship, James P. (1984, Winter). Social work and the liberal arts perspective: A mandate in search of a mission. *New Directions in Teaching and Learning*, 40, 87-95.

The accrediting term, "liberal arts base," does not work because it implies that professional education sits atop or after liberal education. Students learn best if they can apply both social work and nonsocial work course content to the development of professional outcomes.

Winstead, Philip C. (1987). Establishing the planning process for selecting appropriate career programs. *New Directions for Higher Education*, 57, 29-37.

The key steps to establishing a successful career program are presented. They include using an affective planning model, choosing a planning officer, gathering data, and conducting a feasibility study to help establish policies and procedures.

Wisniewski, Richard. (1984, Winter). Linking teacher education and liberal learning. *New Directions in Teaching and Learning,* 40, 39-48.
   Linking teacher preparation to liberal learning is critical to preparing good teachers.

Woditsch, G.A., Mark, A., & Giardina, R.C. (1987, November/December). The skillful baccalaureate: Doing what liberal education does best. *Change,* 19, 48-57.
   The strength of the traditional liberal arts program lies in its ability to produce students that model the effective, independent thinking skills of the intelligent mind at work (IMW).

Wong, Frank F. (1985, Summer). Pilgrims and immigrants: Liberal learning in today's world. *Liberal Education,* 71, 97-108.
   The cosmopolitan character of the world must become a part of the liberal arts curriculum.

Worsham, Toni (1988, September). From cultural literacy to cultural thoughtfulness. *Educational Leadership,* 46, 20-21.
   Content-based instruction is presented as a cause for students being culturally illiterate. Process instruction is proposed as the solution.

Wraga, Williams G. (1989, Fall). Political literacy: Teaching active citizenship. *Educational Horizons,* 68, 46-49.
   The teaching of content material should be coupled with the teaching of political knowledge so that students are prepared to function as competent members of our democratic society.

Yager, Robert E. (1988, September). Achieving useful science: Reforming the reforms of the 60's. *Educational Leadership,* 46, 53-54.
   Ziman's STS (Science/Technology/Society) program allows students to investigate problems that they see around them, thus integrating science with relevant problem-solving activities. Similar programs, such as Jean Solomon's Science in a Social Context (SisCon), continue to see equivalent success. A compilation of alternative, innovative science curricula that have gained national attention are described.

Yager, Robert E. (1989, November). New goals for students. *Education and Urban Society,* 22, 9-21.
   The characteristics that distinguish STS (Science/Technology/Society) based programs from traditional programs are outlined. STS is lauded for promoting more effective goals for students because it focuses on the application of presented material.

Ylvisaker, Paul N. (1988, September/October). *Liberal Education,* 74, 26-36.
   Various educators describe courses and programs which exist to teach the concepts and practice of philanthropy.

Zelenski, Joseph E. (1988, Summer). Articulation between colleges and high schools: Something old or something new? A historical perspective 1828-1987. *Community College Review,* 16, 34-38.

Entrance requirements for college freshmen have historically followed a cyclical pattern throughout history, from the study of classics and a liberal education to mercantile, mechanical, and agricultural concerns. The pendulum seems to be swinging toward a set of required core units in high schools to improve the quality of college freshmen and to increase retention and graduation rates.

Zelhart, P.F. & Markley, R.P. (1985, No. 1). Faculty & student diversity and pluralistic general education program. *Journal of General Education,* 37, 34-46.

A track system is proposed as a way to implement general education that accommodates diverse students and faculty. Suggested tracks include those based on the traditional distribution model, production of research, or interpersonal involvement and group socialization.

Zingg, P.J. (1987, No. 3). Quality in the curriculum: The renewed search for coherence and unity. *Journal of General Education,* 39, 173-192.

During the last ten years efforts to define the issue of quality have led to concern over the lack of curriculum coherence and unity. A Collegiate Seminar Program, based on the Great Books approach, has been developed at St. Mary's College.

Zita, J. (1988, No. 2). From orthodox to pluralism: A postsecondary curricular reform. *Journal of Education,* 170, 58-76.

The College of Liberal Arts at the University of Minnesota implemented a U.S. Cultural Pluralism requirement in 1985.

BIBLIOGRAPHY OF SUB-SAHARA AFRICAN LIBRARIANSHIP, 1989

Compiled by Glenn L. Sitzman

PREFACE

The compilation for 1989 is the third supplement to the "Bibliography of African Librarianship" published in the compiler's *African Libraries* (Scarecrow Press, 1988). The total titles provided in the base bibliography and the three supplements come to approximately 4,000.

The present compilation contains some 477 entries, accounting for approximately 468 titles, with about a dozen titles entered under more than one heading. For example, one article with a title referring to French-speaking Africa actually focuses on three countries. The article is therefore entered under each of the three countries, with no entry under French-speaking Africa. Likewise, a bibliography of a single subject has entries under "Bibliographies" and also under the subject. For whatever value they may be to research in librarianship, historical dictionaries are included in this compilation. A slight change in format has been effected in that works published before 1980 are listed after titles published in 1980 or later, unless there is only one pre-1980 title. In that case it is interfiled.

Advances in Library Administration and Organization,
Volume 10, pages 251-292.
Copyright © 1992 by JAI Press Inc.
All rights of reproduction in any form reserved.
ISBN: 1-55938-460-3

The compiler has again made an effort to search out retrospective titles, though the search is made more difficult by residence in a country with less than minimal library coverage of Africa. Nevertheless, by the use of bibliographies and through the help of various individuals the compiler has added some 175 titles published before 1980. Nearly 300 titles published since 1980 were taken from the indexes *Library Literature, Library and Information Science Abstracts,* and *Information Science Abstracts,* with a few unindexed titles provided by cooperative individuals. Incomplete retrospective citations have been incorporated as found, or as provided by others.

For those who have an interest in statistics it may be pointed out that the 202 entries which have a broader-than-national focus form 42 percent of the total 477. Of the 202, 94 were published before 1980. The 117 entries for Nigeria account for about 25 percent of the total, and of the 117, 31 are pre-1980 publications. Thirty-nine other countries, plus the former Western Sahara, account for 158 entries, or 33 percent of the compilation. Of the 158, 52 entries (or one-third) are pre-1980. These statistics are, for the most part, approximations and are offered only for whatever interest they may provide.

Special thanks are due to W.J. Plumbe for sending citations for all his publications not collected in his *Tropical Libraries* (Scarecrow Press, 1987), as well as for titles by other authors; to Yvette Scheven (University of Illinois) for assistance with titles difficult for the compiler to identify; to Anne Rouget for a list of titles published by the German Foundation for International Development; to Gerard B. McCabe, co-editor of *Advances in Library Administration and Organization,* for his interest in this bibliographical project, his encouragement, and his counsel; and to the University of Puerto Rico Libraries, especially of the Mayagüez Campus, for permission to use their facilities and services.

GUIDE TO ORGANIZATION OF BIBLIOGRAPHY

Africa in General

General and Peripheral
Academic Libraries
Bibliographies and Bibliography
Biographies of Librarians
Book Trade, Printing, and Publishing
Cataloging and Classification
Documentation and Information Science
Library Education and Training
Public Libraries
School and Children's Library Services and Literature
Special Libraries, Materials, and Services

Africana

General
Africana Collections outside the Sub-Sahara
Africana for Children

Inter-Regional and Regional

Inter-Regional
Eastern Africa
General
Bibliographies and Bibliography
Documentation and Information Science
Library Education
School Libraries
Southern Africa
West Africa
General
Bibliographies and Bibliography

International Meetings

1964. Salisbury, Rhodesia, Leverhulme Conference on University Libraries in Tropical Africa
1972. Kumasi, Ghana, International Workshop on Development and Dissemination of Appropriate Technologies in Rural Areas
1973. Nairobi, Kenya, International Conference on Development of Documentation and Information Networks in East Africa
1974. Dakar, Senegal, Conference on the Harmonization of Librarianship Training Programs in Africa
1976. Brazzaville, Congo, Meeting of Experts on Planning Documentation and Library Networks in Africa
Karen-Kairobi, Kenya, Training Course on the Implementation of Modern Documentation
1978. Nairobi, Kenya, Standing Conference of Eastern, Central and Southern African Libraries (SCECSAL)
1979. Nairobi, Kenya, Consultative Meeting on Information Needs for Development, Planning and Investment Agencies in Africa
1982. Paris, France, International Congress on the Universal Availability of Publications
1984. Nairobi, Kenya, General Conference of the International Federation of Library Associations (IFLA)
1989. Tananarive, Madagascar, African Standing Conference on Bibliographic Control (ASCOBIC)

Individual Countries

Angola
Benin
Botswana
Burkina Faso
Cameroon
Cape Verde
Central African Republic
Chad
Comoros
Congo (People's Republic)
Equatorial Guinea
Ethiopia
Gabon
Gambia
Ghana
   General
   Library Education
   Special Libraries
Guinea
Guinea-Bissau
Ivory Coast
Kenya
   General
   Bibliographies and Bibliography
   Library Education
   Academic Libraries
   School and Children's Library Services
   Special Libraries
Lesotho
Liberia
Madagascar
Malawi
Mali
Mauritania
Mauritius
Niger
Nigeria
   General
   Bibliographies and Bibliography
   Book Trade, Printing and Publishing
   Cataloging and Classification
   Cooperation
   Documentation and Information Science

Uganda
  East African School of Librarianship
  Academic Libraries
Western Sahara
Zaire
Zambia
  Public Libraries
  School Libraries
  Special Libraries
Zimbabwe
  Public Libraries
  Special Libraries

Africa—General and Peripheral

"Africa at IFLA." *African Research & Documentation* 45(1987): 27-29.

Bagrova, I. Y. "Natsional'nye biblioteki razvivayushchikhsya stran: voprosy zakonodatel'nogo obespecheniya" [National Libraries of Developing Countries: Questions of Legislation]. *Bibliotekovedenie i Bibliografia za Rubezhom* 111(1987): 3-17.

Banjo, A. Oluboyega. "Library and Information Services in a Changing World: An African Point of View." In *IFLA General Conference, 1987: Papers, Division of Regional Activities,* 1987. ERIC. ED 300 007.

Campbell, Harry C. "Libraries in War, Peace and Revolution." *Canadian Library Journal* 46(1989): 223-224.

Dodds, T. "The Education of Refugees in Africa: The role of Distance and Open Learning." *Media in Education and Development* 211(1988): 39-43.

Iwuji, H. O. M. "Librarianship and Oral Tradition in Africa." *International Library Review* 21(1989): 201-207.

Khan, Reinhild. "Hunger and Überfluss: ein Literaturbericht zur Entwicklungspolitik" [Hunger and Abundance: A Literature Report on Policy toward Developing Countries]. *Buch und Bibliothek* 38(1986): 862-866+.

Mabomba, Rodrick S. "The Development of Librarianship in the Third World: A View from Africa." *Inspel* 21(1987): 181-207.

Mchombu, K. *User Studies: How to Identify Potential and Actual User Needs,* 1987. ERIC. ED 299 978.

Membrey, David. "The Ranfurly Library Service and the Textbooks for Africa Project." *African Research & Documentation* 46(1988): 40-46.

Ng'ang'a, J. M. *Information and Users: How to Bring them Together–the Intermediary Role of the Professional,* 1987. ERIC. ED 299 979.

Nwafor, B. U. "The Costs of Interlending and Document Supply." Paper read at the IFLA Pre-Session Seminar, 1989.

Tawete, Felix K. "The Challenge of Libraries in the Third World." *Libri* 38(1988): 330-339.

Villa, P. "IFLA's Core Programme on the Advancement of Librarianship in the Third World. 2—A Developed Country Librarian's Viewpoint." *Focus on International and Comparative Librarianship* 17(1986): 26-30.

Vol'pe, M. "Biblioteki mira ... Afrika" (Libraries of the World ... Africa). *Bibliotekar* 3(1986): 56-57.

Wijasuriya, D. E. K. "IFLA's Core Programme on the Advancement of Librarianship in the Third World: Orientation, Mechanisms and Priorities." *IFLA Journal* 14(1988): 324-333.

Pre-1980 Publications

Bonny, Harold V. "Notes on Library Development." *Library Association Record* 67(1965): 293-296.

De Benko, Eugene, guest editor. *Aspects of Rural Library and Information Service in Africa.* East Lansing, MI: African Studies Center, Michigan State University, 1978. (*Rural Africana,* New Series, No. 1, Spring 1978).

————. "On Rural Library and Information Service in English-speaking Africa." *Rural Africana,* 1(Spring 1978): 1-3.

Irmler, J. "Rural Libraries: A Comparative International Study." *International Library Review* 2(January 1970): 49-55.

Jessup, F. W. "Libraries and Adult Education." *Unesco Bulletin for Libraries* 27(1973): 306-315.

Lacy, D. M. "Library in the Underdeveloped Countries." *Catholic Library World* 38(1966): 229-237.

Lorenz, J. G. "Role of Libraries in Economic and Social Development." *Unesco Bulletin for Libraries* 16(1962): 226-233.

Mabomba, R. S. "The Role of Archives in National Information Transfer." *ECARBICA Journal* 4(1979): 21-28.

Nwikina, G. N. "Role of the Library in National Development." *West African Library Association News* 4(December 1961): 70-77.

Penna, C. V. "Interaction Between Education, Libraries and Mass Communication, as Seen by a Librarian: The Meeting of Experts on Education Integrated with Rural Development Organized by UNESCO in Lima (Peru), November 26-December 1, 1973." *Unesco Bulletin for Libraries* 28(1974): 311-314.

————. *Planning of Library and Documentation Services.* 2nd ed. Rev. and enl. by P. H. Sewell and Herman Liebaers. Paris: UNESCO, 1970.

Plumbe, W. J. "Africans Must Have More Books." *World Digest* (July 1948).

————. "Commonwealth Libraries and the Net Book Agreement." *The Bookseller* (August 31, 157).

————. "International Librarianship." *Northern Nigeria Library Notes* 1(May 1964).

————. "Libraries for Africans: A Fourfold Plan." *Crown Colonist* (December 1947).

————. "Libraries in British Tropical Africa." Paper presented at Weekend Conference of the London & Home Counties Branch of the Library Association, Eastbourne, October 1946.

————. "Preservation of Books and Periodicals in Arab Countries." Working Paper for Unesco Conference on Libraries and Documentation in the Arabic-speaking

States, Cairo, September 1962. An abbreviated version was published in *Book for Africa* 33(1963): 3. Published in Arabic as "Siyanat al-kutub wal-dauriyat fil'l-bilad al-Arabiyya." *'Alam al-maktabat* 5(1963): 1.

_____. *The Preservation of Books in Tropical & Subtropical Countries*. Kuala Lumpur: Oxford University Press, 1964.

_____. "Tropical Librarianship: Myth or Reality?" *BLATT: Bulletin of the Library Association of Trinidad and Tobago* (June 1962).

Reale, V. "Books by Air." *Unesco Bulletin for Libraries* 18(1964): 300-301.

"Recommendations Relating to School, Public, National, University, and Special Libraries." *International Library Review* 1(1969): 317-332.

SCAUL Newsletter. 1-6? Zaria, Nigeria, etc., Standing Conference of African University Libraries, 1965-71? W. J. Plumbe, first editor of the Newsletter, commented in a recent letter (March 21, 1990) that "While it lasted it was a mine of information mostly unavailable elsewhere but I believe it is now defunct." In a subsequent letter of May 22, 1990, Plumbe provided this history: He edited Nos. 1-5 while he was librarian at Ahmadu Bello University, Zaria, Nigeria; Nos. 1-3 were published at ABU, January 1965-December 1965; Nos. 4-5, edited by W.J.P. at ABU, were "printed, published and distributed by Harold Holdsworth, University College Library, Dar es Salaam, Tanzania, April 1967-March 1968;" No. 6 was edited by Patricia M. Larby and was published at the University of Nairobi, Kenya, in July 1971. Plumbe does not "know what became of the Newsletter after that." Concerning the Standing Conference he clarified for the compiler the seeming confusion of names: "The title of the *Newsletter*, or rather of SCAUL itself, went through a period of uncertainty in 1971. SCAUL was founded in September 1964 and designated 'Standing Committee on African University Libraries.' At a Conference of Librarians from Commonwealth Universities in Africa (not of SCAUL) held in Lusaka in August 1969 it was re-designated the 'Standing Conference of African University Librarians.' At a meeting of SCAUL held in Addis Ababa in February 1971 it was referred to as the 'Standing Conference of African University Libraries' and is its latest name as far as I know although it now has Eastern and Western branches and the parent body may have expired." The list of international meetings in *African Libraries* (pp. 262-266) seems to support the inference that SCAUL no longer exist.

Sharr, F. A. "Functions and Organization of a Rural Library System." *Unesco Bulletin for Libraries* 26(1972): 2-7.

Wainwright, G. "Libraries and Literacy." *Library World* 70(1968): 12-15.

Africa—Academic Libraries

Havard-Williams, P. "Research Libraries in Developing Countries: April, 1987." *Outlook on Research Libraries* 9,8(August 1987): 1.

Ifidon, S. E. *Essentials of Management for African University Libraries*. Lagos: Libriservice, 1985.

Nwafor, B. U. "Funding Third World University Libraries." Paper read in the University Libraries Section of IFLA, 1989.

Plumbe, W. J. "Climate as a Factor in the Planning of University Library Buildings." *Unesco Bulletin for Libraries* 17(1963): 6.

Priestly, Carol. "International Campus Book Link." *COMLA Newsletter* 64(June 1989).

Africa—Bibliographies and Bibliography

Anwar, Mumtaz A. *Information Services in Muslim Countries: An Annotated Bibliography of Expert Studies and Reports on Library, Information and Archive Services.* London: Mansell, 1985.

Bowen, D. N. "Learning Style Based Bibliographical Instruction." *International Library Review* 20(1988): 405-408.

Howell, John Bruce. "Creating a Standard List Online of Books on African Studies for Undergraduate Libraries and Keeping it Up-to-Date." In *Africana Resources and Collections,* ed. Julian W. Witherell, 108-117. Metuchen, NJ: Scarecrow Press, 1989.

Larby, Patricia M., ed. *New Directions in African Bibliography.* London: SCOLMA, 1988.

Polotovskaia, Inna L'vovna. "Natsional'naia bibliografiia v razvivaiushchikhsia stranakh tropicheskoi Afriki" [National Bibliography in the Developing Countries of Tropical Africa]. *Sovetskaiâ Bibliografiiâ* 3(1985): 81-93.

Scheven, Yvette. "Bibliographical Explorers of Africa." In *Africana Resources and Collections,* ed. Julian W. Witherell, 213-227. Metuchen, NJ: Scarecrow Press, 1989.

————. *Bibliographies for African Studies 1970-1986.* London: Hans Zell, Saur, 1988.

Schmidt, Nancy J. "Visualizing Africa: The Bibliography of Films by Sub-Saharan African Filmmakers." In *Africana Resources and Collections,* ed. Julian W. Witherell, 151-177. Metuchen, NJ: Scarecrow Press, 1989.

Sitzman, Glenn L. "Bibliography of Sub-Sahara African Librarianship, 1986-1987." *Advances in Library Administration and Organization* 8(1989): 253-292.

Pre-1980 Publications

Darch, C. and O. C. Mascarenhas. *The Africa Bibliographic Centre (ABC): Towards a Continental Bibliographic and Documentation System for Africa in the 21st Century.* Dar es Salaam, Tanzania: University of Dar es Salaam, 1976.

Guide to National Bibliographical Information Centres. Guide des centres nationaux d'informaton bibliographique. 3rd ed. Rev. and enl. Paris: Unesco, 1970.

McMahon, Susan E., comp. "Rural Library Service in Africa: A Partially Annotated Bibliography." *Rural Africana* 1(Spring 1978): 77-102.

Pantelidis, Veronica S. *The Arab World: Libraries and Librarianship, 1960-1976: A Bibliography.* London: Mansell, 1979.

Africa—Biographies of Librarians

Crossey, Moore. "Hans Panofsky: Biographical Notes and Bibliography." In *Africana Resources and Collections,* ed. Julian W. Witherell, 9-17. Metuchen, NJ: Scarecrow Press, 1989.

Demoz, Abraham. "Hans Panofsky: A Personal Reminiscence." In *Africana Resources and Collections,* ed. Julian W. Witherell, 1-8. Metuchen, NJ: Scarecrow Press, 1989.

Kirk-Greene, A. H. M. "Colonial Service Biographical Data: The Published Sources." *African Research & Documentation* 46(1988): 1-16.

Plumbe, W. J. "Douglas Harold Varley." *SCAUL Newsletter* 5(March 1968).

Africa—Book Trade, Printing, and Publishing

Lambe, Patrick. "Book Hunger in Africa and Worldwide: Recent Journal Articles." *Bulletin of the Association of British Theological and Philosophical Libraries* 2(1988): 14-15.

Montagnes, Ian. "Training Editors in the Third World." *Scholarly Publishing* 20(1989): 162-172.

Seusing, Ekkehart. "The Importance of Publications from Developing Countries and the Implications for Libraries in Industrialized Countries." *IFLA Journal* 15(1989): 118-127.

————. "Research on Development: The Importance of Publications from Developing Countries and the Implications for Libraries in Industrialized Countries." *Inspel* 23(1989): 23-36.

Woodson, Dorothy C. "'Pathos, Mirth, Murder, and Sweet Abandon': The Early Life and Times of *Drum.*" In *Africana Resources and Collections,* ed. Julian W. Witherell, 228-246. Metuchen, NJ: Scarecrow Press, 1989.

Zell, Hans. "African Books Collective: Promoting African Theological Books in Europe and North America." *Bulletin of the Association of British Theological and Philosophical Libraries* 2(1988): 11-13.

Pre-1980 Publications

Kotei, S. I. A. "Some Cultural and Social Factors of Book Reading and Publishing in Africa." Paper presented in Africa: A Dialogue for the Seventies, an International Conference, University of Ife, Ile-Ife, Nigeria, December 16-20, 1973.

Oyeoku, Kalu K. "Publishing in Africa: Breaking the Developing Barrier." Paper presented at Publishing in Africa: A Dialogue for the Seventies, an International Conference, University of Ife, Ile-Ife, Nigeria, December 16-20, 1973.

Africa—Cataloging and Classification

Byrum, John D. and Benny R. Tucker. "Report from the ALA/RTSD Committee on Cataloging: Asian and African Materials." *Library of Congress Information Bulletin* 48(1989): 6-7.

Ejiko, Emmanuel O. "Problems of Classification of African Materials Using the Library of Congress Classification Scheme." *Library Focus* 3(1985): 23-49.

Iwuji, H. O. M. "Africana in LC and DD Classification Schemes: A Need for an Africana Scheme?" *Journal of Librarianship* 21(1989): 1-18.

Pacey, Philip. "The Classification of Literature in the Dewey Decimal Classification: The Primacy of Languagse and the Taint of Colonialism." *Cataloging and Classification Quarterly* 9(1989): 101-107.

Widenmann, Elizabeth A. "Recent Developments in Africana Cataloging in the United States (1973-1988)." In *Africana Resources and Collections,* ed. Julian W. Witherell, 39-61. Metuchen, NJ: Scarecrow Press, 1989.

Pre-1980 Publications

Plumbe, W. J. "Another Appraisal of the Stripdex Catalogue." *Library Review* 21(1968): 5.

─────────. "The Stripdex Catalogue." *Library Association Record* (April 1962),

Africa—Documentation and Information Science

Abate, Dejen. "Libraries and Information Services in a Changing World: The Challenges African Information Services Face at the End of the 1980s." In *IFLA General Conference, 1987: Papers, Division of Regional Activities,* 1987. ERIC. ED 300 007.

Ayala, D. "Boolean Operations Between Solids and Surfaces by Octrees: Models and Algorithm." *Computer Aided Design* 20(1988): 452-465.

Azubuike, Abraham A. "The Computer as Mask: A Problem of Inadequate Human Interaction Examined with Particular Regard to Online Public Access Catalogues." *Journal of Information Science* 14(1988): 275-283.

Bock, G. and Lutz Hüttemann, eds. *Curriculum Adjustments in Information Studies Training Programmes in Africa.* Bonn: German Foundation for International Development, 1987.

Chu, Clara M. and Isola Y. Ajiferuke. "Quality of Indexing in Library and Information Science Databases." *Online Review* 13(1989): 11-35. Focuses on *Library Literature, Library and Information Science Abstracts,* and *Information Science Abstracts.*

"ILCA [International Livestock Centre for Africa] Develops New Database." *Quarterly Bulletin of the International Association of Agricultural Librarians and Documentalists* 33(1988): 139-140.

Kibirige, Harry M. "Development of Information Science [in Developing Countries]." *International Library Review* 21(1989): 157-163.

─────────. *Local Area Networks in Information Management.* Westport, CT: Greenwood Press, 1989.

Massil, S. W. "The Place for Automation in Libraries in Developing Countries." *Journal of Library and Information Science* 11(1986): 38-44.

Morgan, R. M. "Instructional Systems Developing in Third World Countries." *Educational Technology Research and Development* 37(1989): 47-56.

Ouiminga, Ali Krissiamba. "Pour changer la situation documentaire au Sahel" [Changing the Documentation Situation in the Sahel]. *Documentaliste* 24(1987): 230-235.

Owolabi, O. "An Efficient Graph Approach to Matching Chemical Structures." *Journal of Chemical Information and Computer Sciences* 28(1988): 221-225.

Páez-Urdaneta, Iraset. "Information in the Third World." *International Library Review* 21(1989): 177-191.

Vieria, L. C. "Technology for Africa." *Journal of Educational Technology Systems* 17(1988): 103-106.

Pre-1980 Publications

Abedeji, Adebayo. "Requirements of a Numerical and Non-numerical Information and Documentation System (and Network) in Africa." In *Report: Consultative Meeting on Information Needs,* prepared by Francis K. Inganji and T. Moeller, 35-39. Nairobi: Coordinating Centre for Regional Information Training (CRIT), 1979.

Amoa, Kwame. "Some Aspects of the Problem of Information Requirements for Development Planning in Africa." In *Report: Consultative Meeting on Information Needs,* prepared by Francis K. Inganji and T. Moeller, 54-59. Nairobi: Coordinating Centre for Regional Information Training (CRIT), 1979.

Bujra, Abdalla S. "Meeting on Setting up Networks of African Research Institutes on Research Information, Dakar, 1-3 December, 1978." In *Report: Consultative Meeting on Information Needs,* prepared by Francis K. Inganji and T. Moeller, 46-51. Nairobi: Coordinating Centre for Regional Information Training (CRIT), 1979.

Chisupa, R. "National Requirements for Information." In *Report: Consultative Meeting on Information Training (CRIT),* 1979.

Lazar, P. 'Considerations on the Organization and Development of the National Information System in Developing Countries." *Library Herald* 11(1969): 32-43.

Samarasinghe, L. E. "African Data Bank Project—Some Points in Discussion." In *Report: Consultative Meeting on Information Needs,* prepared by Francis K. Inganji and T. Moeller, 42-45. Nairobi: Coordinating Centre for Regional Information Training (CRIT), 1979.

Sidman, Michael. *Documentation Project: Design of an Information Network for PAID [Panafrican Institute for Development] and its Environment.* Panafrican Institute for Development, Central Service for Programmes Support, 1979.

Symposium on Documentation Planning in Developing Countries at Bad Godesberg, 28-30 November 1967. Bonn: German Foundation for Developing Countries, Central Documentation, 1967.

Zaher, Celia. "The Role of Unesco in the Development of Documentation." In *Development of Documentation and Information Networks in East Africa,* 124-135. Bonn: German Foundation for International Development, 1974.

Africa—Library Education and Training

Aina, L. O. "Continuing Education Programmes and the Role of Library Schools in English Speaking Africa." *Training and Education* 6, 2(1989): 43-52.

————. "Education and Training of Librarians for Agricultural Information Work in Africa." *Quarterly Bulletin of the International Association of Agricultural Librarians and Documentlists* 34(1989): 23-25.

Hüttemann, Lutz, ed. *Librarianship and Documentation Studies: Handbook of Teaching and Learning Materials,* 3 volumes. Bonn: German Foundation for International Development, 1985-1987.

Kitambala, Dwan'Essa. "La formation du bibliothécaire africain: réalité acutelle et orientation future" [The Education of the African Librarian: Present Reality and Future Orientation]. In *Théorie et Pratique dans l'enseignement de sciences de l'information,* 61-76. Université de Montréal, Ecole de Bibliothéconomie et des Sciences d l'Information, 1988.

Pre-1980 Publications

Abidi, S. A. H. "Designing a Curriculum for the Training through Refresher Courses of Qualified Library Assistants Working in Special Libraries—'Technical Services'." In *Designing a Curriculum for the Training Through Refresher Courses of Qualified Library Assistants ... Kenya Library Association,* 54-58. Nairobi: Kenya National Academy for the Advancement of Arts and Sciences, 1978.

Bone, Larry Earl. *International Conference on Education for Librarianship, 1967, University of Illinois, Library Education: An International Survey.* Champaign-Urbana: University of Illinois, 1968.

Dean, John. *Planning Library Education Programmes: A Study of the Problems Involved in the Management and Operation of Library Schools in the Developing Countries.* London: Deutsch, 1972.

Inter-University Council for Higher Education Overseas Manpower and Training Committee. "Report of the Working Party on the Training of Library Staff of Overseas Universities." Not published.

Larsen, Knud. "UNESCO Course in Librarianship." *Unesco Bulletin for Libraries* 21(1967): 177-181.

"Leaders or Workers? Library Education in Africa." In *World Trends in Library Education,* ed. G. Bramley, 137-150. Shoe String: Bingley Co., 1975.

"Library Education Policy for the Developing Countries." *Unesco Bulletin for Libraries* 22(1968): 173-188.

Obi, Dorothy S. "Education for Rural Library Service in Africa." *Rural Africana* 1(Spring 1978): 65-75.

Sabor, J. E. "International Cooperation in the Training of Librarians." *Unesco Bulletin for Libraries* 19(1965): 285-290.

————. *Methods of Teaching Librarianship: With an Introductory Study by Richard Nassif.* Paris: UNESCO, 1968.

Thairu, R. Wanja. "Designing a Curriculum for In-service Training of Certified Library Assistants Working in Special Libraries: Suggestions for Technical Services." In *Designing a Curriculum for the Training through Refresher Courses of Qualified Library Assistants ... Kenya Library Association,* 42, 43-53. Nairobi: Coordinating Centre for Regional Information Training (CRIT), 1978.

264   GLENN L. SITZMAN

Africa—Public Libraries

Doust, Robin W. "For Fees." *Unabashed Librarian* 69(1988): 5.
Miyabe, Yoriko. "A Study of Unesco's Activities for the Development of Public
    Libraries in the Developing Countries: The Program in Asia and Africa During
    the First Twenty Years, 1946-1966." *Annals of Japan Society of Library Science*
    34(1988): 49-59. (In Japanese)

Pre-1980 Publications

Chandler, George. "Public Libraries in Development." *International Library Review*
    6(March 1974): 231-235.
International Federation of Library Associations, Public Libraries Section. "UNESCO
    Public Library Manifesto." *Unesco Bulletin for Libraries* 26(1972): 129-131.
Kunz, F. "Die Fahrbibliothek, international gesehen" [Bookmobile from an
    International Point of View]. *Bibliothekar* 19(1965): 1219-1223.
Weimar, V. "Fahrbüchereien auf dem Land, gestern-heute-morgen" [Bookmobiles in
    Rural Regions, Yesterday, Today, Tomorrow]. *Bücherei und Bild* 18(1966): 73-
    77.

Africa—School and Children's Library Services and Literature

Bryan, Ashley. "A Tender Bridge: Readings from Black American Poets, African Folk
    Tales, and Black American Spirituals." In *Pacific Rim Conference on Children's
    Literature* (Third Annual, 1986, University of California at Los Angeles). *A Sea
    of Upturned Faces,* 149-150. Metuchen, NJ: Scarecrow Press, 1989.
Hagen, Inger E. "Barn og litteratur i Afrika" [Children and Literature in Africa]. *Bok
    og Bibliotek* 54(1987): 293.
Ojiambo, Joseph B. "School Library Services in Sub-Saharan Africa." *International
    Review of Children's Literature and Librarianship* 3(1988): 143-155.
Shepherd, J. "Working with Children in a Rural Library." *Library World* 68(1967):
    302-304.
Touchard, W. *Developing African Secondary School Libraries,* 1988. ERIC. ED 297
    781.

Africa—Special Libraries, Services, and Subjects

Abila, B. "Drug Discovery: Need to Explore African Phytoresources." *Drug
    Information Journal* 23(1989): 335-337.
Ali, S. Nazim. "Acquisition of Scientific Literature in Developing Countries."
    Information Development 5(1989): 73-115.
————. "Science and Technology Information Transfer in Developing Countries: Some
    Problems and Suggestions." *Journal of Information Science* 15(1989): 81-93.
Bellamy, Margot. "Bridging the Information Gap in African Agriculture: CABI's
    African Agricultural Literature Service." *Interlending & Document Supply*
    16(1988): 46-50.

Cooney, S. et al. "Information for Agricultural Development: The Role of Literature Services." *Quarterly Bulletin of the International Association of Agricultural Librarians and Documentalists* 33(1988): 79-86.

Kaniki, A. M. "Agricultural Information Services in Less Developed Countries." *International Library Review* 20(1988): 321-336.

Mount, S. D. "Evolutions in Exhibition Catalogues of African Art." *Art Libraries Journal* 13(1988): 14-19.

Mwalimu, Charles. "A Bibliographic Essay Selected Secondary Sources on the Common Law and Customary Law of English-speaking Sub-Saharan Africa." *Law Library Journal* 80(1988): 241-289.

Schmidt, Nancy J. "Visualizing Africa: The Bibliography of Films by Sub-Saharan African Filmmakers." In *African Resources and Collections,* ed. Julian W. Witherell, 151-177. Metuchen, NJ: Scarecrow Press, 1989.

Tabor, R. B. "Integrated Health Care." *Information Service & Use* 8(1988): 13-21.

Tibenderana, P. K. G. "The Role of Audio-visual Media in Solving Some of the Current Problems in Education." *Library Focus* 3(1985): 62-69.

Africana

Barringer, Terry. "Workshop on Photographs as Sources for African History: School of Oriental and African Studies, University of London, 1213 May 1988." *African Research & Documentation* 47(1988): 33-34.

De Benko, Eugene and Patricia L. Butts. *Research Sources for African Studies.* East Lansing, MI: African Studies Center, Michigan State University, 1969.

Easterbrook, David L. "The Archives-Libraries Committee and the Cooperative Africana Microform Project: A Brief History." In *Africana Resources and Collections,* ed. Julian W. Witherell, 18-38. Metuchen, NJ: Scarecrow Press, 1989.

Henige, David. "The Half Life of African Archives." In *Africana Resources and Collections,* ed. Julian W. Witherell, 198-212. Metuchen, NJ: Scarecrow Press, 1989.

Henn, Barbara J. "Securing Asian and African Materials for Library Collections: Practical Advice and Considerations." *Technical Services Quarterly* 5(1988): 41-48.

Howell, John Bruce. "Creating a Standard List Online of Books on African Studies for Undergraduate Libraries and Keeping it Up-to-Date." In *Africana Resources and Collections,* ed. Julian W. Witherell, 178-197. Metuchen, NJ: Scarecrow Press, 1989.

McIlwane, I. C. "The Subject Organisation of Materials on Africa: An overview of Recent Work." *African Research & Documentation* 46(1988): 17-30.

Rowse, Dorothea E. "The Creation of a Book Selection Policy, with Special Reference to African Materials." *Mousaion* 6(1988): 47-56.

Scheven, Yvette. *Bibliographies for African Studies 1970-1986.* London: Hans Zell, Saur, 1988.

Stanley, Janet L. "Documenting African Material Culture." In *Africana Resources and Collections,* ed. Julian W. Witherell, 118-150. Metuchen, NJ: Scarecrow Press, 1989.

Walsh, Gretchen. "African Language Materials: Challenges and Responsibilities in Collection Management." In *Africana Resources and Collections,* ed. Julian W. Witherell, 77-107. Metuchen, NJ: Scarecrow Press, 1989.

Witherell, Julian W., ed. *Africana Resources and Collections: Three Decades of Development and Achievement: A Festschrift in Honor of Hans Panofsky.* Metuchen, NJ: Scarecrow Press, 1989.

Africana—Africana Collections Outside the Sub-Sahara

Datta, Ann. "Beasts, Birds and Bees: Visual Resources for Africa in the Libraries of the British Museum (Natural History)." *African Research & Documentation* 48(1988): 1-22.

Frewer, Louis B. "Resources for African Studies in Rhodes House Library, Oxford." *SCAUL Newsletter* 5(March 1968).

Gray, Beverly A. "Africana Acquisitions at the Library of Congress." In *Africana Resources and Collections,* ed. Julian W. Witherell, 62-76. Metuchen, NJ: Scarecrow Press, 1989.

Africana—Africana for Children

"A Is for Africa." *The School Librarian's Workshop* 9(1989): 1-3.

Inter-Regional and Regional

Information Trends—News Magazine: Review of Developments in Information Studies in the Eastern and Southern African Region. Volume 1—. Bonn, Gabarone: German Foundation for International Development and University of Botswana, 1988—.

Inganji, F. K. *Status of Information and Documentation Services in Eastern and Southern Africa and Future Prospects.* Bonn, FRG: German Foundation for International Development, 1983.

Peters, Heidrun, ed. *Library Training in Eastern, Central and Southern Africa: A Reader; Berlin (West), 1-9 September 1982.* Bonn: German Foundation for International Development, 1983.

Inter-Regional and Regional—Eastern Africa

Hüttemann, Lutz, ed. *Budgeting and Financial Planning: Papers and Proceedings of the Information Experts Meeting; Arusha, 23-27 May 1983.* Bonn: German Foundation for International Development, 1983.

Pre-1980 Publications

Mukwato, L. E. "The Role of Libraries in Adult Education." Paper presented to the Standing Conference of East African Libraries, 1974.

Tambwe, Assia. "New Trends in Librarianship in the East African Community." In *Implementation of Modern Documentation*, ed. Soud Timami, 11-12. Nairobi, Kenya: Coordinating Centre for Regional Information Training (CRIT), 1976.

Inter-Regional and Regional—Eastern Africa—Bibliographies and Bibliography

Abidi, S. A. H. "Libraries and Librarianship in East Africa: A Select Bibliography." *EASL* (*East African School of Librarianship*) *Bulletin* 1, 2(1983).

Mwasha, A. Z. *Librarianship in East Africa: A Selected Bibliography.* Dar es Salaam: National Central Library, 1977.

Inter-Regional and Regional—Eastern Africa—Documentation and Information Science

Hüttemann, Lutz and F. K. Inganji, eds. *Use of Computers in information Handling, Training Workshop, Nairobi, 21 April-2 May, 1986.* Bonn, Addis Ababa: German Foundation for International Development and Pan-African Documentation and Information System, 1986.

Musana, Augustes, ed. *The Impact of DSE/ESAMI* [*Deutsche Stiftung für Internationale Entwicklung/Eastern and Southern African Management Institute*] *Training Programmes. Course Report: Arusha, 21-25 October 1985.* Bonn: German Foundation for International Development and Eastern and Southern African Management Institute, 1985.

Musana, Augustes and Lutz Hüttemann, eds. *Trade Information Services, Seminar Papers: Arusha, 22 April-3 May, 1985 and 24 Oct.-4 Nov. 1988.* 2nd extended ed. Bonn, Arusha: German Foundation for International Development and Eastern and Southern African Management Institute, 1988.

Pre-1980 Publications

Arntz, Helmut. "Possibilities of Improving Documentation Services in East Africa." In *Development of Documentation and Information Networks in East Africa*, 82-92. Bonn: German Foundation for International Development, 1974.

Chimulu, Foster et al. "Design of an Abstracting Service: Final Report [of] Working Group B." In *Implementation of Modern Documentation*, ed. Soud Timami, 129-160. Nairobi, Kenya: Coordinating Centre for Regional Information Training (CRIT), 1976.

Chisupa, R. "Documentation and Information—an Important Asset to the Development of East African Region." In *Development of Documentationn and Information Networks in East Africa*, 56-62. Bonn: German Foundation for International Development, 1974.

Dadzie, E. W. K. "Activities in Africa and International Cooperation in Documentation." In *Development of Documentation and Information Networks in East Africa*, 63-71. Bonn: German Foundation for International Development, 1974.

Deressa, Makonen. "The Role of EDP (Electronic Data Processing) Service in Documentation in East Africa: Panel Discussion; Notes." In *Implementation of Modern Documentation,* ed. Soud Timami, 73-75. Nairobi, Kenya: Coordinating Centre for Information Training (CRIT), 1976.

Gebremedhin, Mehret. "Notes on a Discussion of Aspects of National Information Policy." In *Implementation of Modern Documentation,* ed. Soud Timami, 86. Nairobi, Kenya: Coordinating Centre for Regional Information Training (CRIT), 1976.

Jumba-Masagazi, A. H. K. "Co-ordinate Report of the Working Groups." In *Development of Documentation and Information Networks in East Africa,* 150. Bonn: German Foundation for International Development, 1974.

_____. "Documentation and Information an Important Asset for the Development of the Eastern African Region." In *Development of Documentation and Information Networks in East Africa,* 39-55. Bonn: German Foundation for International Development, 1974.

Lwanga, T. K. "Analytical Comments on County Reports." In *Development of Documentation and Information Networks in East Africa,* 99-102. Bonn: German Foundation for International Development, 1974.

_____. "New Trends in Librarianship—Relevant to Eastern Africa." In *Implementation of Modern Documentation Proceedings,* ed. Soud Timami, 4-7. Nairobi, Kenya: Coordinating Centre for Regional Information Training (CRIT), 1976.

_____. "A Proposal for the Basic Structural Organization of Documentation and Library Services in East Africa." In *Development of Documentation and Information Networks in East Africa,* 72-81. Bonn: German Foundation for International Development, 1974.

Nagarajan, K. S. "The Role of International Organisations in East Africa (Thesis Paper)." In *Implementation of Modern Documentation,* ed. Soud Timami, 101-102. Nairobi, Kenya: Coordinating Centre for Regional Information Training (CRIT), 1976.

Ng'ang'a, James. "Open Forum: The Role of International Organisations in East Africa. Notes." In *Implementation of Modern Documentation,* ed. Soud Timami, 104-105. Nairobi, Kenya: Coordinating Centre for Regional Information Training (CRIT), 1976.

Ochola, Francis W. "National Information Centres or NATIS. Notes on the Discussion." In *Implementation of Modern Documentation,* ed. Soud Timami, 90. Nairobi, Kenya: Coordinating Centre for Regional Information Training (CRIT), 1976.

Tocatlian, Jacques. "Organizational Structure in East Africa in the Framework of the UNISIST Programme." In *Development of Documentation and Information Networks in East Africa,* 136-149. Bonn: German Foundation for International Development, 1974.

Wersig, Gernot. "Documentation and Librarianship in East Africa (Thesis Paper)." In *Implementation of Modern Documentation,* ed. Soud Timami, 3. Nairobi, Kenya: Coordinating Centre for Regional Information Training (CRIT), 1976.

————. "The Role of EDP (Electronic Data Processing) in Documentation in East Africa (Thesis Paper)." In *Implementation of Modern Documentation,* ed. Soud Timami, 71-72. Nairobi, Kenya: Coordinating Centre for Regional Information Training (CRIT), 1976.

————. "The Role of International Organizations in Eastern Africa (Thesis Paper)." In *Implementation of Modern Documentation,* ed. Soud Timami, 103. Nairobi, Kenya: Coordinating Centre for Regional Information Training (CRIT), 1976.

Inter-Regional and Regional—Eastern Africa—Library Education

Mukwato, L. E. "Training of Librarians in East Africa: A Talk to the Zambia Library Association." *Zambia Library Association Journal* 1(1969): 11-18. Published also in *International Journal of Special Libraries (INSPEL)* 4(1969): 91-96.

Inter-Regional and Regional—Eastern Africa—School Libraries

Otike, Japhet N. "The Information Professional's Place in a School Community: A Challenge to the East African States." *School Library Media Quarterly* 17(1989): 78-81.

Inter-Regional and Regional—Southern Africa

Handbook of Southern African Libraries. Pretoria, South Africa: The State Library, 1970.

Inter-Regional and Regional—West Africa

Banjo, A. O. *Social Science Libraries in West Africa: A Directory.* Lagos: Nigerian Institute of International Affairs, 1987.

Sheriff, G. M. *Resource Sharing in West Africa: Some Implications for the Development of National Information Policies,* 1977. ERIC. ED 176 764.

Inter-Regional and Regional—West Africa—Bibliographies and Bibliography

Davies, Helen. *Libraries in West Africa: A Bibliography.* 3rd ed. Oxford: Hans Zell; Munich: K. G. Saur, 1982.

International Meetings

1964. Salisbury, Rhodesia, Leverhulme Conference on University Libraries in Tropical Africa.

Plumbe, Wilfred J. "Leverhulme Conference on University Libraries in Tropical Africa." *Northern Nigeria Library Notes* 2 & 3(October 1964/January 1965).

1972. Kumasi, Ghana, International Workshop on Development and Dissemination of Appropriate Technologies in Rural Areas.

International Workshop on Development and Dissemination of Appropriate Technologies in Rural Areas, Kumasi, Ghana, 1972. *Workshop Report.* Berlin: German Foundation for Developing Countries, Seminar Centre for Economic and Social Development, 1972.

1973. Nairobi, Kenya, International Conference on Development of Documentation and Information Networks in East Africa.

Development of Documentation and Information Networks in East Africa, Nairobi, 24th July-1st August 1973. Bonn: German Foundation for International Development, 1974.

1974. Dakar, Senegal, Conference on the Harmonization of Librarianship Training Programmes in Africa.

Conference on the Harmonization of Librarianship Training Programmes in Africa, Dakar, Senegal, 25-27 February 1974. *Preliminary Report of the Rapporteurs.* Dakar: University of Dakar School of Librarians, Archivists, and Documentalists and UNESCO, 1974. (mimeographed)

1976. Brazzaville, Congo, Meeting of Experts on Planning Documentation and Library Networks in Africa.

Chateh, Peter Nkangafack. *Rapport de la réunion d'experts sur la planification des réseaux de services de documentation en Afrique (NATIS) tenue à Brazzaville, République Populaire du Congo du 5-10 juillet 1976* [Report of the Meeting of Experts on Planning Documentation and Library Networks in Africa (NATIS)]. Présenté et complété par Peter Nkangafack. Yaoundé, 1976.

1976. Karen-Nairobi, Kenya, Training Centers on the Implementation of Modern Documentation.

Implementation of Modern Documentation. Proceedings [of the] Training Course Held in Karen-Nairobi, February 9-March 13, 1976, Sponsored by Unesco, ed. Soud Timami. Nairobi, Kenya: Coordinating Centre for Regional Information Training (CRIT), 1976.

1978. Nairobi, Kenya, Standing Conference of Eastern, Central and Southern African Librarians.

Designing a Curriculum for the Training through Refresher Courses of Qualified Library Assistants Working in Special Libraries: Proceedings of the Pre-Conference Workshop of the Third Standing Conference of Eastern, Central and Southern African Libraries, Held at Kenya Science Teachers College, Nairobi, Kenya, August 20th to 26, 1978, in Co-operation with Kenya Library Association. Nairobi: Coordinating Centre for Regional Information Training, 1978.

Standing Conference of Eastern, Central and Southern African Librarians (SCECSAL) [*Pre-Conference*] *Workshop Document[s].* Nairobi: Kenya Library Association, 1978. (No. 1-8 in 10 parts)

1979. Nairobi, Kenya, Consultative Meeting on Information Needs for Development, Planning and Investment Agencies in Africa.

Report: Consultative Meeting on Information Needs for Development, Planning and Investment Agencies in Africa, Nairobi, Kenya, April 9-13, 1979, prepared by Francis K. Inganji and T. Moeller. Nairobi: Coordinating Centre for Regional Information Training (CRIT), 1979.

1982. Paris, France, International Congress on the Universal Availability of Publications.

Mabomba, R. S. "International Congress on the Universal Availability of Publications, Paris, 3-7 May, 1982: A Report." *MALA Bulletin* 3, 1(1982).

1984. Nairobi, Kenya, General Conference of the International Federation of Library Associations (IFLA).

Pereslegina, Engel'sina Viktorovna. "Itogi 50-i sessii IFLA" (Summary of the 50th IFLA Session). *Sovetskaia Bibliografia* 2(1985): 91-95.

1989. Tananarive, Madagascar, African Standing Conference on Bibliographic Control (ASCOBIC).

M'baye, Saliou. "7th ASCOBIC Seminar in Madagascar." *International Cataloguing and Bibliographic Control* 18(1989): 15-16.

Individual Countries

Angola

Eremina, Z. S. "I Sovetsko-Angol'skii seminar na bibliotechnomu delu na temu 'Massovaya biblioteka i eé sotsial' nye funktsii' (Moskva 4-12 cent. 1986 g.)" [1st Soviet-Angolan Library Seminar on the Topic "The Public Library and its Functions" (Moscow, 4-12 Sept. 1986)]. *Bibliotekovedenie i Bibliografia za Rubezhom* 113(1987): 63-65.

Martin, Phyllis M. *Historical Dictionary of Angola.* Metuchen, NJ: Scarecow Press, 1980.

Benin

Decalo, Samuel. *Historical Dictionary of Benin.* 2nd ed. Metuchen, NJ: Scarecrow Press, 1987.

Marshall, M. R. "Libraries in Dahomey." *Library World* 72(1971): 208-211.

Botswana

Boadi, B. Y., F. Gibbons, K. J. Mchombu, and J. R. Neill. *Introduction to Librarianship and Documentation: Four Teaching and Learning Modules Used During Training Courses at the University of Botswana from 1984 to 1987.* 2nd ed. Bonn, Gaberone: German Foundation for International Development and University of Botswana, 1988.

Breutner, Claus. "The NIR (National Institute of Development and Cultural Research) Documentation Unit, Organisation, Tasks and Contributions to National Development." In *Report on Use of Information ... Gaberone, 1-5 Sept. 1980,* ed. Francis Inganji, 17-25. Gaberone: University College of Botswana, 1981.

Gessesse, Kebede. "Agricultural Library and Information Development in Botswana: A Profile." *Quarterly Bulletin of the International Association of Agricultural Librarians and Documentalists* 33(1988): 117-119.

Hüttemann, Lutz, ed. *Establishment and Management of a National Information Service in Botswana, Workshop Papers: Gaberone, 23-27 February 1987.* Bonn, Gaberone: German Foundation for International Development and Botswana National Library Service, 1987.

Morton, Fred, Andrew Murray, and Jeff Ramsay. *Historical Dictionary of Botswana.* New ed. Metuchen, NJ: Scarecrow Press, 1989.

Neil, J. R. and S. I. A. Kotei. "Towards a National Information System for Botswana." In *Report on Use of Information ... Gaberone, 1-5 Sept. 1980,* ed. Francis Inganji, 36-53. Gaberone: University College of Botswana, 1981.

Raseroka, Helen Kay. "Library Instruction at the University of Botswana: Perspectives and Issues." *Bookmark* 46(1987): 65-68.

Report on Use of Information and Documentation for Planning and Decision Making: A Seminar Held by NIR (National Institute of Development and Cultural Research) and the German Foundation for International Development (DSE), Gaberone, 1-5 Sept. 1980, ed. Francis Inganji. Gaberone: University College of Botwsana, 1981.

Shio, Martin J. "Management of Information in Government." In *Report on Use of Information ... Gaberone, 1-5 Sept. 1980,* ed. Francis Inganji, 26-35. Gaberone: University College of Botswana, 1981.

————. "The Use of Information for Planning and Decision Making." In *Report on Use of Information ... Gaberone, 1-5 Sept. 1980,* ed. Francis Inganji, 8-16. Gaberone: University College of Botswana, 1981.

Sturges, Paul. "International Transfer of Information and National Self-sufficiency: The Case of Botswana." In *ASIS '86: Proceedings of the 49th ASIS Annual Meeting,* eds. Julie M. Hurd and Charles H. Davis, 23: 320-325. Medford, NJ: Learned Information Inc. for the American Society for Information Science, 1986.

Tlou, T. "Opening Speech: Seminar on the Use of Information and Documentation for Planning and Decision-Making." In *Report on Use of Information ... Gaberone, 1-5 Sept. 1980,* ed. Francis Inganji, 3-6. Gaberone: University College of Botswana, 1981.

Burkina Faso

McFarland, Daniel M. *Historical Dictionary of Upper Volta.* Metuchen, NJ: Scarecrow Press, 1978.

Cameroon

Chateh, P. N. "Appropriate Technologies for Libraries in Developing Countries." *Information Technology for Development* 4(1989): 41-52.

Levine, Victor T. and Roger P. Nye. *Historical Dictionary of Cameroon.* Metuchen, NJ: Scarecrow Press, 1974.

Cape Verde

Lobban, Richard and Marilyn Halter. *Historical Dictionary of the Republic of Cape Verde.* 2nd ed. Metuchen, NJ: Scarecrow Press, 1988.

Central African Republic

Kalck, Pierre. *Historical Dictionary of Central African Republic.* Metuchen, NJ: Scarecrow Press, 1980.

Chad

Decalo, Samuel. *Historical Dictionary of Chad.* 2nd ed. Metuchen, NJ: Scarecrow Press, 1987.

Comoros

Lefebvre, Michel. "Documentation et bibliothèques aux Comores" [Documentation and Libraries in the Comoros]. *Argus* 17(1988): 76-85.

Congo (People's Republic)

Danset, F. "Public Reading in French-speaking Africa." *International Library Review* 21(1989): 245-248. (Focus on Mali, Ivory Coast, Congo)

Thompson, Virginia and Richard Adloff. *Historical Dictionary of the People's Republic of the Congo.* 2nd ed. Metuchen, NJ: Scarecrow Press, 1984.

Equatorial Guinea

Liniger-Goumaz, Max. *Historical Dictionary of Equatorial Guinea.* 2nd ed. Metuchen, NJ: Scarecrow Press, 1988.

Ethiopia

Gebremedhin, Mehret. "New Trends in Librarianship in Ethiopia." In *Implementation of Modern Documentation,* Soud Timami, 13. Nairobi, Kenya: Coordinating Centre for Regional Information Training (CRIT), 1976.

Pankhurst, Rita. "Libraries in Post-revolutionary Ethiopia." *Information Development* 4(1988): 239-245.

————. "Library Provision in Post-revolution Ethiopia." *Focus on International & Comparative Librarianship* 19(1988): 15-16.

Prouty, Chris and Eugene Rosenfeld. *Historical Dictionary of Ethiopia.* Metuchen, NJ: Scarecrow Press, 1981.

Gabon

Gardinier, David E. *Historical Dictionary of Gabon.* Metuchen, NJ: Scarecrow Press, 1981.

Gambia

Freeman, Mike. "AAL Aid to The Gambia." *Focus on International & Comparative Librarianship* 19(1988): 27-28.
_____. "A Toubab in West Africa (or Bounding through The Gambia)." *Assistant Librarian* 81(1988): 189-191.
Gailey, Harry A. *Historical Dictionary of The Gambia.* 2nd ed. Metuchen, NJ: Scarecrow Press, 1987.
Harris, Gill. "Branch and Mobile Libraries in The Gambia." *COMLA Newsletter* 64(1989): 6-7. (First published in *Service Point* 41(1989): 14-17.)

Ghana

Alemna, A. A. "Libraries and the Economic Development of Ghana." *Aslib Proceedings* 41(1989): 119-125.
_____. "Management of Libraries in Ghana: Concepts, Practices and Constraints." *Aslib Proceedings* 41(1989): 217-223.
De Heer, A. N. "Rural Library Services in Ghana." *Rural Africana* 1(Spring 1978): 5-19.
McFarland, Daniel Miles. *Historical Dictionary of Ghana.* Metuchen, NJ: Scarecrow Press, 1985.
Osei-Bonsu, M. "Some Aspects of Library Development in Ghana, 1750-1964." *Libri* 38(1988): 221-226.

Ghana—Library Education

"Library Training in Ghana." *Unesco Bulletin for Libraries* 20(1966): 326.

Ghana—Special Libraries

Alemna, A. A. "Special Libraries in Ghana: An Appraisal." *Aslib Proceedings* 41(1989): 23-28.
Udofia, Callix. "Content and Situational Relevance of Agricultural News in the *Ghanian Times* and the *Daily Times* (Lagos)." *Rural Africana* 1(Spring 1978): 51-64.

Guinea

O'Toole, Thomas E. *Historical Dictionary of Guinea (Republic of Guinea/Conakry).* 2nd ed. Metuchen, NJ: Scarecrow Pres, 1987.

Guinea-Bissau

Lobban, Richard and Joshua Forrest. *Historical Dictionary of the Republic of Guinea-Bissau.* 2nd ed. Metuchen, NJ: Scarecrow Press, 1988.

Ivory Coast

Danset, F. "Public Reading in French-speaking Africa." *International Library Journal* 21(1989): 245-248. (Focus on Mali, Ivory Coast and the Congo). Mundt, Robert J. *Historical Dictionary of the Ivory Coast.* Metuchen, NJ: Scarecrow Press, 1987.

Kenya

De Graft-Johnson, K. E. et al. "Library Automation in Support of Training and Operations Research Activities at the Centre for African Family Studies, Nairobi, Kenya." *Library Software Review* 7(1988): 318-324.

Otike, Japhet N. "Indigenous Materials in Libraries and Information Centres in Kenya." *Collection Management* 11(1989): 199-215.

_____. "Library Cooperation in Kenya." *Journal of Librarianship* 21(1989): 36-48.

Pre-1980 Publications

Ndegwa, J. "Documentation Centres and Libraries in Kenya." In *Development of Documentation and Information Networks in East Africa,* 103-110. Bonn: German Foundation for International Development, 1974.

Pfukani, Bilha. "New Trends in Librarianship in Kenya." In *Implementation of Modern Documentation,* ed. Soud Timami, 14-15. Nairobi, Kenya: Coordinting Centre for Regional Information Training (CRIT), 1976.

Kenya—Bibliographies and Bibliography

Maina, Patrick M. "Kenya Librarianship Index, 1969-1980." *Nairobi University Library Magazine* 3(1980): 69-96.

Otike, J. N. "Bibliographic Control in Kenya." *Information Development* (1989): 23-28.

_____. "Bibliographic Control of Literature in Research Disciplines in Kenya." *Inspel* 23(1989): 14-22.

Kenya—Library Education

Musisi, J. S. "A Faculty of Information Sciences at Moi University—Kenya." *COMLA Newsletter* 61(1988): 8-10.

Pre-1980 Publications

Osundwa, J. N. "Designing a Curriculum for In-service Training of Library Administration Course for Library Assistants in Special Libraries in Kenya." In *Designing a Curriculum for the Training through Refresher Courses of Qualified Library Assistants ... Kenya Library Association,* 23-31. Nairobi: Coordinating Centre for Regional Information Training (CRIT), 1978.

Training Course on the Implementation of Modern Documentation. Nairobi: Coordinating Centre for Regional Information Training (CRIT), 1976.

Kenya—Academic Libraries

Pfukani, Bilha. "Report of Visit to the University of Nairobi Main Library." In *Implementation of Modern Documentation,* ed. Soud Timami, 29. Nairobi, Kenya: Coordinating Centre for Regional Information Training (CRIT), 1976.

Kenya—School and Children's Library Services

Nyariki, Lily. "IBBY/Unesco Workshop in Kenya." *Bookbird* 26(1988): 18.

Otike, J.N. "Collection Development in School Libraries in Kenya." *Focus on International & Comparative Librarianship* 19(1988): 16-18.

Kenya—Special Libraries

Otike, J. N. "Research Libraries in Kenya." *Outlook on Research Libraries* 10(June 1988): 5-8.

Tesfaye, Alemayehu. "Report of Visit to the Kenya National Archives Reprographic Centre." In *Implementation of Modern Documentation,* ed. Soud Timami, 109. Nairobi, Kenya: Coordinating Centre for Regional Information Training (CRIT), 1976.

Umbima, William E. "The International Laboratory for Research on Animal Diseases (ILRAD) Library: A Vital Link in Kenya's Mission-oriented Agricultural Research." *Quarterly Bulletin of the International Association of Agricultural Librarians and Documentalists* 34(1989): 30-31.

Lesotho

Ambrose, David P. "A Brief Survey of the Existing Literature on Science and Technology Relating to Lesotho." *African Research & Documentation* 47(1988): 1-27.

Haliburton, Gordon. *Historical Dictionary of Lesotho.* Metuchen, NJ: Scarecrow Press, 1977.

Hüttemann, Lutz, ed. *Coordination and Improvement of National Information Services, Mbabane and Maseru Workshop Papers: Mbabane, 24-28 February 1986 and Maseru, 3-7 March 1986.* Bonn, Mbabane, Maseru: German Foundation for International Development, Swaziland National Library Service and National University of Lesotho, 1986.

Liberia

Dunn, D. Elwood and Svend E. Holsoe. *Historical Dictionary of Liberia.* Metuchen, NJ: Scarecrow Press, 1985.

Madagascar

Nucé de Lamothe, Marie-Simone de. "Services annexes et activités diverses de la Bibliothèque Universitaire de Tananarive" [Auxiliary Services and Varied Activities of the University Library of Tanarive]. *SCAUL Newsletter* 4(April 1967).

Malawi

Crosby, Cynthia A. *Historical Dictionary of Malawi.* Metuchen, NJ: Scarecrow Press, 1980.

Hüttemann, Lutz, ed. *Management of National Documentation Centres, Malawi Workshop Papers: Blantyre 6-14 March 1984.* Bonn: German Foundation for International Development, 1984.

Mabomba, R. S. *A Bibliography of Published and Unpublished Works on Libraries and Related Information Activities in Malawi.* Lilongwe: Malawi National Library Service, 1984.

_____. "The Creation and Development of a Nation-wide System of Libraries in Malawi, with Particular Reference to Public Libraries." Paper presented at the 50th IFLA General Conference (Public Libraries), Nairobi, August 20-25, 1984.

_____. "Developing Library and Information Services to Rural Communities in Malawi." Master's Thesis, College of Librarianship Wales, 1985.

_____. "Education for Librarianship at the Grass Roots Level: What Level of Skills Are Available among the Personnel Required to Deliver Services to Meet Identified Needs?" Paper presented at the Pre-Session Seminar, 50th IFLA General Conference, Nairobi, August 13-18, 1984.

_____. *A Manual for Small Libraries in Malawi.* Lilongwe: Malawi Library Association, 1981.

Msiska, Augustine W. C. "Malawian Librarianship Looks to Training for the Future." *Training and Education* 5(1988): 44-48.

Pre-1980 Publications

Chimulu, Foster Maynards and Foster Garnett House. "New Trends in Librarianship in Malawi." In *Implementation of Modern Documentation,* ed. Soud Timami, 16-17. Nairobi, Kenya: Coordinating Centre for Regional Information Training (CRIT), 1976.

Mabomba, R. S. *Cataloguing Manual.* Zomba: University of Malawi Library, 1974.

Plumbe, W. J. *Annual Report.* Zomba: University of Malawi, 1966-1972.

_____. "University of Malawi." Brief to the architect discussed at a meeting on March 4, 1966.

_____. "University of Malawi Libraries." *SCAUL Newsletter* 4(April 1967); 5(1968).

Mali

Danset, Francoise. "Public Reading in French-speaking Africa." *International Library Review* 21(1989): 245-248. (Focus on Mali, Ivory Coast, Congo).

278   GLENN L. SITZMAN

Imperato, Pascal James. *Historical Dictionary of Mali.* 2nd ed. Metuchen, NJ: Scarecrow Press, 1986.

Mauritania

Gerteiny, Alfred G. *Historical Dictionary of Mauritania.* Metuchen, NJ: Scarecrow Press, 1981.
Kent, F. L. "Training of Librarians and Documentalists in Arabic-speaking Countries." *Unesco Bulletin for Libraries* 21(1967): 301-310.

Mauritius

Riviere, Lindsay. *Historical Dictionary of Mauritius.* Metuchen, NJ: Scarecrow Press, 1982.

Niger

Baldwin, Charlene M. and Robert G. Varady. "Information Access in Niger: Development of a West African Special Library." *Special Libraries* 80(Winter 1989): 31-38.
Decalo, Samuel. *Historical Dictionary of Niger.* 2nd ed. Metuchen, NJ: Scarecrow Press, 1989.

Nigeria

Ahiakwo, O. N. "Forecasting Techniques and Library Circulation Operations: Implications for Management." *Library and Information Science Research* 10(1988): 195-210.
Ajiferuke, Isola. "Model and Measure of Research Collaboration." *Canadian Library Journal* 46(1989): 267-268. (Summary of dissertation).
Alegbeleye, G. O. "The Conservation Scene in Nigeria: A Panoramic View of the Condition of Bibliographic Resources." *Restaurator* 9(1988): 14-26.
Daniel, Cecilia I. "Library and Information Services for the Rural Population in Nigeria." *Library Focus* 5(1987): 1-23.
Dikko, I. "Books and Education." Talk to ATC Students, Ahmadu Bello University, Zaria, Nigeria, 1984.
————. "The Reader and the Non-reader: An X-ray of the Library User." Paper delivered at Kashim Ibrahim Library Seminar, Ahmadu Bello University, Zaria, 1983.
Dosunmu, J. A. "Preservation and Conservation of Library Materials in Nigeria." *COMLA Newsletter* 64(1989): 3-4.
Eyitazo, Adekunle O. "Status Report on the Attitude of Automated Library System Vendors to Investing in Nigeria." *Program* 23(1989): 247-256.
Ishaka, Peter A., A. Agbor, and J. Mba. "You Gotta Cry to Learn: Economic Downturn Hikes the Cost of Education in Nigeria. Illiteracy Is Moving Up." *Newswatch* (May 15, 1989): 56-57.

Ndakotsu, Tsuzom M. "Censorship and the Librarian." *Library Focus* 3(1985): 11-22.
Nweke, Ken M. C. "Educational Objectives, Libraries and Reading in Nigeria." *Information Development* 4(1988): 145-149.
Omoniwa, Moses A. "The 'Newer' Budgeting Techniques as Devices for Better Allocation of Resources in Nigerian Libraries." *Library Focus* 2(1984): 26-54.
Oyewole, A. *Historical Dictionary of Nigeria.* Metuchen, NJ: Scarecrow Press, 1987.
Umo, Margaret G. "A Survey of Legal Deposit Laws in Nigeria." *Library Focus* 4(1986): 1-21.

Pre-1980 Publications

Dikko, I. "Genesis of the Reading Room." *KAGOBNISO Notes* 1(1978): 1-76.
————. "Hausa in the Mass Media: A Preliminary Study in Translation Problems." *The Mirror* (Ahmadu Bello University, Department of English and Modern Languages) No. 2 session (1975-1976): 38-48.
————. "Hausa Language Resources in Nigerian Libraries." Master's Thesis, Ahmadu Bello University, 1978.
————. "Nigerian Librarianship and the Non-literate Majority." Paper read at seminar, Ahmadu Bello University Library Science Department, Zaria, 1979.
Mohrhardt, F. E. and C. V. Penna. "National Planning for Library and Information Services." *Advances in Librarianship* 5(1975): 61-106. (Includes Nigeria).
Rappaport, P. "Library Development in Nigeria." In *Symposium on Documentation in Developing Countries at Bad Godesberg,* 31-37. Bonn: German Foundation for Developing Countries, 1967.
Ukanou, Njoku. "Rural Libraries in Nigeria." *Rural Africana* 1(Spring 1978): 21-28.

Nigeria—Acquisitions

Dikko, I. "Cooperative Acquisitions: A Model for Nigeria." Paper submitted to the National Library of Nigeria's Advisory Committee on Library Cooperation, 1976.

Nigeria—Bibliographies and Bibliography

Afolabi, Michael. *The Periodical Literature on Librarianship in Nigeria, 1979-1985: A Bibliography.* Zaria: Department of Library Science, Faculty of Education, Ahmadu Bello University, 1986.
Aina, L. O. "Bibliographic Control of the Literature of Science and Technology." *International Library Review* 21(1989): 223-229.
Ajayi, John Alufemi. *Library Education in Nigeria 1948-1986.* Zaria: University Board of Research, Ahmadu Bello University, 1987.
Olatunji, A. "Index to Bendel Library Journal vol. 1(1) June 1978-vol. 3(2) December 1980." *Bendel Library Journal* 4(1981): 24-29.

Pre-1980 Publications

Afolabi, Michael. *Library Literature on Nigeria, 1910-1978: A Bibliography.* Zaria: Ahmadu Bello University, 1979.

Dikko, I. "The Hausas: Their Language, Literature, Customs and Folklore: An Annotated Bibliography." Compiled through Physical Inspection of the Resources at the School of Oriental & African Studies Library, University of London, 1965. (Unpublished).

Nigeria—Book Trade, Printing, and Publishing

Dikko, I. "A Peep at Publishing." Paper delivered at Guest Lecture Series, Department of Library Science, Bayero University, Kano, 1985.
_____. "The Production and Supply of Books and International Materials for the New System of Education." *Nigerian Educational Forums* 5(1982): 127-128.
Nwoga, D. I. "Onitsha Market Literature." *Transition* (Kampala) 19(1965): 26-33.

Nigeria—Cataloging and Classification

Aina, Joseph O. "Cataloging and Classification of Nigerian Government Publications: Survey Report of the University of Ibadan and Obafemi Awolowo University Libraries." *Government Publications Review* 15(1988): 137-145.
Dieneman, W. W. "The Cataloging of Haus Names." *Northern Nigeria Library Notes* 1(May 1964).

Nigeria—Cooperation

Batubo, F. B. "Library Co-operation." *International Library Review* 20(1988): 517-532.

Nigeria—Documentation and Information Science

Adeniram, O. R. "Bibliometrics of Computer Science Literature in Nigeria." *International Library Review* 20(1988): 347-359.
Ajiferuke, Isola Y. and Clara M. Chu. "Quality of Indexing in Online Databases: An Alternative Measure for a Term Discriminating Index." *Information Processing & Management* 24(1988): 599-601.
Daniel, James O. "The Knowledge Base for Library Automation Personnel." *International Library Review* 21(1989): 73-82.
Soyibo, Adedoyin and Wilson O. Aiyepeku. "On the Categorization, Exactness and Probable Utility of Bibliometric Laws and their Extensions." *Journal of Information Science* 14(1988): 243-251.

Nigeria—Libraries and Education

Dikko, I. "The Educational Role of Libraries in the Northern States vis-à-vis the University Community." *Northern States Library Notes* 6(1972): 11-15.
_____. "Libraries and Illiteracy." *Northern States Library Notes* 9(1975): 36-47.

Nigeria—Library Education

Agumanu, Joan N. "Education and Training for Nonprofessional Library Staff in Nigeria." *Journal of Education for Library and Information Science* 30(1989): 68-69.

Ajayi, John Alufemi. *Library Education in Nigeria 1948-1986.* Zaria: University Board of Research, Ahmadu Bello University, 1987.

Nzotta, Briggs C. "Research and Education for Research in Nigerian Library Schools." *Education for Information* 6(1988): 123-143.

Ochogwu, M. G. "Issues in Education for Librarianship in Nigeria." *Training and Education* 5(1988): 64-71.

Ogunsheye, F. A. "New Proposals for Structure of Library Personnel and Curricula for the Various Levels or Categories." Paper presented at the Colloqium on Education and Training for Librarianship in Nigeria, University of Ibadan, Nigeria, March 15-19, 1974. (Mimeographed).

Nigeria—Library Education—Ahmadu Bello University

Afolabi, Michael. "Postgraduate Education in Librarianship at Ahmadu Bello University, Zaria, Nigeria." *Library Focus* 2(1984): 99-120.

Mohammed, Zakari. "Teaching Reference and Information Service in the Department of Library Science, Ahmadu Bello University, Zaria." *Library Focus* 3(1985): 70-89.

Onadiran, G. T. "Reactions of Past Students to the Bachelor of Library Science Degree of Ahmadu Bello University, Nigeria." *Education for Information* 6(1988): 39-59.

Nigeria—Library Education—Bayero University

Ibrahimah, M. Z. "The Teaching of Preservation and Conservation at Bayero University, Kano, Nigeria." *Restaurator* 9(1988): 51-60.

Nigeria—Library Education—University of Ibadan

Aiyepeku, W. G. *Teaching Research Methods to Potential Graduate Librarians,* 1987. ERIC. ED 299 974.

Nigeria—Library Education—University of Maiduguri

Nweke, Ken M. C. "Information Technology Used for Education in the Maiduguri Library School, Nigeria." *Education for Information* 7(1989): 43-49.

Nigeria—Professional Associations

Dikko, I. "The Nigerian Library Association: Past, Present and Future." Lecture delivered to Class of Assistant Library Officers, College of Administrative and Business Studies, Kaduna Polytechnic, June 9, 1978.

Plumbe, W. J. "Presidential Address, Annual Conference of Nigerian Library Association, 3 April 1965." *Nigerian Libraries* 1(1965): 4.

Nigeria—Academic Libraries

Adikwu, C. C. A. "A Survey of University Archives in Five Universities in Nigeria." *Library Focus* 5(1987): 24-37.
Aina, Joseph O. and Briggs C. Nzotta. "The Use of Subscription Agency Services by Nigerian University Libraries." *Serials Librarian* 14(1988): 147-162.
Alafiatayo, Benjamin O. "Reader Malpractices in Nigerian University Libraries." *Library Focus* 4(1986): 51-69.
Ampitan, Edwards J. "A Survey of Professional Opinion on Academic Status of Libraries in Nigerian Universities." *Library Focus* 5(1987): 99-109.
Mohammed, Zakari. "A Survey of Computer-based Circulation Control Systems in Nigerian University Libraries." *Library Focus* 5(1987): 68-79.
Nigeria. National Universities Commission. *Executive Secretary's Report on Tour of Nigerian Universities,* 1987.
Nwafor, B. U. "Library Services for Postgraduate Education in Nigeria in the Late Eighties." Paper read at the Meeting of the Deans of Postgraduate Schools of Nigerian Universities, Jos, November 16, 1987.
Onadiron, G. T. "Book Theft in University Libraries in Nigeria." *Library and Archival Security* 8(1988): 37-48.
Ononogbo, Raphael U. "User Satisfaction in a Depressed Economy." *International Library Review* 21(1989): 209-221.
Salaam, Monso O. "Inter-library Cooperation through Gifts and Exchange among Nigerian University Libraries." *Library Focus* 2(1984): 72-98.
Strategies for Survival by Nigerian Academic and Research Libraries during Austere Times: Proceedings of a National Seminar, eds. S. M. Lawani et al. Nigerian Association of Agricultural Librarians and Documentalists and Academic and Research Libraries Section of the Nigerian Library Association, 1988.
Unomah, J. I. "User Education in Academic Libraries: The Nigerian Situation." *Journal of Library and Information Science* 13(1987): 111-132.

Nigeria—Academic Libraries—Abubakar Tafawa Balewa University

Antwi, I. K. "The Problem of Library Security: The Bauchi Experience." *International Library Review* 21(1989): 363-372.

Nigeria—Academic Libraries—Ahmadu Bello University

Afolabi, Michael. "Exhibition in Nigerian University Libraries: A Case Study of the Kashim Ibrahim Library, Ahmadu Bello University, Zaria." *Library Focus* 4(1986): 42-50.
Bozimo, Doris O. "Basic Library Knowledge and Extent of Previous Library Use among Nigerian University Freshmen: A Preliminary Study at Ahmadu Bello University." *Library Focus* 4(1986): 22-41.

Pre-1980 Publications

Cave, Roderick G. J. M. "Education & Training of Library Staff in Ahmadu Bello University." *Northern Nigeria Library News* 2 & 3(October 1964).
Plumbe, W. J. "Ahmadu Bello University Libraries: The First Three Years." *Nigerian Libraries* 3(1967): 46-62. [First published in *Northern Nigeria Library Notes* 4(October 1965)].
————. "Ahmadu Bello University. Programme for Library Building, Zaria Site, 4 October 1963." Brief to the architect.
————. *A Guide to the Libraries of Ahmadu Bello University.* Zaria: Ahmadu Bello University, 1964.

Nigeria—Academic Libraries—Federal University of Technology, Makurdi
[Merged with University of Jos, 1984]

Plumbe, W. J. *Annual Report.* Makurdi, Nigeria: Federal University of Technology Library, 1982-1983.

Nigeria—Academic Libraries—Rivers State University of Science and Technology

Decor, Sunday K. "Attitudes and Perceptions of Student Patrons." *International Library Review* 21(1989):: 373-385.

Nigeria—Academic Libraries—School for Arabic Studies, Kano

Galadanci, Shehu Ahmed Said. "The Library of the School for Arabic Studies, Kano." *Northern Nigeria Library Notes* 2 & 3(October 1964).

Nigeria—Academic Libraries—University of Ibadan

Azubuike, Abraham A. and Monica A. Graves. "The Reference Services of a Research Library." *International Library Review* 21(1989): 237-246.

Nigeria—Academic Libraries—University of Maiduguri

Agaji, Abayomi. "Effects of a Harsh Climate on Audiovisual Services in Libraries in Arid Regions: The Case of the Media Unit of Maiduguri University Library." *Audiovisual Librarian* 14(1988): 126-128.

Nigeria—Children's Library Services

Lawal, O. O. "Children in Fiction: The Nigerian Perspective." *Bookbird* 27(1989): 9-12.
Osiobe, Stephen A. et al. "Theme and Illustrations as Correlates of Literature Performances among Nigerian Primary School Pupils." *Library Review* 38(1989): 45-52.

Scharioth, Barbara. "Book and Reading Promotion Activities." *Bookbird* 27(1989): 12-13.
Segun, Mabel D. "The Image of Old Age in Nigerian Children's Literature." *Bookbird* 27(1989): 5-9.

Nigeria—Public Libraries

Ajibero, Matthew Idowu. "Public Relations and Publicity in Nigerian Public Libraries." *Library Focus* 5(1987): 38-48.
Dikko, I. "The Library Board and Public Library Services." Paper delivered at NLA Borno State Annual Conference, Maiduguri, 1982.
————. "The Potential Users of the Public Library in Nigeria." Conference paper delivered at the Plateau State Division of the Nigerian Library Association, Jos, 1979.
Nzotta, Briggs Chinkata. "The Administration of Branch Libraries in a Developing Country: A Case Study." *Public Library Quarterly* 9(1989): 47-60.

Nigeria—Public Libraries—Former Midwestern State

Nigeria. Midwestern State. *Midwest Library Board Edict 1970;* Edict No. 4 of 1971. Supplement to *Midwestern State of Nigeria Gazette,* 8, 10(February 18, 1971).

Nigeria—Public Libraries—Former Northern Region

Allen, Joan. "Books Mean Progress: The Public Library and N. A. (Native Authority) Reading Rooms in Northern Nigeria." *West African Library Association News* 4(October 1961): 4-10. (This entry corrects an error in *African Libraries,* p. 414.)
————. "Early Days in the Northern Regional Library, Kaduna." *Northern Nigeria Library Notes* 2 & 3(October 1964).
————. "Summary of the Sharr Report." *Northern Nigeria Library Notes* 1(May 1964).

Nigeria—Public Libraries—Anambra State

Ezennia, Steve E. "Problems and Achievements in Collection Building and Management in Anambra State, Nigeria." *Collection Management* 10(1988): 157-168.

Nigeria—Public Libraries—Kaduna State

Boman, Daniel D. "Library and Information Services in Kaduna State Library Board." *Library Focus* 5(1987): 49-67.
Dikko, I., Committee Chairman. *Report of the Committee Appointed to Look into the State's Library Services, Library Board of Kaduna State,* 1978.
————. "The State Library Services." Lecture delivered at the 9th Annual Conference of Principals, Zaria, 1979.

Nigeria—School Libraries

Oni-Orisan, B. A. "The Role of Governance and School Authorities in the Development of School Libraries." *Library Focus* 5(1987): 1-10.

Nigeria—Secondary School and College Libraries

Obokoh, N. P. "Alternative Revenue and Material Sources for Secondary School Libraries in Nigeria." *Library Focus* 3(1985): 50-61.
Ogunleye, Gabriel Olubunmi. "Manpower Aspects of Secondary School Libraries in the 6-3-3-4 Education System in Nigeria: The Case of Ondo State." *Library Review* 37, 4(1988): 28-34.

Nigeria—Special Libraries, Materials, and Services

Agaji, Abayomi. "Effects of a Harsh Climate Audiovisual Services in Libraries in Arid Regions: The Case of the Media Unit of Maiduguri University Library." *Audiovisual Librarian* 14(1988): 126-128.
Fatuyi, E. O. A. "The Plan, Design and Set-up of the Leather Research Institute of Nigeria (LERIN) Library." *Library Focus* 5(1987): 80-98.

Nigeria—Special Libraries, Materials, and Services—Agriculture

Adedigba, Y. A. "Budgeting in the Agricultural Libraries and Documentation Centres in Nigeria." *International Library Review* 20(1988): 215-226.
Akhibge, Funmi, O. "Kolanut: The Characteristics and Growth of its Literature in Nigeria." *Quarterly Bulletin of the International Association of Agricultural Librarians and Documentalists* 33(1988): 47-52.
Ibekwe, G. O. "The Present Constraints to the Realization of the Role of Nigerian Agricultural Libraries in Food Production and Prospects for Fulfillment." *Quarterly Bulletin of the International Association of Agricultural Librarians and Documentalists* 33(1988): 121-133.
Udofia, Callix. "Content and Situational Relevance of Agricultural News in the *Ghanaian Times* and the *Daily Times* (Lagos)." *Rural Africana* 1(1978): 51-64.

Nigeria—Special Libraries, Materials, and Services—Handicapped

Ayalogu, Meg C. "Meeting the Reading Needs of the Blind in Nigeria: Problems and Challenges." *Education Libraries Bulletin* 31(1988): 7-13.
Dikko, I. "Public Library Services: The Case of Audiovisual Materials." Seminar on Library Services for the Handicapped Persons in the 80s, Kaduna State Library Board, 1981.

Nigeria—Special Libraries, Materials, and Services—Law

Ifebuzor, Christopher C. "Centralization versus Decentralization of Law Libraries and Law Library Services in Nigerian Universities." *Law Library Journal* 80(1988): 605-617.

Okewusi, Peter Agboola. "Law Libraries in the Western Region/State of Nigeria."
    International Library Review 20(1988): 227-232.
————. "Library Services for Lawyers in the Ministry of Justice of Oyo State of
    Nigeria." *State Librarian* 36(November 1988): 33-35.

Nigeria—Special Libraries, Materials, and Services—Medicine and Health Sciences

Ekweozoh, Christopher N. "The Research Library of the Federal Department of
    Veterinary Research, Vom, Northern Nigeria." *Northern Nigeria Library Notes*
    2 & 3(October 1964).
"UCH Medical Students in Dilemma." *Nigerian Observer* (July 19, 1987): 1.

Nigeria—Special Libraries, Materials, and Services—Newspapers

Aina, L. O. "Newspaper as a Tool in Educational Research in Nigeria." *Inspel* 21(1987):
    163-167.
————. "Researchers' Attitudes to Newspaper Indexing in Nigeria." *Indexer*
    16(1988): 97-98.
Alegbeleye, G. O. "Newspaper Preservation and Access with Particular Reference to
    University Libraries in Nigeria." *Libri* 38(1988): 191-204.
Nwakaby, Martina. "Portrait of a Newspaper Library in a Developing Country." *Serials
    Librarian* 14(1988): 121-128.

Nigeria—Special Libraries, Materials, and Services—Science and Technology

Aguolu, Christian Chukwunedu. "Scientific and Technical Information in Nigeria."
    International Library Review 21(1989): 395-409.
Alabi, G. A. "The Citation Pattern of Nigerian Scientists." *International Library Review*
    21(1989): 129-137.
Ehikhamenor, F. A. "Perceived State of Science in Nigerian Universities."
    Scientometrics 13(1988): 225-238.
Gupta, D. K. "Scientometric Study of Biochemical Literature of Nigeria, 1970-1984:
    Application of Lotka's Law and the 80/20 Rule." *Scientometrics* 15(1989): 171-
    180.

Rwanda

Borchardt, Peter, ed. *Gestion des Services d'information, Rapport d'un stage realisé
    à Kigali, 20-31 octobre 1986* [Management of Information Services, Report of
    a Training Program Carried out at Kigali, October 20-31, 1986]. Bonn, Kigali:
    German Foundation for International Development and Organisation for the
    Management and Development of the Kagera River Basin, 1987.

Senegal

Colvin, Lucie G. *Historical Dictionary of Senegal*. Metuchen, NJ: Scarecrow Press,
    1981.

M'baye, Saliou. "Le réseau archivistique national au Sénégal" [The National Archival Network in Senegal]. *Information Development* 5(1989): 29-31.

Senegal—Library Education

Kane, Kalidou. "L'écart entre la théorie et la pratique dans l'enseignement de la science de l'information: l'expérience d l'EBAD" [Distance Between Theory and Practice in Teaching Information Science: The Experience of EBAD (Cheik Anta Diop University of Dakar)]. In *Théorie et pratique dans l'enseignement des sciences de l'information,* 95-121. Université de Montréal, Ecole de Bibliothéconomie et des Sciences de l'Information, 1988.

Thiam, Mbaye. "Evolution du profil des étudiants et des enseignants en sciences de l'information au Sénégal: évolution et perspectives" [Evolution of Students' and Professors' Profile in Information Science in Senegal: Evolution and Perspectives]. In *Théorie et pratique dans l'enseignement des sciences de l'information,* 397-401. Université de Montréal, Ecole de Bibliothéconomie et des Sciences de l'Information, 1988.

Pre-1980 Publications

"Regional Centre for the Training of Librarians at Dakar." *Unesco Bulletin for Libraries* 18(1964): 101-104.

"School for Librarians, Archivists, and Documentalists in Senegal." *Unesco Bulletin for Libraries* 22(1968): 106.

Seychelles

Jackson, F. "Natsional'naya biblioteka Respubliki Seishel'skie Ostrova" [The National Library of Seychelles]. *Bibliotekovedenie i Bibliografia za Rubezohm* 111(1987): 41-43.

Sierra Leone

Foray, Cyril Patrick. *Historical Dictionary of Sierra Leone.* Metuchen, NJ: Scarecrow Press, 1977.

Mansary, M. L. "Information Technology in Government: The Sierra Leone Experience." *Information Technology for Development* 3(1988): 275-296.

Sierra Leone—Bibliographies and Bibliography

Thompson, J. S. T. *Library Development, Bibliographical Control, Archives and Book Development in Sierra Leone: A List of References,* 1978.

Sierra Leone—Public Libraries

Ogundipe, O. O. "Rural Libraries in Sierra Leone." *Rural Africana* 1(Spring 1978): 29-33.

Somalia

Castagno, Margaret F. *Historical Dictionary of Somalia.* Metuchen, NJ: Scarecrow Press, 1975.

Kerrison, R. J. "Prospects for NATIS in the Somali Democratic Republic." Master's thesis, Loughborough Uniersity, 1977.

Sudan

Ahmed, Munir D. "Die Ausbildung von Bibliothekaren und Archivaren im Vovderen Orient" [The Training of Librarians, Documentalists and Archivists in the Near East]. *Auskunft* 8(1988): 277-286. (Includes Sudan).

Pre-1980 Publications

Bannaga, Ali Mohayad. "The Democratic Republic of the Sudan Country Report on Documentation and Libraries in Documentation and Information Network in East Africa." In *Development of Documentation and Information Networks in East Africa,* 111-114. Bonn: German Foundation for International Development, 1974.

Kent, F. L. "Training of Librarians and Documentalists in Arabic-speaking Countries." *Unesco Bulletin for Libraries* 21(1967): 301-310. (Includes Sudan).

Plumbe, W. J. "An African Library." *Eastern Caribbean Library Review* 2(March 1952).

————. *Annual Report.* Khartoum, Library of Research Division, Ministry of Agriculture, 1949-1952.

————. "A Library in the Sun." *The Torch* (Durham County Library) (Summer 1951).

Voll, John O. *Historical Dictionary of Sudan.* Metuchen, NJ: Scarecrow Press, 1978.

Swaziland

Hüttemann, Lutz, ed. *Coordination and Improvement of National Information Services, Mbabane and Maseru Workshop Papers: Mbabane, 24-28 February 1986 and Maseru, 3-7 March 1986.* Bonn, Mbabane, Maseru: German Foundation for International Development, Swaziland National Library Service, and National University of Lesotho, 1986.

Tanzania

Hüttemann, Lutz, ed. *Management of Information Services, Workshop Papers: Arusha, 9-20 May 1983.* Bonn: German Foundation for International Development and Eastern and Southern African Management Institute, 1983.

Hüttemann, Lutz and Augustes Musana, eds. *Information Services for Rural Development and Industry, Workshop Papers, Arusha 3-7 Oct. and 10-21 Oct. 1983.* Bonn: German Foundation for International Development and Eastern and Southern African Management Institute, 1984.

Lahti, Marjatta. "Kirjastotyötä Tansaniassa—vuorotellen malarian ja ameeban kourissa" [Librarianship in Tanzania—in the Grips of Malaria and Amoeba]. *Kirjastolehti* 80(1987): 78-79.

Mascarenhas, Ophelia C., chief ed. *Establishment of a National Information and Documentation Network in Tanzania. Papers of the Seminar Held in Dar es Salaam 16 to 24 February 1989.* Bonn and Dar es Salaam: German Foundation for International Development, University of Dar es Salaam, 1989.

Musana, A., J. N. Kiyimba, and L. Hüttemann, eds. *Management of Information Services: Workshop Papers, Arusha, 11-22, April 1988.* Bonn, Arusha, Kigali: German Foundation for International Development, Eastern and Southern African Management Institute, and Organisation for the Management and Development of the Kagera River Basin, 1988.

Nawe, Julita. "The Impact of a Dwindling Budget on Library Services in Tanzania." *Library Review* 37(1988): 27-32.

Pre-1980 Publications

Baregu, M. L. M. "Rural Libraries in Functional Literacy Campaigns in Tanzania." *Rural Africana* 1(Spring 1978): 35-43. [First published in *Unesco Bulletin for Libraries* 26(1972): 18-24].

Mascarenhas, O. C. "Country Reports—Tanzania." In *Development of Documentation and Information Networks in East Africa,* 115-120. Bonn: German Foundation for International Development, 1974.

Newa, John. "New Trends in Librarianship in Tanzania." In *Implementation of Modern Documentation,* ed. Soud Timami, 18-20. Nairobi, Kenya: Coordinating Centre for Regional Information Training (CRIT), 1976.

Tanzania—Bibliographies and Bibliography

Darch, Colin M. "The Library Literature of Tanzania." *Someni* 5(1977): 91-102.

Tanzania—Public Libraries

Lahti, Marjatta. "Kehityshteistyötä—Mazibum kirjastoprojekti" [Development Cooperation—the Mazimbu Library Project]. *Kirjastolehti* 79(1986): 226-229.

Yamada, Nobue. "Tanzanian Public Libraries: A Visit to Moshi Regional Library." *Toshokan Zasshi* 81(1987): 730-734. (In Japanese).

Tanzania—Special Libraries

Mbwana, S. S. "The Role of Agricultural Information in Research and Training in Tanzania." *Journal of Library and Information Science* 12(1987): 38-45.

Mbwana, S. S. and K. Gessesse. "The Scientific Literature Service in Tanzania." *Focus on International & Comparative Librarianship* 19(1988): 30-31.

Musana, A. and Lutz Hüttemann, eds. *Management of Agricultural Information Services, Course Material; Arusha, 19-30 October 1987.* Bonn, Arusha: German

Foundation for International Development and Eastern an Southern African Management Institute, 1988.

Togo

Decalo, Samuel. *Historical Dictionary of Togo.* 2nd ed. Metuchen, NJ: Scarecrow Press, 1987.

Uganda

Kiregeya, Emmanuel. "New Trends in Librarianship in Uganda." In *Implementation of Modern Documentation,* ed. Soud Timami, 21. Nairobi, Kenya: Coordinating Centre for Regional Information Training (CRIT), 1976.

Lwanga, T. K. "Country Report [Uganda]." In *Development of Documentation and Information Networks in East Africa,* 121-123. Bonn: German Foundation for International Development, 1974.

Uganda—East African School of Librarianship

"East African School of Librarianship." *Unesco Bulletin for Libraries* 18(1964): 105-109.

Otike, Japhet N. "The Training of Information Personnel in East Africa." *Libri* 39(1989): 110-126.

Uganda—Academic Libraries

Sitzman, Glenn L. "Makerere University College of Libraries." *SCAUL Newsletter* 4(April 1967): 147-151. ["Main Library" by G. L. Sitzman; "Albert Cook Library" by Margot Thompson; "National Institute of Education Library" by Mrs. P. Umbima].

Western Sahara

Hodges, Tony. *Historical Dictionary of Western Sahara.* Metuchen, NJ: Scarecrow Press, 1982.

Zaire

Bobb, F. Scott. *Historical Dictionary of Zaire.* Metuchen, NJ: Scarecrow Press, 1988.

Zambia

Hüttemann, Lutz, ed. *Management of a National Information and Documentation Network in Zambia: Workshop Papers, Lusaka, 15-24 February 1988.* Bonn, Lusaka: German Foundation for International Development and Zambia Library Association, 1988.

Pre-1980 Publications

Brown, E. M. "Letter." Zambia Library Association Journal 5(1973): 37-38.
Mushipi, Clifford. "New Trends in Librarianship in Zambia (National Council for Scientific Research)." In *Implementation of Modern Documentation,* ed. Soud Timami, 22. Nairobi, Kenya: Coordinating Centre for Regional Information Training (CRIT), 1976.
Mwanakatwe, J. M. *The Growth of Education in Zambia Since Independence.* 2nd ed. London: Oxford University Press, 1975.
Ogundipe, O. O. "Rural Libraries in Zambia." *Rural Africana* 1(Spring 1978): 45-49.
"Zambia Library Service." In *Zambia. First National Development Plan* (Chapters 22 and 23).

Zambia—Public Libraries

Msadabwe, E. M. "Ranfurly Library Service Helps the Branch Library at Kalabo, Zambia." *Library Association Record* 90(1988): 661.

Pre-1980 Publications

Kent, Penelope. "Zambia Library Service in Luapula Province." *Zambia Library Association Journal* 5(1973): 71-73.
Sleath, C. V. "Public Library Statistics." *Zambia Library Association Journal* 2(1970): 6-7.
Spillers, R. E. "Development of Public Libraries in Zambia." *Zambia Library Association Journal* 6(1974): 87-89.

Zambia—School Libraries

Blancharde, B. J. M. "The Library in the Zambian Secondary School." *Zambia Library Association Journal* 3(1971): 13-21.
Bwalya, Marcel. "The Case for Children and School Libraries in Zambia." *Zambia Library Association Journal* 5(1973): 11-16.
Lungu, Charles. "The Fate of School Libraries in Zambia: What Can We Do?" *Zambia Library Association Journal* 5(1973): 65-70.

Zambia—Special Libraries

Czajkowski, Franciszek. "Zambia uruchamia krajowa biblioteke dla niepeinosprawnych" (Zambia Has Set up a National Library for the Handicapped). *Bibliotekarz* 54(1987): 28-29.
Lundu, Maurice Chimfwembe and Charles B. M. Lungu. "Acquisition of Scientific Literature in Developing Countries: Zambia." *Information Development* 5(1989): 99-107.

Zimbabwe

Hüttemann, Lutz, ed. *Establishment, Function and Management of a National Library and Document Service: Workshop Report, Harare 6-15 March 1985*. Bonn: German Foundation for International Development, 1985.

————. *"Manpower Training News": Proceedings and Papers of the Information Experts Meeting, Harare, 18-21 March 1985*. Bonn: German Foundation for International Development, 1985.

Kadungure, Rodwell. "Libraries are Like Chameleons: They Take After the Complexion of Society." *Zimbabwe Librarian* 19(December 1987): 60-62.

Made, Stanislaus M. "Library Situation in Zimbabwe: An Historical Background to the Establishment of the National Library and Documentation Service (NLDS)." *Wits Journal of Librarianship & Information Science* 5(1988): 171-197.

Zimbabwe—Public Libraries

Doust, Robin W. "Books on Wheels: The Bulawayo Bookmobile." *Zimbabwe Librarian* 19(December 1987): 41-43.

Zimbabwe—Special Libraries

Chimulu, F. M. "The ARIPO (African Regional Industrial Property Organization) Approach to Patent Search and Examination." *World Patent Information* 11(1989): 71-75. (The library is at Harare).

Hava, Jarmila. "The Library at the National Gallery of Zimbabwe." *Art Libraries Journal* 11(1986): 30-43.

Hungwe, K. "Culturally Appropriate Media and Technology: A Perspective from Zimbabwe." *Tech Trends* 34(1989): 23-23.

Mabaso-Kwalo, Sylvia. "Zimbabwe's First Steps towards the Year 2000: Establishing a National Focal Point (NFP) for Health Information Services." *Zimbabwe Librarian* 19(December 1987): 53-59.

BIOGRAPHICAL SKETCHES
OF THE CONTRIBUTORS

James R. Coffey is a reference librarian at the Camden Library of Rutgers University.

Patricia A. Etter is Assistant Archivist for Information Services and Head of Reference for the Department of Archives and Manuscripts, Arizona State University, Tempe. She is a specialist on overland journeys and southern trails to California in the 1840s and is author of *An American Odyssey* (University of Arkansas Press, 1986) in addition to numerous journal articles, bibliographies, and book reviews. She received her MLS from the University of Arizona.

Sandra E. Goldstein received her MLS from the University of Michigan. She worked as a library associate at the University of Michigan's Chemistry Library for two years. She is currently working on a Ph.D. at UCLA's Graduate School of Library and Information Science.

Larry Hardesty is Director of Libraries at Eckerd College in St. Petersburg, Florida.

Robert M. Hayes, Professor GSLIS/UCLA (1964-present), Dean (1974-1989), received his Ph.D. in mathematics at UCLA in 1952, and worked in industry from 1949-1964. He is President ASIS, ISAD/ALA; Vice-President AAAS' advisor WCHLIS chairman NCLIS task force, ALA/COA, NIM advisory panel. His publications include two basic texts and he received the following awards: National Lecturer (ACM, ASIS, NFAIS, Illinois University), Beta Phi Mu, UCLA alumni, ALISE, Zagreb University.

Theodora T. Haynes is a reference librarian at the Camden Library of Rutgers University.

Faith Jack, employed as an English teacher by the Washington County (MD) Board of Education, is on a leave of absence while she pursues a Master of Science in Library Science degree at Clarion University of Pennsylvania. Admitted to Clarion's Certificate of Advanced Studies Program, she plans to prepare for a career in academic librarianship.

Rashelle Karp is an Associate Professor of Library Science at Clarion University of Pennsylvania. Her teaching responsibilities include business reference sources and services, collection development, and library services to disabled populations.

Ellsworth Mason is a library building consultant following a long and distinguished career in librarianship.

Polly Mumma is currently employed as a cataloger at Collier Library, University of North Alabama.

Glenn L. Sitzman is a retired librarian from Clarion University of Pennsylvania.

Thomas J. Waldhart is an Associate Professor and Dean at the College of Library and Information Science, University of Kentucky. He received his Ph.D. degree from Indiana University in 1973 and for several years his research interests have focused on cost justification in libraries.

Sandra Yaegle received a bachelor's degree in elementary education and English from Houghton College in 1972, and a master's degree in special education from Indiana University of Pennsylvania in 1977. She taught second and third graduate students for four years, then specialized in teaching primary and secondary level special education students.

INDEX

Advances in Library Administration and Organization

Edited by **Gerard B. McCabe,** *Director of Libraries,*
Clarion University of Pennsylvania and
Bernard Kreissman, *University Librarian Emeritus,*
University of California, Davis

REVIEWS: "Special librarians and library managers in academic
institutions should be aware of this volume and the series it initiates.
Library schools and University libraries should purchase it."
— *Special Libraries*

"... library schools and large academic libraries should include this
volume in their collection because the articles draw upon practical
situations to illustrate administrative principles."
— *Journal of Academic Librarianship*

Volume 1, l982, 148 pp. $63.50
ISBN 0-89232-2l3-6

CONTENTS: Introduction, *W. Carl Jackson.* **Continuity or
Discontinuity-A Persistant Personnel Issue in Academic
Librarianship,** *Allan B. Veaner.* **Archibald Cary Collidge and
"Civilization's Dairy: Building the Harvard University Library",**
Robert T. Byrnes. **Library Automation: Building and Equipment
Considerations in Implementing Computer Technology,** *Edwin B.
Brownrigg.* **Microforms Facility at the Golda Meir Library of the
University of Wisconsin, Milwaukee,** *William C. Roselle.* **RLIN and
OCLC - Side by Side: Two Comparison Studies,** *Kazuko M. Dailey,
Jaroff Grazia, and Diana Gray.* **Faculty Status and Participative
Governance in Academic Libraries,** *Donald D. Hendricks.*

Volume 2, 1983, 373 pp. $63.50
ISBN 0-89232-214-4

CONTENTS: Introduction, *Bernard Kreissman.* **Management
Training for Research Librarianship,** *Deanna B. Marcum.* **Subject
Divisionalism: A Diagnostic Analysis,** *J.P. Wilkinson.* **Videotext
Development for the United States,** *Michael B. Binder.* **The
Organizational and Budgetary Effects of Automation on Libraries,**
Murray S. Martin. **The Librarian as Change Agent,** *Tom G. Watson.*
Satellite Cable Library Survey, *Mary Diebler.* **Deterioration of Book
Paper,** *Richard G. King, Jr.* **Evaluation and the Process of Change
in Academic Libraries,** *Delmus E. Williams.* **Towards a Reconcep-
tualization of Collection Development,** *Charles B. Osburn.*
**Strategies and Long Range Planning in Libraries and Information
Centers,** *Michael E.D. Koenig and Leonard Kerson.* **Project
Management: An Effective Problem Solving Approach,** *Robert L.
White.* **A Preliminary and Selective Survey of Two Collections of
Juvenilia,** *Michele M. Reid.* **Biographical Sketch of the
Contributors.**

J A I P R E S S

Volume 3, 1984, 320 pp. $63.50
ISBN 0-89232-386-8

CONTENTS: Introduction, *Gerard B. McCabe.* **International Exchange and Chinese Library Development,** *Priscilla C. Yu.* **Measuring Professional Performance: A Critical Examination,** *Andrea C. Dragon.* **The Turnover Process and the Academic Library,** *James G. Neal.* **Subject Bibliographers in Academic Libraries: An Historical and Descriptive Review,** *John D. Haskell, Jr.* **University of California Users Look at Melvyl: Results of a Survey of Users of the University at California Prototye Online Union Catalog,** *Gary S. Lawrence, Vicki Graham, and Heather Presley.* **Job Analysis: Process and Benefits,** *Virginia R. Hill and Tom G. Watson.* **College Library and Nonusers,** *Nurieh Musavi and John F. Harvey.* **David Milford Hume, M. D., 1917-1973,** *Mary Ellen Thomas.* **The Association of Research Libraries 1932-1982 50th Anniversary. The Impact of Changes in Scholarship in the Humanities Upon Research Libraries,** *Ralph Cohen.* **The ARL at Fifty,** *Stephen A. McCarthy.* **ARL/LC: 1932-1982,** *William J. Welsh.* **The Influence of ARL on Academic Librarianship, Legislation, and Library Education,** *Edward G. Holley.* **Biographical Sketch of the Contributors.**

Volume 4, 1985, 233 pp. $63.50
ISBN 0-89232-566-6

CONTENTS: Introduction, *Bernard Kreissman.* **The Third Culture: Managerial Socialization in the Library Setting,** *Ruth J. Person.* **Public Library Unions: Bane or Boon?,** *Rashelle Schlessinger.* **Satisfaction with Library Systems,** *Larry N. Osborne.* **Budgeting and Financial Planning for Libraries,** *Michael E.D. Koening and Deidre C. Stam.* **Library Support of Faculty Research: An Investigation at a Multi-Campus University,** *Barbara J. Smith.* **Staff Development on a Shoestring,** *Helen Carol Jones and Ralph E. Russell.* **The Impact of Technology on Library Buildings,** *Rolf Funlrott.* **Whither the Book? Considerations for Library Planning in the Age of Electronics,** *Roscoe Rouse, Jr.* **Attempting to Automate: Lessons Learned Over Five Years, Pittsburgh Regional Library Center,** *Scott Bruntjen and Sylvia D. Hall.* **Annotated Bibliographer of Materials on Academic Library Service to Disabled Students,** *Rashelle Schlessinger.* **Biographical Sketch of the Contributors.**

Volume 5, 1986, 307 pp. $63.50
ISBN 0-89232-674-3

CONTENTS: Introduction, *Gerard B. McCabe.* **A Longitudinal Study of the Outcomes of a Management Development Program for Women in Librarianship,** *Ruth J. Person and Eleanore R. Ficke.* **Volunteers in Libraries,** *Rashelle Schlessinger Karp.* **The History of Publishing as a Field of Research for Librarians and Others,** *Joe W. Kraus.* **The Respone of the Cataloger and the Catalog to Automation in the Academic Library Setting,** *Joan M. Repp.* **Accredited Master's Degree Programs in Librarianship in the 1980s,** *John A. McCrossan.* **Collection Evaluation - Practices and Methods in Libraries of ALA Accredited Graduate Library Education Programs,** *Renee Tjoumas and Esther E. Horne.*

Volume 8, 1989, 302 pp. $63.50
ISBN 0-89232-967-X

CONTENTS: Introduction, *Bernard Kreissman.* Quality in Bibliographic Databases: An Analysis of Member-Contributed Cataloging in OCLC and RLIN, *Sheila S. Intner.* The Library Leadership Project: A Test of Leadership Effectiveness in Academic Libraries, *Eugene S. Mitchell.* Applying Strategic Planning to the Library: A Model for Public Services, *Larry J. Ostler.* Management Issues in Selection, Development, and Implementation of Integrated or Linked Systems for Academic Libraries, *Elaine Lois Day.* Acquisitions Management: The Infringing Roles of Acquisitions Librarians and Subject Specialists-An Historial Perspective, *Barbara J. Henn.* Development and Use of Theatre Databases, *Helen K. Bolton.* The Academic Library and the Liberal Arts Education of Young Adults: Reviewing the Relevance of the Library-College in the 1980s, *Peter V. Deekle.* College Libraries: The Colonial Period to the Twentieth Century, *Eugene R. Hanson.* Library Administrators' Attitudes Toward Continuing Professional Education Activities, *John A. McCrossan.* A Core Reference Theatre Arts Collection for Research, *Sharon Lynn Schofield, Helen K. Bolton, Rashelle S. Karp, and Bernard S. Schlessinger.* The Library Buildings Award Program of the American Institute of Architects and the American Library Association, *Roscoe Rouse, Jr..* Bibliography of Sub-Sahara African Librarianship, 1986-1987, *Glenn L. Sitzman.* Bibliographical Sketches of the Contributors. Index.

Volume 9, 1991, 262 pp. $63.50
ISBN 1-55938-066-7

CONTENTS: Introduction, *Gerard B. McCabe.* Administrative Theories, Business Paradigms and Work in the Academic Library, *Allen B. Véaner.* Whatever Happened to Library Education for Bibliotherapy: A State of the Art, *Alice Gullen Smith.* Three Libraries: Use of the Public Library Planning Process, an Analysis Accompanied by Recommendations for Future Users, *Annabel K. Stephens.* Book Piracy and International Copyright Law, *Serena Esther McGuire.* Investigation of the Motivational Needs of Corporate Librarians: A Framework, *Sohair Wastawy-Elbaz.* Libraries, Technology, and Access: the Statewide Automation Planing Process in New York, *Frederick E. Smith and George E.J. Messmer.* The National Szechenyi Library Budapest - Hungary, *Elizabeth Molnar Rajec.* The Royal Scientific Society Library of Jordan, *Nahla Natour,.* A Collection for a Brokerage Firm Library, *Kris Sandefur, Lori Rader, Bernard Schlessinger, and Rashelle Karp.* Bibliography of Sub-Sahara African Librarianship, 1988, *Glenn L. Sitzman:* The I.T. Littleton Seminar - Introduction, *Cynthia R. Levine and D.F. Bateman.* Perspectives on the Information Needs of the Agricultural Researcher of the 21st Century, *J. Edmond Riviere.* Computing Technology and Libraries, *Henry E. Schaffer.* Biographical Sketches of the Authors. Index.